Photographs of the racing plates in which
Desert Orchid won his fourth King George VI
Rank Chase at Kempton Park, Boxing Day
1990. The front plates are reproduced here
actual size. Pieces of Kempton Park mud and
woodshavings still adhering to the plates have
been left in place.

THE GREY HORSE
The true story of
DESERT ORCHID

THE GREY HORSE
The true story of
DESERT ORCHID

RICHARD BURRIDGE

PELHAM BOOKS

PELHAM BOOKS

Published by the Penguin Group
Penguin Books Ltd,
27 Wrights Lane, London W8 5TZ
Viking Penguin Inc., 375 Hudson Street, New York, New York 10014, USA
Penguin Books Australia Ltd, Ringwood, Victoria, Australia
Penguin Books Canada Ltd, 10 Alcorn Avenue, Toronto, Ontario, Canada M4V 3B2
Penguin Books (NZ) Ltd, 182–190 Wairau Road, Auckland 10, New Zealand

Penguin Books Ltd, Registered Offices: Harmondsworth, Middlesex, England

First published in 1992

Copyright © Richard Burridge 1992

Typeset in 12/13½ pt Garamond
Printed in England by Clays Ltd, St Ives plc

A CIP catalogue record for this book is available from the British Library.

ISBN 0 7207 1923 2

To my father, without whom none
of this would have happened.

CONTENTS

PART FOUR: *At Full Stretch*

PART FIVE: *Turning for Home*

PREFACE

A FEW WEEKS BEFORE I finished this book, I went to a small electrical shop in London I'd been to over the years to buy a new belt for a vacuum cleaner. As the grey haired lady behind the counter got my change, I realised she was looking at me, thoughtfully. Then she smiled. 'I'm sorry,' she said, 'I do hope you'll forgive me. I don't know your name. But are you anything to do with . . . him?'

I looked at her, and her hopeful, friendly expression didn't change. 'Yes,' I said. 'I suppose I am.'

'I thought so,' she said. 'I thought you were. Wish him the very best of luck, won't you?' She gave me my change, and pressed my hand for luck, too.

What has happened to us over the years will not happen again, and it has been sometimes easy to forget just how unbelievably lucky we have all been.

Desert Orchid has meant so much to so many people, he has touched so many lives and left so many memories. I cannot hope to reach all those memories, nor would I want to try.

These are merely mine.

Richard Burridge.

January 1992

ACKNOWLEDGEMENTS

I'd like to thank four people in particular for making this book possible: James Burridge for breeding Desert Orchid, David Elsworth for training him, Rodney Boult for teaching him to be a racehorse, and George Armatage for keeping him straight. There are so many others who have played a large part: his jockeys Colin Brown, Simon Sherwood and Richard Dunwoody, and also Richard Linley, Graham Bradley and Brian Rouse; and his owners, Simon Bullimore and, in particular, Midge Burridge, for all the work she has done with the fan club.

I'd also like to thank all those who've looked after him at Whitsbury over the years, in particular, Gary Morgan, Jackie Paris (now Young) and Janice Coyle; everybody who rode him at work: Melanie Leonard, Jim Davies, Ross Arnott, Martin Chilton, Paul Holley, Alan McCabe, and many others; all those who took him racing: Peter Maughan, Martyn Jenkins, Andy Larkin and Simon Elsworth; and the many people behind the scenes at Whitsbury, including Chris Harper, Charlie Elsey, David Townsend, Dominic ffrench Davis, Derek Brown, Shirley and Simone Boult, Bert Morrow and particularly Jane Elsworth for making us all so welcome over the years Chris Hill, who put in hundreds of unpaid hours answering enquiries about Desert Orchid.

I'd like to thank the farriers who have shod those fragile feet, Paul Henderson, John Allington and John and Michael Haykin, and the vets, Richard Watson, Jan Puzio, Edmund Collins and John Patterson.

All those who looked after Desert Orchid when he was not at Whitsbury: Ruth and Jack Jackson, Jim Stone, P. J. Swarbrick, Frances Burridge, Sally Buck, Clare Holland, Kathy Osborn,

Pauline and Harold Hall, Alistair Clarke, Clare Pears, Trevor Lowe, Henrietta Sedgwick, Celia Hammond, Carol Milburn, Jane Milburn and Thalia Gordon Watson.

I'd especially like to thank my brothers Simon and Johnnie Burridge for their help with this book and for making going racing so much fun over the years, also Camilla and Felicity Burridge; Pony, Amy and Milo Burridge; Hugo, Caroline and Tim Seely; my mum Anne and her husband Jack; Juliet, Becky, Gemma, Alice and Thomas Bullimore; Phillip and Audrey Burridge; Lucy Watson and Kath Owen; and Annie Brown, Lucy Sherwood and Carol Dunwoody.

To Myles Hildyard for providing a home away from home, and for keeping quiet about it, too. To all the others who've helped me in Yorkshire: Wendy and Bernard Hodgson, Ken and Dot Macdonald, Tom and Maureen Caffrey, Dick Atkinson, Tommy Calvert and Mary Reveley. To Rachel Neale, Nancy Armatage, Bill Owen, Mary Haykin, Margaret Matheson, Geoff Lowe, Juliet Naylor and Jill Deane.

To all the racecourse managers who made the grey horse so welcome, in particular, Tim Neligan, Michael Webster, Ian Renton, Edward Gillespie and Roy Craigie.

To all the TV and radio commentators, in particular, Peter O'Sullevan, Graham Goode, Julian Wilson, John Inverdale and Peter Bromley. To all the journalists, especially John Oaksey, Geoff Lester, Brough Scott and Michael Seely. To all the photographers, in particular, Ed Byrne and Ed Whitaker.

To all those who have worked so hard for the fan club, especially Johnny Hippisley, Haydyn Bainbridge, Jan and Peter Yolland, Penny and Paul Mercer, the Greet family, Jane Bertram, Tessa and John Smith, and Anna Hunt.

To my publisher Roger Houghton for his great patience in waiting till Desert Orchid's career was over to publish this book. To Arianne Burnette for her encouragement and professionalism. To Annie and Susan at Vail Library.

To Michael Sissons and Anthony Jones for their support over the years.

To all the trainers we have raced against over the years, in particular, David Nicholson, Nicky Henderson, Josh Gifford and Jenny Pitman. To all the owners, jockeys and horses who have

taken Desert Orchid on. To all the people who have watched him and cheered him and backed him and backed against him. To all those
I have mentioned, and those I have not, and most of all to Desert Orchid.

You know who you are. Thank you.

PHOTOGRAPHIC ACKNOWLEDGEMENTS

❧

THE AUTHOR AND PUBLISHERS are grateful to the following for permission to reproduce copyright photographs: Gillian Armatage, 41; David Ashford, 48; Kenneth Bright, 14, 19, 22, 27, 28c; Burridge Family, 1, 2; Richard Burridge, 5, 20; Ed Byrne, 37; Gerry Cranham, 24, 42, 47; Mark Cranham, 10; Desert Orchid Fan Club 23; John Elliott, 33; Simon Elsworth, 36, 45; Ronald Fain, 40; Mel Fordham, 3; Robert Hallam, 44; David Hastings, 46a, 46b, 46c; Alan Johnson, 12, 16; Caroline Norris , 38; Paddock Studios, 7, 13, 15, 17, 31, 43; Bernard Parkin, 21, 28a, 32; George Selwyn, 4, 6, 9, 34, 35; Solo Syndication, 29; South Coast Press Agency, 30; Sporting Pictures, 28b; Colin Wallace, 8, 11; Ed Whitaker, 39; Sue Wingate, 25, 26; R. H. Wright, 18.

PART ONE

At the Start

I

The Stuff That Dreams Are
Made Of

Imagine this.

A London solicitor sits in a stuffy, overheated office above Holborn Viaduct. A long legal document is open in front of him but he is paying no attention to it. Instead he is dreaming of breeding a great racehorse. It is a curious idea that has wound itself through the seams of his life. Now, as he approaches his sixties, time is running out. His breeding stock is hardly extensive, consisting of a ten-year-old mare who won two small races, but he has not given up. Not for the first time that day, he puts aside the legal document and picks up a favourite and well-worn book. It is Federico Tesio's *Breeding the Racehorse*.

At the same time a hundred miles away in the small market town of Devizes, a cheerful man in his late thirties is setting up a fabric stall. This is not how he intended to spend his life, but things have been difficult lately, in fact they have been a bit of a struggle since the word go. At first glance there is nothing unusual about him: about five foot eight, medium build, he already has a few grey hairs. But on a closer look, and something about him invites a closer look, there is an unusual quality here. With his twinkling eyes, and his restless, infectious energy, he remains indifferent to adversity, and gives the impression he will succeed at anything he puts his hand to.

Meanwhile a tall man of twenty-six is lost somewhere in St John's Wood. He is the relief boardman at a large bookmaking chain and is wandering around the narrow streets trying to find

3

where he is supposed to be going, knowing that the first race is about to start. It would be a problem if he was fired, to say the least. He is broke and, besides, his job allows him to keep in touch with racing at somebody else's expense, as it is highly unlikely that he will ever be able to do it at his own.

Eleven years later these same three people were in the middle of one of the greatest sporting celebrations anyone could ever remember. Grown men were weeping openly, and even hardened journalists were wiping away tears. The event made the front page of eight national newspapers. It was the lead item on the television news and was later talked about in the House of Commons and discussed from Hong Kong to West Virginia. But for the participants it seemed that it could not really be happening. It seemed that it must be a dream, a fairy tale.

It seemed that way to most people, and if you'd suggested eleven years earlier that these three people might be, respectively, the breeder, trainer and principal owner of a grey horse that had just won one of the most emotional horse races of all time, they would have said it was a dream. And of course it *was* a dream. And it still is a dream.

About Desert Orchid.

Just imagine that.

2

Useless?

FOR ANYONE NOT FAMILIAR with the finer points of jump racing, it should perhaps be pointed out that success is often built on an unlikely cobweb of hopes, dreams, accidents and surprises. But even by those standards the genesis of this story is so strewn with coincidences, set-backs and collisions of chance and ambition that it almost defies the imagination . . .

On 11 April 1979, a bay colt was born in Goadby in Leicestershire. When I say bay, I mean he appeared to be bay, but anyone of any experience could have said that he would, in fact, eventually be grey. This was lucky, because that was about the only nice thing most people could think to say about him.

'Oh that's nice, he's grey,' they would say, and then change the subject. It wasn't that there was anything wrong with him, it was just that in some indefinable way he looked odd. He had a large, common head, a pink nose, and shot up one end, then the other, but never quite looked as if the bits belonged together. Perhaps as a result of this, he also had a permanently surprised expression on his face. The groom who looked after him, Ruth Jackson, tried to offset his oddness by giving him the most normal name she could think of. She called him Fred.

When he was two, Fred was proudly paraded by his breeder before a local trainer to see what he thought of him. At the time one of Fred's legs was the size of a small tree.

'Useless,' concluded the trainer. 'Send him to the sales.' Where he would barely have raised the price of the petrol taking him there.

Fred's breeder tried not to be disappointed. He was a London solicitor called Jimmy Burridge, and for years he had dreamt of breeding horses. His whole life had been punctuated by short, intensely exciting periods with horses, interspersed with much longer and rather less exciting periods thinking about them.

He first rode at the age of three in India. His father Tom had been a major in the Sikh Regiment till he had lost an arm fighting in Afghanistan, and was seconded to run a military grass farm. When he moved to Lucknow, Tom helped build the polo ground, then turned his attentions to the grass racetrack. He was an accomplished horseman, and managed to win enough good races with moderate, but well-backed, horses to pay for his children's education, and passed on his love of horses to his son. At seven, Jimmy rode out a grey Arab called Hudson and when Hudson won a big race, Jimmy was pushed forward by his father to receive the prize.

At eight Jimmy returned to Budleigh Salterton, and horses disappeared from his life. The money spent on his education had not been wasted though, and a brilliant academic and sporting career was interrupted only by the war. He fought with the 11th Hussars, then in 1946 he found himself an Assistant District Commissioner in the Sudan. Once again he was surrounded by horses. He played polo and raced Arab horses. When his wife Anne flew back to England to have her first child in 1951, Jimmy galloped along the dusty air strip, waving her goodbye till her plane had disappeared into the brilliant blue sky.

My birth, and the subsequent arrival of my twin brothers, then obliged him to concentrate on earning a living in London. He could no more contemplate owning a horse than he could building an aeroplane, but a great friend from the war came to his rescue.

Myles Hildyard had a wonderful house at Flintham, near Newark, and he offered Jimmy the use of a couple of boxes. Jimmy hunted borrowed horses for a while, but then one day he heard there was a ten-year-old mare who had won the Cottenham point-to-point for sale for £175.

On a cold February day Jimmy went to see her, but found her field empty. She had jumped into the next field and was standing with icicles hanging off her. She was an almost white thoroughbred, very Arab looking, with a wonderful head carriage and a fierce eye. Her name was Grey Orchid.

He liked her, but his first ride lasted less time than it took to spell her name. She reared over backwards, and landed on top of him on a muckheap. He thought it unwise to try that again, so he lunged her in a field and jumped on again, this time kicking her forward so she wouldn't give an encore. Instead, she threw her head up and almost knocked him out, then did several laps of the field before he could recover sufficiently to pull her up. Still, for £175 you couldn't expect perfection, so he bought her.

The process of making her rideable, however, proved hazardous, and he didn't receive much encouragement. One day he was lungeing her to warm her up, when a relation of Myles's wandered up and considered him. 'Mark my words,' she concluded, 'nothing but harm will come from that horse.'

Jimmy decided not to mark her words and started hunting Orchid. When he realised how good she was, he decided to point-to-point her. He spent most of his spare time in Turkish baths to lose weight, and by the time his first race, the Brocklesby, came round, he was feeling so ill he could barely stand up.

Grey Orchid hit the third fence and he fell off. Unfortunately he had become addicted to the adventure of the whole thing, the pain as much as the pleasure, and he became a familiar ghostly and exhausted figure in the paddock. His application was not rewarded.

One time Grey Orchid spread a plate, then another she was brought down when challenging at the third last. Finally, having hurt his back, he asked a younger rider, David Peake, to substitute for him in the Quorn Adjacent. Of course, she won.

The following season Jimmy did manage a second place in a two horse race, but it was a good second, he used to say proudly. They *were* in the air together in the air at the second last.

Grey Orchid's legs finally packed up and he decided to breed from her, as he loved her and thought she had class. However, he was obliged to spend more time consulting a map than a book of pedigrees. He picked the closest stallions, and the cheapest, and not necessarily in that order. Again it proved hard going. Grey Orchid's first foal, by Blackness, died in the field at two, and she slipped the second, by Fleche Bleu, but the third, by the H.I.S. stallion Brother, who stood in Lincolnshire at the princely sum of £20, bore fruit. Jimmy was pleased with the name he gave the filly. Flower Child, by Brother out of Grey Orchid.

The only problem was that he didn't own her – technically this foal was Myles's, but Myles was happy to swop her for Orchid's next foal, which was by a Hanoverian, which suited Myles better.

Flower Child turned out to be a brilliant hunter, but she was as wild as the wind, and by the time she was eight, Jimmy found himself staring out of the window hoping that snow or fog or anything would cancel the day's hunting. He just didn't enjoy it any more. Then a burly young chap called Doug offered to point-to-point her, but after Doug had put up an average of a stone and a half overweight in three efforts, with predictable results, Jimmy decided to give point-to-pointing a miss.

By this time he had married again. He had met Midge, a tall, very attractive brunette, when he went to her father's surgery in Connaught Square. Midge was a real racing fan, the kind of committed nut who could rattle off the winners of big races at will. In particular, she loved the jumpers.

So when she met Jimmy, she was rather impressed that here was someone who actually *owned* racehorses, and who had ridden in point-to-points! Jimmy used to, as he put it, 'swank' about his point-to-point career. One day he was telling her how he'd come second on his own horse in a point-to-point a few weeks earlier, when her father Fraser smiled, and peered over his spectacles. 'How many runners were there?' he asked.

'Two,' said Jimmy.

Their relationship survived, and after they'd been married a few years and had moved to Leicestershire, Jimmy was pondering his next move with Flower Child. Midge encouraged him to put her into training and at the age of nine, Flower Child went into training with Charlie James in East Garston.

Jimmy knew nothing about 'proper' racing, and so anxiously awaited his trainer's verdict on his charge, but after Charlie had had her for a few weeks, he said she couldn't jump, marvellous sort of animal, etc, but he wouldn't like to risk his professional (Gerry McNally) on her. At the last moment Charlie saw that she had actually run in three point-to-points without falling, so Gerry McNally was duly engaged for her first chase at Taunton. They finished down the field, but Gerry said she'd jumped well. She clearly hadn't regarded schooling fences as jumps, and had ignored them. Encouraged by this, Charlie ran her in a novice chase at Leicester. She came second. Wild celebrations ensued.

Flower Child then became a regular early season performer, especially at Fontwell and Plumpton, and Jimmy and Midge celebrated in style whenever she got placed. She never really looked like she'd win, though, because despite Charlie's earlier fears, all she really liked doing *was* jumping, and as soon as it was clear there were no more fences, she lost interest. This was rather an unfortunate quirk from a racing point of view, as finishing straights are notable for their lack of obstacles. She was frequently challenging at the last, but despite Gerry's urgings, usually managed to come second or third.

The occasion of Flower Child's first victory, at Plumpton, was hardly calculated to attract the attention of the international racing press, but it was entertaining enough all the same. Flower Child had been locked in a series of titanic battles all autumn with a horse called Mouldy Old Dough, and Mouldy Old Dough had always prevailed, due to Flower Child's lack of interest on the run in. On this occasion, however, a novice two mile chase, the gods had decreed that it should be a two horse race, and Mouldy Old Dough did Flower the favour of falling, leaving Flower to come home alone.

Gerry was grinning from ear to ear as he rode into the winner's enclosure to a smattering of sarcastic applause. Jimmy had not realised that this was also one of Charlie James's first winners, and the celebrations endured long into the evening.

Flower did win another chase, but years of carrying Jimmy's thirteen and a half stone around the hunting field, let alone Doug's fourteen stone in point-to-points, had blunted what speed she might once have had. Then her legs went, and this time Jimmy decided to take breeding more seriously. Her racing career had given him a kick, and he realised she was much better than her form figures suggested. He bought all the breeding books he could lay his hands on, and for weeks the dining table was covered with sellotaped charts tracing obscure horses' parentage back through the generations.

One day Jimmy decided to check his homework with a local breeding expert; he invited him to lunch and announced he was thinking of going into breeding.

'What have you got?' asked the expert.

'Well, thought I'd start off with my mare Flower Child,' he said, proudly pointing to her in the field.

'I see,' said the expert, after studying the mare. 'If you want my advice, I'd shoot that one and start again.'

Jimmy plugged on. To date his total capital outlay had been £175 for Grey Orchid and £20 for the mating to Brother, but this time he was prepared to splash out up to £400, provided that the stallion stood in Britain. He slogged through the pedigree books trying to find evidence of earlier generations of matings that had worked, and finally came up with a stallion whom he was really pleased with.

Grey Mirage had not been far below top class on the flat, winning 2,000 Guineas trials at Kempton and Ascot, and coming second to Brigadier Gerard in the Lockinge Stakes. But knee problems had curtailed his career and he now stood at £350. He was by Double-U-Jay, who was descended from Fair Trial, out of a Prince Chevalier mare. The dam was also a great-granddaughter of Nearco (the grandsire of Northern Dancer), and Brother was a grandson of Nearco via Nasrullah. So in March of 1978 Flower Child was duly despatched to Grey Mirage in Shropshire, and Jimmy awaited the results with interest.

I had encouraged Jimmy's breeding enterprises with the reckless courage of the non-combatant, because I had other things on my mind, most of which involved trying to earn a living. I hadn't sat on a horse for years, though I had backed a few.

So when he showed the gawky yearling to me, I was expected to be more positive than everybody else. Unfortunately, I wasn't; I just made the usual polite noises and excused myself.

I did like the fact that he was grey, as I had more or less grown up at Flintham, and almost all the horses we'd had, or borrowed, were greys. The ponies my brothers and I learnt to ride on were greys, and I had a grey Arab pony called Harry whom I adored. Everybody who ever rode him fell off. He had no mouth and liked to gallop flat out then stop dead, because the only thing he really liked doing was eating, and he found that easier without some snotty kid on his back. Riding Harry was the most exciting thing I'd ever done, and after I became too big for him, I cast my eyes enviously at the point-to-pointing scene. However, we didn't have any horses, and I certainly couldn't have persuaded anyone else to put me up – I may have been brave, but I was equally incompetent.

So I turned to racing. I was already addicted to the Grand National, in fact my whole family was so obsessed by it that we had evolved a complicated set of rules: you were not allowed to keep asking 'what's happened to my horse?' and you were not allowed to start screaming at your horse, if you still had one, till after they crossed the Melling Road for the last time.

I went racing with Midge and my stepfather Tim and then started going regularly on my own. My three years at Cambridge convinced me that apart from the normal adolescent preoccupations, I was only really interested in movies and horse racing, and later, at the National Film School in Beaconsfield, I actually became a 'professional' gambler for a few months in order to supplement my grant. I say professional, but it was pretty pathetic, and though I managed to take a regular sixty quid a week off the bookies for a few months, I found myself so involved by the whole thing that I didn't do anything else. So I gave that up, and went to work as a relief boardman in a betting shop.

I continued to be told about Fred, though, as things were always going wrong. He lost a tooth which wouldn't grow back, and Ruth Jackson, who turned up with a carload of Alsatian dogs every day to look after Jimmy's horses, discovered that the business of raising horses was taking a toll on Jimmy's nerves. He saw disaster around every corner.

Ruth soon had problems of her own. The attempt to insert a bit into Fred's mouth was fiercely resisted, and with Ruth holding on to his neck, he used to carry her around the stable as she struggled to squeeze the offending implement past his clenched teeth. The first time she climbed on his back, though, was sufficiently uneventful for her to proceed to walking, then trotting over cavallettis. Encouraged by Fred's performance, she decided to stack two on top of each other. Fred shot so high into the air at this obstacle, that he also shot Ruth out of the saddle.

In late September of his second year, Fred was gelded, and recovered sufficiently quickly to jump into an adjoining field where he apparently considered the grass looked better. Then one day

Jimmy got a phone call. Did he own a young iron grey horse? Jimmy cautiously admitted he did. The caller said he thought so, and Jimmy might like to know it had recently been seen galloping down the main road to Melton Mowbray.

Jimmy spent most of his life anticipating disasters like these, though when they actually happened, he was usually more surprised than anyone else. Fred was eventually recaptured after several close shaves with a Barton's bus and a cement wagon.

Ten days later, though, a hind leg started to swell up alarmingly and was soon as thick as a lamp post. Richard Watson from the Gibson practice was called in, and decided to take Fred back to his surgery in Oakham to X-ray him. Fred was given a general anaesthetic, and Richard Watson eventually dug out a tiny thorn the size of a pinhead out of the fetlock joint.

Jimmy, Midge and Ruth nursed him back to health, but Jimmy was gloomier than ever, thinking whatever chance his horse might have had of one day winning a small race had now gone. He became preoccupied by feeding, and became something of an authority on the subject. Meanwhile Fred continued to be cheer-fully indifferent to people's opinion of him, and continued to behave eccentrically. On an early venture out on to the roads, Fred, ridden by Ruth and accompanied by Midge on her grey hunter, encountered a hedge-cutter. Fred backed off, snorting at it, and feeling his backside against a four foot hedge, promptly jumped the hedge from a standstill, sideways. Midge was rather surprised to see Fred and a rather white-faced Ruth on the other side of the hedge.

In the spring of 1982 Jimmy started to wonder what to do with Fred, and I sold my first script. I got £5,000 for it, and as I had been broke for years, it seemed like a fortune. I cleared my debts, vaguely thought of buying a car, and a month later went with my girlfriend Rachel to stay with my dad. As usual he asked me whether I'd like to see Fred. I walked to the field with him – it was the first time I'd seen the horse outside, he'd always been in a box before. We stood at the gate considering the dark grey gelding. For the first time he started to look like a real horse, or perhaps it was the first time I'd taken a proper look at him, I don't know. He suddenly seemed rather well proportioned, and correct. Then something happened, I'm not quite sure what. Something must have been bothering him – a wasp, a bee perhaps – and he tossed his head, wheeled, started to trot, then cantered, bucking and kicking. A bell was ringing so loudly at the back of my head I couldn't think.

'What do you think?' Jimmy asked. By now he was so used to uncomplimentary remarks that he probably dreaded the answer.

'He can certainly move, Dad,' I said.

'Can he?' said Jimmy, sounding interested, 'I'm not very good at judging these things. Can he really?'

Could he move? He was sensational. My heart was pounding.

'Is he for sale?'

Jimmy turned and looked at me suspiciously. 'Have you got any money?'

We negotiated terms on the way back from the field. I'd pay £2,000 for a controlling fifty per cent interest, which gave me the right, after due consultation, to make the decisions on his racing career.

Half an hour later, the folly of my gesture came home to me. I had just received a windfall which was not at all certain to repeat itself, and I had just blown most of it on a horse of debatable value who would cost more to keep than my average earnings over the past three years.

'I think I've just done something rather stupid,' I said to Rachel.

'What?' she asked.

'You know that carpet I said we might buy, and that holiday we might take . . . ?'

'Yes,' she said, suspiciously.

'Well . . . I think I've just bought a racehorse.'

3

Partners

I'D ONLY BOUGHT HALF OF HIM. Jimmy wanted to keep one leg himself, and one leg had already been sold to one of the unlikeliest candidates for racehorse ownership imaginable, Simon Bullimore.

Simon was forty. He was a partner in the same firm of London solicitors as Jimmy, Lovell White & King. Jimmy had known him for years, and knew he was only interested in boats. Building them and sailing them. About five foot seven, very bright, with twinkling, perceptive eyes, he was one of the most cheerful people I'd ever met.

But he knew nothing about racehorses. What he did know was that he wanted to persuade Jimmy and Midge to come sailing round the Mediterranean. Not a particularly unpleasant offer on the face of it, but Jimmy had better things to do. Bullimore persisted. 'Right,' thought Jimmy, 'two can play at this. If I've got to take part in his bloody hobby, he can take part in mine.'

'All right,' said Jimmy, 'I'll come sailing with you.'

'Wonderful!' said Simon.

'But there's a condition.'

'Go on,' said Simon, a little suspiciously.

'You have to buy a leg in a horse I've bred.'

'How much?' asked Simon.

'A hundred pounds,' said Jimmy. Fred was a foal at the time.

'And is it a good horse?' asked Simon.

'Of course it's a good horse,' said Jimmy, 'I bred it.' And then added, 'Not that you could tell the difference anyway.'

'Deal,' Simon laughed. 'We sail in three weeks.' Jimmy's bluff had been called.

Without giving the matter much thought, Simon sort of

assumed the horse would run in the Grand National and then the Derby. Or maybe the other way round.

As events turned out, he got rather the best of the deal. Jimmy and Midge were caught in a terrible mistral for three days, during which Jimmy was constantly seasick, and Simon Bullimore became the owner of one leg of an unnamed grey gelding who, at the age of three, had cost him £100 plus a quarter of three years' keep, making a total of £850.

It was one of the few consolations, if not the only one, that Jimmy derived from any disparaging remarks thrown in Fred's direction. 'This'll teach Bullimore,' he thought murderously, whenever it occurred to him that the grey gelding might in fact turn out to be useless. 'He'll learn!' he thought, as he recalled regurgitating his breakfast for the third time in as many days.

Simon remained cheerful. Drily advised by Jimmy that it was 'not particularly likely' that Fred would turn out in the Derby and the Grand National, at least not in the same season, he still looked forward to hearing about what was going to happen to him. Whatever it was, he was convinced that the horse would be a success. He was an optimist. But despite this, he thought it might be wise not to tell his wife Juliet, not for the time being, anyway.

So now the horse had three owners, and we needed to give him a name. We went to the stable and looked at Fred. He looked back blankly. No help there. Then a famous poem came to mind, Thomas Gray's 'Elegy Written in a Country Churchyard', and the passage 'Full many a flower is born to blush unseen,/And waste its sweetness on the desert air'. It had the desert from Mirage and the flower from Flower. And it had the ironic insinuation, if Fred did turn out to be completely useless, that his gifts would remain 'unseen', that Flower's progeny would, in effect, have wasted its talents on the desert air of National Hunt racing. We checked the book of registered names, and the name was available. 'Desert Air'.

A week later Jimmy rang. We couldn't have the name 'Desert Air'. Some bright spark at Weatherbys had noticed there was already a 'Desert Heir', and from a commentating point of view this could be confusing in the unlikely event of both horses being in the same race. Back to square one. We all agreed that no good horse ever had a bad name. You had to imagine it being shouted home by a commentator. 'And it's Desert Air challenging at the last, and it's Desert Air going away . . .'

'Let's keep the "Desert" anyway,' I said. We agreed. There was a pause.

'I really loved Grey Orchid, you know,' said Jimmy, 'and she *was* the start of all this.' We thought about it for a moment. Desert Orchid. It seemed perfect, and the name was available.

Now the serious stuff: when should, er, Desert Orchid go into training.

'This season,' I said. Jimmy frowned.

'But he's only three,' he protested. 'He can't go chasing when he's three.'

'He can go hurdling,' I said.

'Hurdling?' Jimmy asked, as if I'd just suggested he drink bleach.

'What's wrong with hurdling?'

'He's not a hurdler. He's a chaser.'

'If he's going to be any good as a chaser then he'll probably be some good as a hurdler,' I said. 'It's better than leaving him in the field.'

The idea still seemed ridiculous to Jimmy, so we made some ground rules. We would put an upper spending limit of £3,000 on the enterprise. If Desert Orchid hadn't shown any signs of ability by the time we'd spent that, we'd put him back in the field for a couple of years. Then again, even if he was any good as a hurdler, we'd give him a maximum of three seasons hurdling before we sent him chasing.

There still remained the question of the trainer. I had given this some thought, but wanted to make sure I was on firm ground.

'I am entitled to chose the trainer?' I asked. 'That was our agreement?' Jimmy agreed. I took a deep breath.

'I'd like to send him to David Elsworth,' I said. There was a short pause. Jimmy frowned.

'Who?' he asked.

4

The Wizard of Whitsbury

I HAD GRADUALLY BECOME AWARE of David Elsworth over the past two seasons, but he made an even bigger impression on me when he won the Triumph Hurdle with Heighlin.

The Triumph Hurdle is the first race on the third day of the Cheltenham Festival meeting, and is one of the most hyped, argued-over, and speculated-on races in the entire calendar; it's also a graveyard for ante-post punters. David had bought Heighlin for the race the autumn before and had actually won it. Pretty impressive for a small trainer, I thought. Pretty impressive for any trainer. Then there was Lesley Ann, who was making a name for herself over fences, and Raffia Set and Ferryman on the flat.

As it had never occurred to me till now that I might ever own a racehorse, I looked up David's record in an old *Timeform Chasers and Hurdlers Annual*. It was a year out of date, but his win total over the last few years made interesting reading: it went 4:7:18:24. He was obviously hungry enough to win small races with moderate horses, but good enough to win big races with good horses. I liked the idea that he didn't train in a big centre like Lambourn or Newmarket, though admittedly I had no idea where Lucknam Park, his address given in *Timeform*, actually was. As he was also not a big nor a fashionable trainer, I thought there was a reasonably good chance he'd take Desert Orchid.

I pitched all this to Jimmy, who said he'd like to meet David. Events then slowed to a full stop. I carefully composed a letter to David, exaggerating the virtues of 'Desert Orchid' (it looked a bit odd in print) and asking if he'd possibly consider training him. The letter received no answer. I waited a month. Still nothing. I waited another month. I called the Jockey Club and asked whether they had his number. They did. Had he moved lately? They said he'd moved about nine months ago. I wondered if I'd sent the letter to the wrong address, but I couldn't remember what address I had sent it to.

Hoping that David hadn't been so dismayed by the prospect of getting our horse that he'd simply decided not to reply, I tried telephoning him. It was now September.

'Whitsbury Stables,' went a gruff Mancunian voice on the other end of the phone.

'Have I got the right number for David Elsworth?' I asked, a little nervously.

'Yes, I'm Mr Elsworth's secretary, Chris Hill. Can I help?' the voice went.

'Er, yes, my name's Richard Burridge. Did you get a letter from me?' There was a pause.

'What was the letter about?' he asked.

'About a horse. Desert Orchid?' There was another pause.

'Desert what?'

'Desert Orchid. I sent you a letter about him.' There was another long pause. You could tell Chris Hill was being cautious here.

'When did you send it?'

'About two months ago, but I may have sent it to the wrong address. What is the address there?'

'Whitsbury Manor Stables, Whitsbury, near Fordingbridge, Hants. Was that it?'

It certainly didn't ring any bells. 'I'm not sure.'

Chris was obviously losing patience with this. 'Well would you mind me asking what the letter said?'

'I wanted to know whether he'd take a horse.'

'Hang on.'

There was the sound of somebody entering the room and a short conversation. Then another voice. 'David Elsworth here.'

'Oh, Mister Elsworth, hello. My name's Richard Burridge, and I wondered whether you'd consider taking a horse. He's a three-year-old gelding, and he's the first . . .'

'Sure, send him down, Robert.'

'You'll take him?'

'Yes, that's what we do here, train horses.' He laughed. 'Where are you based?'

'Well I'm ... well the horse is in Leicestershire. But we don't know whether he's any good.'

'I'll soon tell you.'

'Right. Good. Only could we come down and see you first?'

'Any time, Robert. Just give us a call the day before. Thanks for calling.'

Jimmy, Midge and I went to see him in Hampshire two weeks later. As I drove into the carpark by the top yard, I recognised a man of about five foot eight, in his mid-forties with hair starting to turn grey, dressed in a windcheater and wellies, giving a bollocking to a tiny stable lad.

We got out of my car looking self-conscious. Then David patted the lad on the back and the lad walked off, and I realised David hadn't been giving him a bollocking, just explaining something in a very emphatic manner. We introduced ourselves and David smiled. There was an overwhelming directness about him, as if he knew who we were, and knew we must be in this for the same reasons as he was. A kind of shared joke, like isn't this crazy, but somebody's got to do it. A man of great charm.

'That your car?' he asked, studying my battered Citroën. 'I won't lower the fees if you're poor, you know. We're all poor here.' He grinned, and offered us a tour of the top yard.

The thatched, brick and wood-framed stables were magnificent, and David obviously enjoyed showing us round, walking into each box, purring through his lips like a horse snorting, explaining the horse's breeding and taking its rugs off. We didn't get a word in, but we didn't need to. It was a one man show.

The yard had been built by William Hill, the legendary bookmaker, and was now owned by his nephew, Chris Harper, who ran the adjoining Whitsbury Stud. Gordon Richards had trained there, then Bill Marshall (who had trained Grey Mirage), and when James Bethell had moved out the year before, David had moved in from Lucknam Park. It was not a move he could have anticipated five years before.

David's rise to prominence in the racing world had been unconventional. As a child he had had nothing to do with horses. In 1955 he was about to leave school at fifteen when his class had to write an essay on what their fathers did for a living. David had been brought up by his grandparents, but Pat Macklin, who sat beside him, wrote an essay on her father, and the teacher made her read it out. Her dad was a 'lad' at Alec Kilpatrick's yard in Collingbourne Ducis and looked after the great chaser Galloway Braes. David thought this sounded interesting, so he packed a bag and hitched over to Kilpatrick's yard and asked for a job. He was quartered in a poorly insulated Nissen hut, and froze his behind off all winter, getting such bad chilblains when turning over mountains of carrots that his hands were scarred for life. But he was a bit of a know-all, watching and learning all the time, and deep down he began to think he knew more than Kilpatrick. The years passed, and David applied for his apprentice's licence and rode winners, but he'd decided what he really wanted to do was train horses himself.

In 1971, with the support of owner John Duffy, he rented some boxes from Colonel Ricky Vallance, and trained a few horses under his licence. He also rode them, and when the double of Will Oblige and Indulgent went in at Newton Abbot in 1972, he was physically sick with nerves. His biggest success was Red Candle, who won the 1972 Hennessey. Then it all went wrong when Well Briefed won at Newton Abbot after being pulled up the week before at Fontwell.

The case was referred to the Jockey Club, Colonel Vallance's licence was suspended, and David was told he need not bother applying for a licence for two years. David would admit that jobs are occasionally 'pulled' in racing, but that wasn't one of them. They had backed Johnny Haine on Well Briefed at Fontwell the time before.

Thrown out of racing, with a wife and family to support, he took on odd jobs, including night watchman at Stonehenge and selling fabric off a market stall in Devizes, but with no talent for surrender at all, he never abandoned his determination to get back into racing.

A year later he set up a livery yard, and scraped by rejuvenating the 'sick, the lazy and the lame'. The following year he was given a break, if break is the right word for being pardoned for something he had never done in the first place. He was granted a licence.

He got together about a dozen horses and some owners, rented a yard at Lucknam Park, and immediately gained a local reputation for being a shrewd, clever man with an uncanny insight into horses' minds. He started to be sent better horses, and made his mark on the flat; sprinters and steeplechasers came alike to him.

In 1980 he decided he needed better gallops. He had been to Whitsbury as a child and now heard that James Bethell was moving. He took an enormous punt, though by no means the biggest of his life, and took on the lease. Of course we didn't know any of this at the time. He was a line in a newspaper: D. R. C. Elsworth, frequently followed by C. Brown.

We rattled up in his Land Rover to watch second lot. The centuries-old Whitsbury gallops were wonderful, like foam rubber. As David's horses galloped past, he kept up a running commentary, littering his comments with one-liners and elaborate metaphors as if he really identified with his horses and tried to see things from their point of view.

He was living in one of the stud houses at the time and invited us in for coffee afterwards. His wife Jane, an attractive woman in her early thirties wearing enormous glasses, appeared beaming at us.

'Janie,' he said, 'this is Simon, Michael and Midge. Barrows.' He always got the girls' names right.

'Hello, Midge,' said Janie. 'Simon.'

'Richard,' I said.

'Sorry,' said David. 'Richard, Michael and Midge Barrows.'

'Jimmy,' said Jimmy.

'Burridge,' grinned Midge.

'Right,' said David, smiling. 'Tell me about this horse.'

Three months later Jimmy was asked by friends in Leicestershire why he'd sent Desert Orchid to David Elsworth in Hampshire. 'Nothing to do with me really,' he smiled, then added, 'I can only presume Richard picked the trainer who was furthest away from here.'

But there had been one particular thing that had endeared David to him. We had been sitting in David's living room and Jimmy had been torn between praising his gangling three-year-old to the skies and apologising in advance for what would evidently turn out to be his severe shortcomings, and anybody less used to contradictions than David would have been confused. But David clearly understood the cocktail of realism and wild optimism that was being presented to him. Jimmy finished by saying that Desert Orchid had a common head.

'I rather like a common head,' said David.

Whether David had any inkling at that time of what would eventually happen I don't know, but several weeks later Mikey Seely, the future racing correspondent of *The Times* and my stepfather Tim's brother, dropped in at Ab Kettleby and Jimmy went off to find him a phone number.

'What are you up to?' asked Mikey, when he saw me.

'Not much,' I said, 'I've come to see my horse.'

'That's good,' he said, drumming his fingers on the table. Jimmy seemed to be taking a bloody long time to find a phone number.

'As a matter of fact, we're about to put him into training. That grey out in the field. Flower Child's first foal.' He looked at me as if I were mad. There was a long pause.

'Who are you sending him to?'

'David Elsworth,' I replied. He looked a bit more interested.

'David Elsworth, hmm, interesting character, David Elsworth. Once or twice he's threatened to make the big time, but he's never quite made it yet.'

'Well this horse will make all the difference.'

'Oh yes,' replied Mikey, as drily as he could, which is very drily indeed, 'I'm sure he will.'

By now we no longer referred to him as Desert Orchid. It was too much of a mouthful, so I abbreviated it to Des, and then occasionally lengthened it to Dessie. This, if I remember rightly had something vaguely to do with Dessie Hughes who had just won the Champion Hurdle on Monksfield.

The decision made, it was simply a matter of getting the horse to Whitsbury, which wasn't simple at all. Jimmy didn't have a horsebox and it was a six- to seven-hour journey. My mother and Tim offered to lend us their horsebox, and as their house near Bicester was directly en route between Ab Kettleby and Whitsbury, they suggested we break the journey and stay the night.

In November, Rachel and I picked up the horsebox from Bicester, and drove to Ab Kettleby. Desert Orchid considered the arrival of the horsebox suspiciously: it was clear something was up, and he was not stupid. Though this was only his fourth winter he knew that around now, when the nights got shorter, he got put out in a field. But this year he had continued to stay in his box, and he was still being ridden. He didn't like the look of the horsebox at all; the last time he'd been in one he'd been taken to Oakham and given a general anaesthetic. It was all highly suspicious, so he put up a stiff resistance as we tried shoving, pulling and coaxing him into the horsebox. We finally got him in, but he whinnied continuously as we set off, and within twenty minutes he was drenched in sweat. We stopped and tried to calm him down, but he whinnied all the way down the motorway, and when we hit the winding roads to Bicester, there was a loud crash as he fell over. When we arrived at Tim's stables, the joys of racehorse ownership were already beginning to pall slightly, especially when he refused to come out of the horsebox. So we pulled, shoved and coaxed him out, and finally got him into a box for the night, though we were not looking forward to getting him back in again the next morning, particularly if Tim got involved.

Tim has been riding all his life, and is an accomplished horseman and rider to hounds, but, unfortunately, loading horses into horseboxes was not his strong suit. So Rachel, my mother and I snuck out of the house before breakfast confident that Tim would be busy feeding the sheep for at least twenty minutes. Unfortunately Des showed not the slightest inclination to get back into the horsebox, and Tim took rather less time to feed the sheep than usual. He cheerfully hove into view after ten minutes. 'Having trouble? I'll move the horsebox against the barn.' He did. 'And I'll put these hurdles against this side.' He did. 'And now he'll walk straight in.' He didn't.

'Let me take him,' he said.

'Er no, I think it would be better . . .'

But a steely glint had appeared in Tim's eye. So Tim took one side while I took the other. 'Now come on, Des, in you go.' We all tensed. 'Come on, Des, in you go, good boy.' Des planted himself solidly about three yards away from the box, and right on cue, Tim exploded with an imaginative stream of invective.

In the ensuing chaos, Des reared up, knocking my mother against the stanchion of the barn, breaking her finger; all the other horses in the yard started whinnying, and all the dogs started barking. Eventually the smoke cleared. 'Would you like some breakfast, darling?' my mother suggested.

'All right,' said Tim, and marched off, shaking his head.

In the course of a bacon sandwich we coaxed Des into the

horsebox, and set off to Whitsbury. Within twenty minutes Des had started trying to kick the horsebox to pieces. Rachel was calmly buried in a book. 'I'll go in the back and read to him,' she said. So she did, and I didn't hear another squeak out of Des all the way to Whitsbury. Plenty of people have tried to find out exactly what Rachel read to him that day, but apparently they have not yet offered enough money . . .

We eventually pulled into the lower yard at Whitsbury. There was no one around, so I lowered the ramp and Des stuck his head out and whinnied. David duly pulled up in his Mercedes and got out.

'Hello, Brian, so this is the horse. A grey.' He looked at him. 'Let's have him out.'

I untied Des's lead rope while David talked to Rachel. It was soon clear, however, that Des had no intention of leaving the horsebox. David considered this development. 'Problems?' he asked.

My nightmare was coming true. I'd sold this horse as hard as I dared, but now I couldn't even get him out of the horsebox. 'I'm sure he'll come out,' I offered unconvincingly.

'He ever do this before?' asked David.

'No,' I lied.

'All right,' said David, and walked up the ramp, turned Des round in the box, and backed him out. David smiled and handed him back to me. 'Walk him round the yard a couple of times.' I walked him round the yard. 'All right,' said David, 'put him in here', as he opened the door of a box. Three yards short of it Des stopped dead and looked curiously at David. I tugged at his head. Nothing. I turned him round in a circle. Still nothing. David was considering him, expressionless.

Again he took the lead rope, turned Des around and backed him into the box. He took off the headcollar, and handed it to me. 'Well,' I attempted casually, 'what do you think of him?'

David looked at me, and looked back at the horse. 'He's a bit backward,' he grinned, and walked out.

The only other opinion I got was from Jane Elsworth. She poked her head over the stable door, and smiled. 'He's a big Roly-Poly, isn't he?' she said.

5

A Baptism of Fire

I DON'T KNOW IF DAVID formed an opinion about Roly-Poly straight away, but I doubt it. He saw a close-coupled, unfinished iron grey gelding of about 16.1 hh, with clean limbs and a scar on the right rear fetlock joint, and before he could find out whether he was any good, he had to train the horse to be trained. He gave him to a thin, gangly lad called Gary Morgan to look after. Gary was known as Cooperman, and he was as happy to look after the grey gelding as any other horse, providing he didn't kick him or bite him too often. He obviously liked horses, but when you have to get up at 6.30 am every day to muck them out, ride two lots, groom them, feed them and present them for evening stables five days a week, and every other weekend as well, it's easy to see sentiment doesn't play the greater part in the job, especially in the middle of the winter. Cooperman had come with David from Lucknam Park, and was serving his time, waiting for his chance; his ambition was to be a jockey.

David appointed Melanie Leonard as the grey's work rider, and drove up to the gallops every day to watch him and his forty or so other horses go through their paces. Although it was impossible to be definite about these things, he'd indicated it would be at least three months before Des would see a racecourse.

As to what Des thought of it all, I presume it must have been a bit of a shock after spending all his life in the same place, but anything beat going back in that horsebox. After a few days he seemed to be getting the hang of the routine, and it started to feel like fun. Having a canter on the all-weather gallops certainly seemed more amusing than trotting round roads. He became pretty enthusiastic about the whole thing – too enthusiastic. To the team at Whitsbury who were used to horses coming and going, he was just a grey gelding, until one day he picked up his bit and carted Melanie right off the end of the all-weather, which was unusual. David later concluded that at least he didn't have to worry about Desert Orchid's enthusiasm for training. The problem with most horses was persuading them to put a hundred per cent into their training. The problem with this horse was stopping him putting in 110 per cent.

I had returned to London after dropping the horse off at Whitsbury, but if I thought it was going to be as easy as that, I had to think again. I arrived back to a phone call from my father.

'Well?' he demanded. 'What did David say?'

'He said he was a bit backward.'

Unfortunately, my father, who has a wonderful sense of humour, was not amused. 'He must think we're complete idiots!'

'Dad,' I said, 'I'm sure he does. All trainers think owners are complete idiots.'

'Well, yes,' he conceded, 'but . . . but . . .' he exploded again, 'he's not some sort of hooligan. You've given him the wrong end of the stick. I'm going to ring him up and tell him.'

It occurred to me that it would not be a particularly auspicious start to the horse's racing career if one of the owners had a row with the trainer within six hours of the horse arriving in the yard.

'I don't think that's a very good idea, Dad. David will make up his own mind.'

'I don't care about that, he's my horse, I bred him, I nursed him when he was sick, I broke him.'

In the end he did ring up, and presumably had a perfectly civil phone call. At any rate, David was friendly when I next called him. And I had learnt a lesson: don't tell anybody anything unless you have to – it only gets you into trouble.

So I told precisely no one else of my involvement in the Sport of Kings, particularly not my bank manager. Somehow I did not think the overdraft I was living on would look too good if it was found to be supporting a racehorse.

My contact with David was confined to a call every other Sunday morning. David seldom called me, or any of his other owners, except to tell us about some disaster. I was a little surprised, and instantly apprehensive, therefore, when Chris Hill called me after about six weeks. It turned out there was a problem with the partnership agreement, as Jimmy was no longer a registered owner. I said I'd sort it out. 'And by the way,' Chris added, in his dead-pan fashion, 'what the hell have you sent us?'

I went slightly pale. I didn't know how to deal with this enquiry at all. I managed to clear my throat and eventually offered a rather hoarse but, I hoped, non-committal 'Why?'

'He's just pissed all over Buckbe and Vivaque on the gallops. Bye.'

For anyone not familiar with racing this might not have seemed a glowing tribute. But when I have been asked since, and I often have, when it first occurred to me that Desert Orchid might be any good, it was actually in that precise moment. Buckbe and Vivaque were the acknowledged star novice hurdlers at David's yard, and Roly-Poly, the backward fatty from Leicestershire, had beaten them on the gallops after only seven weeks in training. My head was spinning. For days I walked about with a happy grin on my face – he'd beaten Buckbe and Vivaque on the gallops!

David put me in my place when I next saw him, which was at Dessie's first race at Kempton. 'I, er, gather,' I offered hopefully, 'that he's been showing you something on the gallops. I hear he beat Buckbe and Vivaque.' David looked at me curiously for a moment, as if he wondered where on earth I'd heard that.

'Mmm, well maybe,' he said, 'but I don't believe it.' And he walked off. Had I known David better I would have been able to interpret this as an example of his sense of humour, but it is also a lesser known part of training racehorses that you have to train their owners. Nothing is a bigger problem for a trainer than an owner who *expects* his horse to win. David, in other words, believes in educating owners for failure.

The race in question was the Walton Novices Hurdle at Kempton, and suddenly things had started to happen rather quickly. We hadn't really been expecting anything before February, but just before Christmas I got a note from Chris saying Des had been entered. David confirmed that he probably would run. 'He's got to run sometime.' I couldn't argue with the logic of this, but I was confronted with all sorts of problems.

For a start, what was I going to wear? I had never considered myself owner material before and the problem temporarily paralysed me. I plumped for some brown corduroy trousers and a tweed jacket but still didn't feel like an 'owner'.

Chris Hill's enquiry about Jimmy's registration led to a reshuffle in the partnership. Although Jimmy's owner's registration had lapsed, Midge's had not, so they agreed to transfer the leg between them. The partnership was now split fifty per cent to me, twenty-five per cent to Simon Bullimore and twenty-five per cent to Midge. Jimmy technically had no part in the horse at all, but it seemed a small thing at the time.

I also had to register my colours. I imagined I would have to settle for some complicated confusion involving stripes, stars, crosses of Lorraine and so on, so I was surprised when I got exactly what I asked for: dark blue, grey sleeves and cap. I thought it was a good omen and had some colours knitted by a shop in Westbourne Grove.

The days counting down to Des's first race were intensely, distractingly exciting. For some reason the prospect completely gripped me, and though perhaps this reflected rather negatively on my life up to that point, I could not remember contemplating anything as exciting. I could not explain it, but as owning a racehorse is plainly an irrational thing to do anyway, there probably was no explanation ... I started a scrapbook into which I filed everything: entries, five-day declarations, the overnight runners in the *Evening Standard* – hopeless. In one sense I suppose I was excited because if Des was ready to run so soon, it justified the decision to send him into training as a hurdler, but that didn't go anywhere near explaining the kick it gave me to read in the paper: '18 Desert Orchid (R. Burridge) D. R. C. Elsworth 110... C. Brown'.

To David, Cooperman and travelling head lad Peter Maughan this was probably just a normal working day, barring the ridiculous struggle they had had getting the horse into the horsebox. But to us it was a red letter day, and the Burridges were out in force: Jimmy and Midge, my brothers Simon and Johnnie, Simon Bullimore, who had finally told Juliet that he owned a racehorse, my mum, Rachel and I. We sweated nervously through the rest of the meeting, then congregated by the pre-parade ring.

Out of the thin January light there emerged this black-maned, black-legged thing, looking much lighter than before, as he had been clipped for the first time, and appearing to be extremely pleased with himself. He seemed to be surveying the opposition in a jaunty, contemptuous fashion, though it would be reasonable to suppose, as events subsequently proved, that he had no idea at all what he was doing there. He just gave the impression that whatever it was he was supposed to do, he was sure he could do it better than this lot. I'm ashamed to say we did not share his confidence.

His jockey Colin Brown walked up to us in the paddock, tipping his cap and I shook his hand. 'Hello there.'

'Hello, Colin.'

David looked at him oddly, then turned to me. 'Are those your colours?' he asked.

'Yes,' I replied weakly.

'Oh,' said David. 'Anyway,' he resumed to Colin, 'You've seen him at home. He's a bit fresh. Do what you can to teach him something.' As the bell sounded to mount he walked off and we said good luck.

It was the first time we had met Colin, though I had seen him hundreds of times on TV. A short, heavily built man – for a jockey that is – he had a badly crooked nose. He was very cheerful and friendly, and it was easy to see why he was one of the most popular figures in the weighing room.

Colin was another reason why I had sent the horse to David. In the previous two seasons he had ridden some amazing finishes, and though he'd never win prizes for style, horses really ran for him. At that time he probably occupied pretty much the same position within the racing pantheon as David did: not particularly fashionable or well supported, but a grafter who was more than good enough to win a big race with the right horse. Over the years he had established himself as a West Country specialist, and though he had the occasional ride for Fred Winter and Fulke Walwyn, David's arrival had been a big boost for him.

This was not the first time he had sat on Des. As David's stable jockey, he had schooled the grey over hurdles. Warned beforehand by Melanie about what a tearaway Des was, Colin lined him up for the four schooling hurdles. This was always a nervous time for the trainer, because if the horse didn't jump, he was unlikely to be a success over hurdles, and for the jockey, because if the horse didn't jump, he was liable to end up on the floor. Desert Orchid eyed the obstacles with interest. When Colin let him go, he shot towards them, accelerating all the time, and flew them as if he'd been jumping hurdles all his life. He was so impressive David didn't school him again. He was a natural. Of course, there are lots of naturals on the gallops, but not quite so many on the racecourse. It was a good sign.

Colin jumped on Des, and Cooperman led them out to the course. Des looked like Jack the Lad, really pleased with himself, with a gleam in his eye, and took a fierce hold as he tanked off to the start and vanished into the gloom. We all took up our positions in the grandstand. David and Jane seemed to have disappeared.

The tension before the start was almost unbearable. We questioned our sanity. We were all spending money we didn't have and there had been a long period during which nothing had happened. Now the day had dawned, the moment when we were reaping the rewards, and it was so intensely, painfully exciting that we almost prayed for it to be over. We were also about to learn a lesson. There were to be no boring races with this horse.

The starter called them in and by this time my binoculars were shaking so badly I couldn't see a thing. Discounting the possibility that there had been a major earthquake in the Sunbury area, I had to lower my glasses and watch without them – and for the first two flights could see precisely nothing, as Colin had Des tucked in behind a wall of horses, and it was only after the field pelted past the stands that we could confirm that he had jumped the first two hurdles without mishap. But another thing was also clear, and that was that Colin was having his arms pulled out as he fought to restrain Des and tuck him in behind the other runners to teach him to settle.

He was still pulling hard at the back at the third hurdle, then at the fourth, Bloemfontein, ridden by Robert Stronge, fell in front of him; Des took off and landed on Robert Stronge's head! Colin was horrified, convinced he'd killed Robert. Des, however, promptly took advantage of a certain slackening of the reins resulting from Colin's backward glances, and started pulling himself towards the front.

Gradually the field began to thin out, and we could see him progressing to about sixth place. Jumping the third last, on the outside, he still seemed to be full of running, and for the first time the words 'Desert Orchid' were mentioned during the race. That was enough of a thrill, but now it looked like he might actually be involved in the finish. A line of horses approached the second last, and for a few moments Des hit the front. We started screaming for all we were worth. He looked like he might win!

Halfway to the last hurdle he 'blew up', and as the others accelerated he gradually began to fall back. Colin dropped his hands and tried to nurse him over the last. He looked like he'd be about fifth or sixth. But Des wasn't about to be nursed; he lunged blindly at the last hurdle, crashing into it, and somersaulting on landing, lay still. 'Oh shit,' I thought. 'He's fallen.'

I stayed watching the last hurdle while Boardmans Crown and Butlers Pet fought out the finish, and waited for Des to get up, then a cold hand tightened on my insides. Des wasn't moving, he was just lying flat out on the grass. A flag was being raised, summoning the vet and the meat wagon. 'Oh God,' I thought.

I set off towards the last hurdle. Jane Elsworth saw me coming and tried to stop me, obviously fearing the worst, but I tore past her. It looked very bad. There was a crowd round the horse and Colin was staring down at Des. Midge had not been far behind me, but Jane managed to stop her, and she broke down in tears.

I leapt over the rail and ran towards the hurdle. Des was lying flat out, not moving. David was considering the horse as a vet checked his legs to see if they were broken. Colin pulled his tack off and stood staring down at the apparently stricken horse, and murmured, 'I'm sorry, I tried to make him take it easy but he was just too brave.' It sounded like an epitaph.

Des's belly was heaving, the whites of his eyes rolling. The vet gave him a shot to relax him, but still no diagnosis was forthcoming. We stood around watching helplessly, while the vet and two others turned him over. Most of the others had stayed in the stands, and though Simon Bullimore was reassuring everyone it would be all right, no one believed him as they all knew he knew nothing about racing. Still the horse made no attempt to get up. He looked as if he couldn't get up. It had been the last race of the day and most of the racegoers were leaving, though a few were standing around on the rails, staring at the horse that seemed to have only moments to live. Five minutes had passed since the fall, then seven minutes, then ten minutes. Nobody was saying anything, but David put an arm around my shoulder, and said, without much conviction, that he was sure he'd be all right. The rest of the family were drifting up and staring at Des. Nobody wanted to be there if he had to be shot; neither did they want to leave. All the hopes and fears we had had for him, all Jimmy's breeding plans, all those weeks and years of looking after him and breaking him, all the excitement we'd felt over the last few weeks seemed so tragically misguided, that it should end here on a grey, dismal January day at Kempton.

The vet said he'd try to turn him over one more time, and he was halfway through this when Desert Orchid shook his head, arched his neck, hauled himself to his feet and stood trembling, looking at the anxious faces around him breaking into ridiculous grins of relief. 'Bloody hell,' his expression seemed to say, 'was I knackered!' Cooperman led him around a few times and he seemed to be sound.

A spontaneous round of applause broke out, and we all grinned stupidly and patted Des on the neck. David said, 'He's all right, he was just winded.' And Des wandered nonchalantly off towards the stables.

The bars were closing down but David coaxed several large whiskys out of them and incongruously we found ourselves celebrating. Jimmy looked like he'd aged about twelve years in that twelve minutes, but everyone was congratulating Simon for being such 'a brick'. Even Simon realised that this horse had taken more of a strain on his emotions than he had bargained for, and hoped his next race would not be quite so 'exciting'.

David checked Des over thoroughly and next morning pronounced him a hundred per cent. A few days later I bought *Timeform* to see if they had anything to say about him. 'Sturdy, useful-looking colt.' That was nice, though obviously he wasn't a colt. But it was the last paragraph that caught my eye: 'Sure to win races over hurdles if he's none the worse for his fall.' Sure to win races. . .?! A few days later I came across the 'For Your Notebook' section at the back of the Timeform book. 'Another horse to make a very favourable impression at Kempton was Desert Orchid . . .' It made me giddy. Desert Orchid was indeed a racehorse. It was official.

David intended to run him next at a novice hurdle at the Schweppes meeting at Newbury, but it was lost to the frost. A week later he was going to run at Chepstow over two and a half miles in the valuable Persian War Novices Hurdle, but that, too, was abandoned. In between, he briefly put in an appearance in the Triumph Hurdle betting at 66–1.

Finally, a month later, Des turned out for his second race, the Mere Maiden Hurdle at Wincanton. This was to be a 'confidence restorer', and Colin was again instructed to try to settle him at the back. Desert Orchid's confidence, to be honest, didn't look in much need of restoring as he bounced jauntily out on to the track and promptly tried to cart Colin – I suspect David meant that *our* confidence needed restoring.

Before the Newbury race, alerted by the freezing weather forecast, I had bought myself a brown overcoat, the only one whose arms were anything like long enough, and wore it for the first time at Wincanton. The forecast was for thick fog, and for once it was right: you could hardly see a damn thing, and neither Des's colour nor my racing colours did much to help. From the grandstand you could just about see the last hurdle in one direction and halfway round the bend in the other, and most of the race was run in silence as the commentator wasn't much wiser. But even with what you could see, there was something to remember.

The field of twenty-two came into view as they crashed over the second hurdle. Eventually I picked out Des towards the back, and as they approached the stand, I could see Colin having his arms pulled out. As the leaders turned into the bend, Colin felt that, as he had now got Des tucked in behind a wall of horses, it was safe to let out a reef to ease his screaming muscles. Des, about a length and a half behind the horse in front, reacted to this new-found freedom with a characteristic lack of subtlety. To Colin's amazement, Des just shot forward and collided with the horse in front. With Colin hastily hauling back on the reins again, they disappeared into the fog.

About three minutes later they reappeared – at least the leaders did – with Raise the Offer staying on to beat Hollymount and Ikoyi Sunset. Several hundred yards later, Desert Orchid and C. Brown trailed in. Colin had the haunted, haggard look of a man who had just done something he would not care to repeat, but at least Des hadn't made any notable mistakes.

David considered putting him away for the season, as it seemed he would have an easier time the following year if he were still a novice, but then announced he had found a 'really bad race' for him. With Des's Triumph Hurdle quote pinned to my wall, I wasn't sure this was exactly what I wanted to hear, but David said we had to take our chances when they came, and on that confident note we set off excitedly for Sandown.

The Lilac Novices Hurdle (Div 2) at Sandown was not a particularly inspiring event, as it was limited to horses which 'at the start of the current season have not won a hurdle, and which, at starting, have not run in a flat race'. Of the sixteen runners, only two, Aerialist and Diamond Hunter, had even been placed. Augur in *The Sporting Life* was unwise enough to tip him, and Des went off fourth favourite at 7–1.

Again, it was a murky day, and the iron grey was hard to pick out down the back straight at Sandown. It was only when Aerialist, Emperor Charles and Diamond Hunter kicked on on the final bend and stretched the field behind them, that you could actually see him. He was an impossible distance behind. The air around me was filled with the sound of betting tickets being torn up, then suddenly he began to run on. Still about twenty lengths behind at the second last hurdle, the commentator called him for the first time five strides off the hurdle. Emperor Charles was fading now, but Diamond Hunter and Aerialist were a length ahead of him at the last. Des, with his ears laid back, was still running on! He passed Emperor Charles, and Diamond Hunter began to hang to his left. We started to yell – all thoughts of 'preserving his novice status' had vanished entirely. Des plugged on, he was upsides Diamond Hunter now, he was ahead, then he hit the final incline of the Sandown hill, and Diamond Hunter, on a straight course again, rallied in the last strides and beat him by a neck.

The each way Tote tickets were sellotaped together again, and in the end it was the perfect result. We had won the princely sum of £347.20; we had glimpsed, for a few brief seconds, the prospect of victory – and Des had retained his novice status. David said he'd had a few quid on him as it had been such a bad race, but he seemed as pleased as the rest of us. Cooperman was grinning like an idiot.

Thirteen days later, Des turned out at Newbury. The going was heavy, and though no one attached any significance to it, it was Des's first visit to a left-handed track.

The form summary afterwards read 'Pecked first, headway fourth, every chance sixth, weakened approaching two out'. Des trailed in seventh behind Applejo, Destiny Bay and El Mansour. He'd never even remotely looked like winning, and as Colin jumped off him he said, 'He's gone, put him away.' David agreed and that was it. He wasn't disappointed. He felt he'd got Des's first season just about right, and the fact that he hadn't won could be seen as a bonus. We all celebrated and decided that we would in fact keep the horse in training for another season. If he could learn to settle, who knows, he might actually win a race.

6

A Boult from the Blue

DES STARTED HIS SUMMER BREAK at a farm down the road from David, but a few weeks later came home and joined Flower Child's second foal, Ragged Robin, who was also being prepared for a season with David. Ragged was owned principally by my brother Johnny (whose colours, yellow chevrons on black, look like a road sign), and was by Baragoi, more of a stayer than Grey Mirage. He was a bay, smaller and finer than Des, and Jimmy and Midge initially thought he was the better of the two.

Jimmy believed in the old-fashioned plan of walking and trotting round the roads to harden up the legs, and Midge, Jimmy, Ruth and my thirteen-year-old sister Frances used to take turns riding the horses round the narrow lanes. Jimmy did whatever he could to prepare his horses for training, and though I'm not sure David believed in roadwork, it didn't do any harm, and none of the horses Jimmy sent to Whitsbury ever developed leg problems. But while Desert Orchid was hacking round the lanes, there was a more significant development at Whitsbury – the arrival of a new head lad, Rodney Boult.

David had known Rodney for years. They had been claiming jockeys together in Doug Marks's stable at Winkfield, both doing their three and hustling for rides. It was David who introduced Rodney to his future wife, Shirley. In 1959 David was bombing around in a bubblecar. One Sunday when they had nothing to do, he drove Rodney down to a friend's house, and Shirley was there. Rodney married her a few months later. When David moved to Ricky Vallance, Rodney went to Tom Masson at Lewes, but it didn't work out, so he went back to Liverpool to run a nightclub for his father. At the moment he quit, Rodney was probably at the height of his powers in terms of ability and experience. He had started in the Fifties as an apprentice with Major Sneyd, ridden a few winners on the flat, then put on weight, switched to the jumps and had about thirty wins over hurdles. But he was never going to make the big time as a jockey, and now he was married he needed a regular income. Fortunately, after six years in Liverpool, the lure of the racing world proved too strong, and he returned to racing, first with Dick Hern, then with Jackie Astor and eventually with John Dunlop at Arundel.

In the spring of 1977 he was given the job of educating a hot Mill Reef colt. Rodney is one of the most wonderful horsemen I have ever seen, and though the colt threatened to be a hooligan, Rodney rode him in all his work, going to Ireland with him before the Irish 2,000 Guineas. The colt was called Shirley Heights, and after winning the Irish 2,000 Guineas, won the Derby.

Rodney was promoted to second travelling head lad, but he missed the horses and the endless travelling bored him. He was too gentle a soul to complain immediately, but when he did, John Dunlop was not prepared to move him. Rodney left for Whitsbury, where David had said there was always a job waiting for him. It was Arundel's loss and David's gain.

There has always been a family atmosphere at Whitsbury; it is something that visitors always remark on, and this despite the frequent bollockings handed out by D. Elsworth before breakfast. I suspect practically everybody has been fired at some stage, only to be rehired later, but Rodney and David made a natural partnership. As David seems to see inside a horse's mind, so Rodney has an uncanny ability to relax horses.

When Desert Orchid returned in September, Rodney could immediately see there was something odd here. Des was the only horse in the yard to have his manger on his door rather than in the corner. The horse also seemed to be extremely interested in everything, with his ears pricked continually as he stared at one thing after another, as if he owned the place. When he'd arrived at Whitsbury, having his manger at the back of the box didn't tie in at all with his self-appointed role of stable busybody, and he would take a mouthful of food, then rush back to the door to see what was going on, spilling most of the food en route. So David had had a manger fixed to his door, and if you ever went into the lower yard at feeding time, you would only see one horse. While the others were munching away at the back of their boxes, one grey head was buried in a manger by his door, one black eye watching everything . . .

What made even more of an impression on Rodney was the sight of Des running away with his new work rider, Jackie Paris, on the gallops every morning. 'What the hell's wrong with you, Jack?' he asked. 'Hold him up!'

Jackie was by now completely exasperated by this tearaway. 'If it's so easy, *you* do it,' she told him. And so a famous partnership was born.

They became a regular sight at first lot, leading the string down to the gallops. And the miracle started to happen: Desert Orchid, in Rodney's hands, was learning to settle. He was learning to conserve his energies until the effort was required of him. Rodney could see his wildness was due to natural exuberance rather than wilful misbehaviour, and gently, but firmly, calmed him down. As David trained his horses' *minds* to enjoy the hard work, so Rodney gave them confidence, and in this sense Rodney was David's perfect foil. Not that he was a miracle worker – not every horse he ever rode turned into a champion. But every horse he rode improved. Desert Orchid, like Shirley Heights before him, was lucky to have him. The jigsaw was falling into place.

Des got fit quickly. David said he was naturally athletic and well balanced, and was the sort of horse who probably never became very unfit. In six weeks he was ready for his first race, the Haig Whisky Hurdle at Ascot. This was a series for novice hurdlers who have never run on the flat, and was designed to encourage National Hunt horses. It meant they could start without having to take on hot shots off the flat. In other words it was designed to be a gentle introduction. But there was nothing very gentle about Desert Orchid on that day.

The ground was firm, but David felt Des had such a good action it wouldn't be a problem. He was really starting to like this horse, who seemed to have exactly the right attitude: bold, aggressive, and enthusiastic. There were only four runners, and only two real contenders: Des and Lucky Rascal, a four-year-old grey gelding trained by Josh Gifford. Lucky Rascal's owner Peter Hopkins passed David in the carpark before racing and said David's horse would have to go a bit to beat his. David smiled.

Clipped for action, Des was noticeably lighter than the previous year. I don't think it occurred to us that he might win, but I'm not quite sure what we did think. In spite of our experience of the previous season, or perhaps because of it, rational thought seemed elusive on race days. It was a glorious autumn day, and the participants milled about at the start for what seemed to be an age. Then they were under starter's orders, the tapes went up, and Colin was immediately plunged into the familiar battle – only this time with a difference.

None of the four horses in the race wanted to make it, and four strides off the first hurdle, about a length in front of Lucky Rascal, Colin had to give Des his head if he was going to see the hurdle, let alone jump it. The sense of freedom, combined with the sight of a hurdle, acted like an electric shock. Des *shot* forward, lengthening at each stride, and flew the hurdle. Three strides after it he was suddenly fifteen lengths ahead; he flew the second hurdle and hurled himself round the bend twenty lengths in the lead. Going down the back, he seemed to be accelerating, and he was hurdling brilliantly. Colin let him go. Coming into Swinley Bottom he was still going strongly, and jumping the last before the straight he started to get a little tired. But he had been so far ahead I hadn't looked at the other horses. I did now, and saw that his only serious pursuer was Lucky Rascal, and he was under pressure, but Des was still going strong. Richter scale 3 on the binoculars became 9, a full scale earthquake. My binoculars were shaking so much I couldn't see a thing. Jimmy and Midge weren't much better. We certainly couldn't breathe. Des was in the home straight now, and Lucky Rascal seemed to be gaining. But Lucky Rascal was out on his feet, rolling all over the place. Des skipped over the second last and pulled away from Lucky Rascal. He had just one more hurdle. Time seemed to stop. One more hurdle. Colin was going easy on him now, trying to make him be sensible. Des was approaching the hurdle, one stride, two strides – then he put in another stride, and crashed through the top of it. There was a gasp from the crowd, but Des managed to get his feet out, and came cantering past the post, pulling up to win by twenty lengths from an exhausted Lucky Rascal, with the others a hurdle behind.

There is nothing like winning a race. It is such a pure rush of adrenalin, such an overwhelming, uncomplicated, exhilarating high, nothing comes near it. And that moment that your horse passes the post is the sweetest of all. The feeling is so strong that it can slightly overwhelm you. You find yourself searching for that moment for the rest of the day or the rest of the week, and you can never quite recapture the exhilaration of that frozen moment. Of course when it's your first winner that makes it even better.

Des was blowing like a train as Jackie Paris, who was deputising for Cooperman, led him into the winner's enclosure. His eyes were rolling, he was nodding his head, shaking off pats to his head, while we stood around grinning like idiots. David stood back. 'Your first winner?' he asked. I nodded and grinned from ear to ear. 'Well done,' he smiled, in typically modest fashion, and patted me on the back.

An hour later, Jim Davies, who worked for David but had ridden Monkton Rill in the race, joined us with some weighing room gossip. Richard Rowe had been astonished. Lucky Rascal had been impressive at home, but as he turned into the straight his horse had been 'drunk' with exhaustion. It began to dawn on us Des might not be just a racehorse, but a good racehorse.

We floated away on a cloud. David said he should come on for the race, and Jimmy couldn't contain himself, rubbing his face and saying repeatedly, 'He's won a race, I just can't believe it, he's actually won a race.' It was probably one of the best days of his life.

We were still celebrating three weeks later, when David ran him again at Ascot, in the Bingley Novices Hurdle on 18 November. The continuing firm ground had reduced the field to three runners, but a comment in the *Raceform Handicap Book* was wonderful.

> Few horses have made a more favourable impression this autumn than Desert Orchid, who led throughout at Ascot to score by twenty lengths, and on his return to the course it is impossible to oppose him in the Bingley Novices Hurdle. This grey gelding will be an exhilarating sight if he bowls along at the head of affairs on the fast ground he relishes.

Over £15,000 went on him and he started at 1–2. The race turned into a carbon copy of his previous race, with one heartstopping exception.

He shot off, accelerated into the first hurdle, went clear and, turning into the straight, had galloped his rivals Don Giovanni and Gillie's Prince into the ground. He was cantering away with the race when he came to the second last hurdle, stepped at it and crashed through it. For a second his nose was on the ground, but Colin was ready, and sticking on like glue, managed to pick him up and coaxed him over the last hurdle to win by fifteen lengths. 'Made all, soon clear, blundered two out, ran on well' ran the round-up in *The Sporting Life*. He had won *two* races. We would die happy.

David thought Des's blunder was due to the fact that he hadn't seen another horse either at home or on the racecourse and had lost concentration. He decided to run Des in the two and three-quarter mile December Novices Hurdle at Sandown next. The distance was clearly further than he'd gone so far, but David said he thought Des was tough enough, and that was that.

Des looked good in the paddock – harder, tougher – and he seemed to have grown up. As usual he sweated up, but the cockiness had been replaced with an altogether more purposeful look. Colin let him get the steam out of him, then settled him a couple of lengths in front. Round the back he was flying and was still in the lead turning into the straight. He didn't seem to be having any problem with the distance, and Colin held him together over the second last, then went for everything over the last. It was one of the best jumps of a hurdle I'd ever seen, and he was about three lengths in the lead starting up the hill. But out of the pack came a big chestnut called Catch Phrase – and in the dying strides of the Sandown hill he was too good for Des. Though Des stayed on, Catch Phrase went on and beat him by three-quarters of a length. David was totally dismissive of a journalist's suggestion that he didn't stay. 'If he didn't stay, what about the horses behind him?' He was ten lengths clear of the rest. Then on the way back to the winner's enclosure, a front plate came off. Funnily enough, a photo taken by Mel Fordham showed the plate clearly hanging off on the last hurdle first time round. So he had galloped at least a circuit with a loose plate, and had torn it off on the run in. We weren't too disappointed.

David decided to run next at Kempton on Boxing Day, but before that we got compensation for Sandown. Ten days later we were at Newbury to watch Ragged Robin. Ragged Robin was unplaced, but a couple of races later Catch Phrase was running in the Challow Hurdle over three miles. We watched Des's Sandown conqueror with interest and were delighted to see Catch Phrase pulverise his rivals and win by thirty lengths. I was watching the race beside David, and afterwards he turned to me. There was a strange light in his eyes, and he looked rather serious.

'You know something, Richard,' he said, staring at me. 'You know something? You've got a bloody gold mine!'

PART TWO

❦

Gathering Speed

7

A Cloud of Dust

Before Kempton I owned up to various friends that I had a racehorse, because what was happening was so exciting I needed to tell somebody! I coyly suggested to my agent, Anthony Jones, that if he wasn't doing anything on Boxing Day he might tune in to the 1.10 at Kempton – this was the first time Des was on television. Anthony had been my agent for about a year, and had had a beneficial effect on my finances.

'You own a racehorse?' he asked.

'Half one.'

'Good,' he said, 'that'll keep you poor.'

My brothers were particularly pleased this race was on a holiday, because they were running out of excuses to get out of their offices on race days. Simon had evolved a sophisticated routine. He told people that he was at a 'meeting' all day, omitting to mention it was a race meeting, or that he was 'on a course' all day, omitting again to mention that it was a racecourse. The family certainly saw more of each other at the track than anywhere else and on Boxing Day we had the perfect excuse to get out of the usual Christmas festivities. We were going to Kempton!

Colin had to choose between riding Des at Kempton and Buckbe at Wincanton, and chose Buckbe. She had been nominated as a stable star at the start of the season and was living up to expectations.

David offered the ride on Des to Richard Linley, who as the retained jockey for Sheik Ali Abu Khamsin rode Gaye Brief, the reigning Champion Hurdler. Richard was a friend of Colin's, and Colin had rung him up with some simple advice. 'Let him go. You'll think he'll never stop but once he gets far enough ahead he'll drop the bit and settle.' It took a certain amount of courage to follow these instructions, but Richard did, to the letter.

By now, Desert Orchid's eighth race, he was getting the hang of this racing business. He arrived at the course three or four hours before his race; he was led into a racecourse box, and rolled. He loved rolling, and one of the perks of Whitsbury was a sand pit which David occasionally let horses roll in after they'd done their morning's work. This was fun for Des, but not quite so much fun for Gary who then had to clean him up. Every morning after Gary had put fresh shavings in his box, he rolled again. When he went racing he had to roll yet again, and Gary frequently found himself having to pinch more shavings from neighbouring boxes. Demanding horse, this.

Half an hour before his race, Des was walked around the pre-parade ring, and after the jockeys had weighed out, David and Peter Maughan tacked him up. This was when the fun started. By now Des understood what lay ahead, and trembled with excitement. He couldn't do with any pats of encouragement, either, and usually tried to bite anyone who attempted such familiarity. When the girths were tightened, he exploded, kicking the box or laying back his ear and swinging his head at David or Peter. This was a good sign. The fitter he was, the more dangerous he got. If he floated down to the start, looking relaxed, that was another good sign. If he threw his head around and was too free, that was a bad sign. He usually sweated up, but that didn't really mean anything. It just meant he knew what was about to happen.

Des was favourite, but the well-backed second favourite was an expensive Irish import of Fred Winter's called Ihaventalight, ridden by John Francome, who was having his first run in this country. Timeform now rated Des 124p and had added to his summary, 'quick jumper'. That was something of an understatement. At Kempton he put in an identical performance to his two previous two mile outings. With Peter Maughan on duty at Wincanton, Des wasn't plaited, and with his mane and tail flying, he blasted off, was soon twenty lengths clear, and finished pulling up to win by fifteen lengths from Ihaventalight and Derby Dilly. Richard Linley was impressed, though he did say that he didn't know if Des would be quite as good on soft ground.

But the ground remained fast, and with his next race slotted in two weeks later at Sandown in the Tolworth Hurdle, Des got the headline 'Desert Orchid to Bloom at Sandown' in *The Weekender*. If I'd received a quid for every time I read 'Desert Orchid to Bloom' since, I wouldn't be paying off a mortgage now, but at the time it seemed wonderful. On the morning of the race, the *Daily Express* ran the headline 'Do not desert Orchid'. These two headlines pretty much formed the pattern for the coming years.

The Tolworth was a valuable Grade 2 two mile novice hurdle in which Des's rivals included the four-year-old Triumph Hurdle favourite Dodgy Future, the unbeaten Keelby Kavalier and Ihaventalight, who was now opposing on ten pounds worse terms. Fred Winter thought that John Francome had 'let him get away' at Kempton, and told him to lay up closer this time.

David was a little concerned beforehand. This was the horse's fifth run in under three months, and though he appeared to be as well as ever, he didn't want to ask too much of him at this stage. Initially we were a little concerned when Des couldn't shake off Ihaventalight; John Francome managed to stay on Colin's tail all the way round the back straight. But approaching the second last hurdle, Colin shook the grey up, and he stayed on to win by eight lengths and fifteen from Ihaventalight and Horn of Plenty. Oliver Sherwood, then Fred Winter's assistant, said later that this completely demoralised Ihaventalight. Afterwards David was standing in the gents' when he felt a piercing gaze on him. He turned round and there was Fred Winter glaring at him. He said, 'That *is* a bloody good horse, isn't it?'

Des's form now read 11211, and Cheltenham beckoned. At the start of the season I suppose we'd just wanted to win a race, any race. But now we were seriously considering Cheltenham, and at that stage he might even have started favourite for the Waterford Crystal Supreme Novices Hurdle. So instead of taking things one race at a time, we decided to give him a break and lay him out for Cheltenham in March.

But a week later David said he wanted to run Des again in a couple of weeks at Ascot, and then almost as an afterthought, suggested that as well as the Supreme Novices, he also wanted to enter him for the Champion Hurdle. The Champion Hurdle is the top race for hurdlers in the country. David said he always felt he might have made a mistake when he ran Lesley Ann in the staying novice chase at Cheltenham, the Sun Alliance, rather than the Gold Cup. She had won the Sun Alliance, but David felt she might have won the Gold Cup, and didn't want to make the same mistake twice. So Desert Orchid was now in the Champion Hurdle.

The press started to write about him in earnest, and his first champion was John Oaksey. Oaksey's writing was always shot through with an uncomplicated, enthusiastic joy in horses, and Desert Orchid was his kind of horse. Des appeared on the front cover of *Pacemaker* before his next race, the two mile Datchet Novices Hurdle at Ascot, though a good many judges felt he could not concede ten pounds to the Michael Dickinson-trained Santella King, who had won five out of his last six. David had had a bad run too, with seven favourites going down, and was a little worried that his horses might not be right.

However, Des showed no signs of his hard race at Sandown, and though the previously unraced Hill's Pageant did put up a fight, Des won by eight lengths. He was clearly as tough as old boots. David thought he should put Des away and bring him back in the Champion Hurdle. We all got stuck in at 66–1, and settled back in a warm, but slightly disbelieving glow of anticipation.

We met again a week later when Ragged Robin came third at Windsor, and David had changed his plans. Des was so well, he wanted to run him in the Kingwell Hurdle at Wincanton a few days later. The Kingwell is an established Champion Hurdle trial, and it is *not* a novice event. It is one of the top hurdle trials in the calendar, and several Champion Hurdle hopefuls, notably Very Promising and the mare Stans Pride, were also due to run. If he could manage a place it would confirm that he was ready to take on the big boys. On the other hand, we were more or less committed now to the Champion Hurdle, and it was fresh horses who did well on the slogging grounds of Cheltenham. Running in the Kingwell would mean that Des would not have had a break since October, and would also have run seven times, more than any other horse in the Champion Hurdle. As a five-year-old, and the youngest horse in the field, he would need all his strength to have a chance against the likes of Dawn Run and Gaye Brief. In the end David decided to have a go in the Kingwell, but I had a problem. I was due to go to Texas to research a script with a friend, Geoff Lowe, and would miss the race.

I was in a filthy mood as I dropped in on Geoff's house in Chiswick on the way to the airport on the Sunday before the Kingwell. Geoff was still in the bath. I told him the plane left in an hour. 'We'll make it,' he said calmly. Ten minutes later Geoff appeared and started to make breakfast.

We arrived at the check-in desk with half an hour to go. Geoff slapped the tickets on the desk, and was told the flight had closed twenty minutes earlier. Geoff made some frantic phone calls. 'We can go tomorrow,' he said.

'You go tomorrow,' I grinned. 'I'll come on Friday.' The Kingwell was on Thursday. And Des was favourite.

We converged on Wincanton not quite believing what had happened in the intervening year. Last year, at the same meeting, Desert Orchid had been unplaced in the novice hurdle. Today he was favourite for the Kingwell Hurdle. Heady stuff, though with the exception of Return to Power, Des was now actually *bottom* rated by Timeform. In the paddock, Des seemed to be rising to the occasion and was undergoing something of a transformation. The previous night at evening stables he had been so relaxed he was lying down, and only after considerable prodding and shoving could he be persuaded to present himself for inspection.

Colin was rather more excited. All jockeys dream of riding really good horses, and Des's rise to the top had been exhilarating by any standards. It had happened so quickly that none of us had had much of a chance to let it sink in. Colin thought Des might be one of the best horses he had ever ridden, but this was the crunch: he knew he would not be able to shake off these brilliant hurdlers as easily as his previous rivals, and decided to ride him slightly differently.

He set off in front, but didn't try to stretch the field. They were hunting him, looking as though they could take him whenever they liked. They still looked like that going into the far bend. They didn't look like that coming out of the bend. Coming up the slight incline to the second last hurdle only Admiral's Cup, Stans Pride and Very Promising were in striking distance, but as Colin gradually wound up the pace, only Stans Pride had a chance. The mare, to whom Des was giving five pounds, jumped the second last upsides, but Des ran on. Des jumped the last on the inside; Stans Pride jumped it right on the outside rail. For a moment the optical illusion generated by the split made it seem like Stans Pride was gaining, but as they flashed past the post, Des was going away, and won by four lengths with Very Promising twelve lengths away in third.

Delirium. Big wide ridiculous grins were pasted over our faces as we drove home, and I was still grinning the next day, as armed with all the papers, I read and reread them all the way to Houston. Des was now third favourite for the Champion Hurdle. I rang home to see how things were going, and Rachel told me Gaye Brief was out of the Champion Hurdle and we were now second favourite. Second favourite for the Champion Hurdle . . .

It was incredibly exciting. Jimmy got the award for the Bisquit Cognac Pacemaker International Stud Farm of the month, and though some people were wondering whether Des's stamina would be up to the uphill finish at Cheltenham, plenty of others thought he might be the only horse who could beat the great Irish mare Dawn Run. Des was now firmly in the public domain, and there was a growing rooting section for him in the press. P. Mechen wrote to *The Sporting Life* saying that for him 'the highlight of the current National Hunt campaign had been the performances put up by Desert Orchid'.

A week before the Champion Hurdle we got an offer of £70,000 for Des from an owner of Fred Winter's. Seventy thousand pounds. Tax free. We turned it down, but not till we'd savoured the moment. It's not every day you get the chance to say no to a tax-free seventy grand.

Jimmy stayed rooted to the Oracle weather map on TV and it looked like we'd get the fine weather we were praying for. Fast ground would definitely help.

The hot favourite was Dawn Run, who had won four of her five starts that season, and was a year older than Des. She was the pride of the Irish, and the Irish take Cheltenham very seriously. The Cheltenham Festival is the Mecca of the jumping world. It lends structure to the whole jumping calendar, and as the Festival approaches, excitement reaches fever pitch. The Irish converge in force, as does practically anyone interested in racing who can get the day off. Traffic jams the roads before and after racing; the place itself is so crowded it's almost impossible to get a drink, and seeing the horses in the paddock, then reaching the ring to place a

1 Desert Orchid, a.k.a. Fred, as a foal in the summer of 1979.

2 Jimmy Burridge, in his pyjamas, proudly showing off his yearling in the summer of 1980.

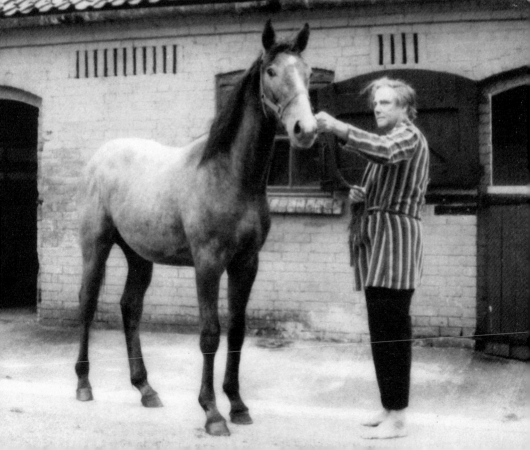

3   Desert Orchid, ridden by Colin Brown, looks like Jack the Lad as he is led out by Gary Morgan for his first race at Kempton in January 1983.

4   A baptism of fire. He crashes at the last and doesn't get up for ten minutes.

5   Magic hands. Rodney Boult becomes Desert Orchid's regular work rider in October 1983, and teaches him to calm down . . . a little.
6   Desert Orchid, ridden by Colin Brown, hurling himself over a hurdle on his way to his first win in the Haig Whisky Hurdle at Ascot in October 1983.

7 The winner's enclosure at Ascot after Des's first win. Both owner and winner bred by Jimmy Burridge. From left to right: Jackie Paris deputises for Gary Morgan, Richard Burridge, Simon Bullimore, Jimmy Burridge.

8 Four months later Des is third favourite for the Champion Hurdle after winning the Kingwell Hurdle at Wincanton. He is led in by Gary Morgan who is about to leave Whitsbury.

9 February 1985, Des storms to his only win of the season in the Oteley Handicap Hurdle at right-handed Sandown.

10 Des takes a fall when leading at the last in the Trillium Hurdle at Ascot in April, and doesn't get up for five minutes. Not encouraging for a horse about to jump fences.

11 Jumping his first steeplechase fence in public before going on to win his first novice chase at Devon & Exeter by twenty-five lengths.

12 Desert Orchid showing his enthusiasm for fences as he wins his first four novice chases by a total of sixty-four lengths.

13 A winning team. Desert Orchid, David Elsworth and Jackie Paris become a regular sight in the winner's enclosure at Ascot.

14 Jane Elsworth.

15 Johnnie Burridge and, in the foreground, Simon Elsworth.

16 The big time. Simon Sherwood and Desert Orchid make it look easy as the grey storms to a fifteen length victory in his first ever three mile chase, the King George VI Chase at Kempton on Boxing Day, 1986.

bet requires planning of military precision. It is completely unique, one of the glories of the English sporting scene, and as impossible to explain to foreigners as the lbw rule.

David was a veteran of the Festival and had had several winners over the years. He tried to help us keep the whole thing in perspective, but we didn't want to keep it in perspective. We let our imaginations rip. Des was the second favourite for the Champion Hurdle, and though Dawn Run looked unbeatable, and physically towered above Des, we felt we had a chance.

There was a change today. Cooperman had left Whitsbury after getting an offer to ride as an apprentice. He was sorry to abandon Des, but he had to take his chances when they came. Jackie Paris took over. She had ridden Des in the early days and was an obvious candidate. She had been at Whitsbury with James Bethell before David arrived and was one of three 'lads' who had stayed behind. About five foot two, with a serious, slightly anxious expression, she'd been plunged in at the deep end at the Champion Hurdle. But she looked comfortable with Des, as he arched his neck in the parade and looked purposeful. Our mouths started to get dry as he cantered down to the start with Colin doing his best to restrain him.

It's impossible to see anything clearly at Cheltenham unless you've got a box or a seat in the stand, so I settled for a percentage position. Being tall helped, as I stood on the grass halfway up the run in.

The starter climbed on to his rostrum, and the tapes went up, and they were off, for the 1984 Champion Hurdle. Des and Dawn Run hit the front immediately, but the mare had the inside rail and pressured Des over the first two. At the third Des outjumped her, and was ahead at the fourth, but not, a little worryingly, appearing to go with quite his usual freedom. His ears were back. He was still just ahead at the fifth, but as soon as they turned into the bend, Dawn Run overtook him, then Buck House, then Very Promising, and his grey form disappeared into the wall of horses.

There is a dull thud that hits you when you realise something you've dreamed of is not going to happen, when all those dreams, those castles on cobwebs, evaporate. For a few moments you feel empty. Desert Orchid finished eleventh.

There were incredible celebrations after Dawn Run's victory. Charmian Hill, the mare's owner, was given the bumps in the winner's enclosure, and these wild celebrations formed the backdrop to our postmortems.

Of course it was disappointing. Disappointment is just the other side of elation. It was possible Wincanton had taken the edge off him; it was possible he was over the top; it was possible he just wasn't tough enough or good enough. But the disappointment didn't last long. We went to the bar and toasted the great Irish mare, and concluded after a very short time, that it had been a wonderful season, beyond our wildest dreams. We had started the season hoping to win a race, any race, and had ended up as second favourite for the Champion Hurdle. We had a lot to look forward to. Maybe even, who knows, the Champion Hurdle next year.

8

Coughing up

THAT YEAR DES WENT TO Flintham for the first time. Myles Hildyard had offered Jimmy a wonderful field with a running spring and overgrown hedges which gave horses shelter from the wind whichever way it blew. It was the same field Flower Child grew up in, so Des now spent the winters where his father had been trained, and the summers where his mother grew up. He was turned out with a cousin, Gemini, an Anglo-Arab/Irish draught cross, who formed an instant affection for him, poring the ground whenever separated from him. Myles's ex-groom, Jim Stone, offered to keep an eye on the horse, and in the middle of May he was turned out for twelve weeks, day and night.

Considering Des's achievements in the previous season, you would think these were happy days for Jimmy, but, in fact, his anxieties increased. Two or three times a week he made the forty-minute trip over from Ab Kettleby in a car full of over-excited dogs, and leant over the gate, fully expecting Des to have, as he put it, 'lost a leg or a head or something'. He regarded the business of having horses out at grass as one of the most thankless tasks conceivable, as the best that could happen was that nothing would happen. It didn't get much better when he came back to Ab Kettleby, and Des and Ragged started their roadwork. Several near misses with corn trailers were not good for his health, and if he wasn't out himself, and Ruth was ten minutes late, he was virtually scrambling the paramedics. Des survived this anxiety with no difficulty at all, ambling his way round the lanes, happily stopping and posing for anybody who recognised him. There did seem to be some way in which he had grown from his triumphs; he realised he was something special. In a field he was always top dog, and in the stable he was furious if any other horse received more attention. He compensated by being so enthusiastic and inquisitive about everything. He had enormous charm.

We elaborated a complicated procedure for taking him back to Whitsbury, which involved taking him to Kempton on a race day, and switching him into David's horsebox; it meant we didn't have to go all the way to Whitsbury. David surveyed the horse, who by now was going much lighter, and was polite enough not to make any comments on the size of his belly.

Perhaps it was David's remark about a gold mine, I don't know, but I surveyed the meetings book happily, worked out how much money I was going to make, and turned down three scripts. I had something I wanted to write, but I didn't want anyone to commission it, and I needed eating money in the meantime. This was not really a problem, I concluded, because this horse was obviously going to support me!

In October, I went down to Whitsbury with Jimmy. It was one of the many joys of having a horse with David, those autumn mornings when the season was all before us: getting up at five to be there by half-past seven, letting the dogs out for a run in the New Forest as the mist cleared, being caught up in the bustle of a racing yard as it geared up for another day, then driving out to the gallops with David and getting a running commentary on the horses as they galloped past, followed by one of Jane's wonderful breakfasts. As Des had a leisurely pick of grass after work, Rodney said he was pleased with him, though he did mention that the guv'nor was not entirely happy, and 'he was usually right about these things'. David said it was nothing he could put his finger on, but Des just didn't seem to have quite the same bounce. You believe what you want to believe of course, but it's unwise to dismiss David's feelings about horses.

We reconvened at Kempton for Desert Orchid's first race of the season in the Captain Quist Hurdle. He was no longer a novice, so he had to run in conditions races or handicaps. The Captain Quist was perfect: an early season conditions race, it put the accent on fitness. Meanwhile Des had started to become a legend over the schooling hurdles. Colin was amazed when on his one and only schooling session, he took off a car's length in front and landed two cars' length the other side of the hurdle.

At Kempton Des had to give Very Promising ten pounds, which considering their last two meetings seemed a lot. Timeform thought Very Promising would beat him by twenty lengths, but we thought Des should have improved during the summer. I had a decent bet on him, but Des didn't attack his hurdles with his usual fire, and although he was still well ahead turning into the straight, the writing was on the wall. Ra Nova and Janus swept past him after the second last and beat him a length and a half and four lengths, with Very Promising a further half length behind in fourth.

It wasn't that disappointing, but compared with last season it seemed somehow uncharacteristic. David put it down to his needing the race, and we moved on confidently to Sandown for the Holsten Pils Hurdle. Des's reputation scared off a lot of horses, and there were only three opponents for this £10,000 added race – Allten Glazed, Cut a Dash, and Rushmoor.

I walked the course and the going seemed perfect. I walked back up to the grandstand and bumped into Simon Bullimore. I was halfway through a sandwich when I heard a voice over the PA. 'Will Richard Burridge please go to the weighing room?' I couldn't think why, but I didn't think it could be anything serious.

David was waiting in the entrance to the weighing room. 'He coughed,' he said. It took a moment for this to sink in. 'Jackie said he coughed twice as he got out of the horsebox. I'm afraid we'll have to withdraw him.'

'Of course,' I said, hollowly. We were now standing in the winner's enclosure, which seemed pretty incongruous. Something about my expression must have got to David. 'Come on,' he said sympathetically, 'let's take a look. Just to make sure.'

David signed me in to the stables and we walked to Dessie's box. Jackie was looking worried. 'Let's have him out,' said David. Jackie put a headcollar on Des and, inquisitive as ever, he walked out . . . and coughed three times.

'At least we heard it,' said David, 'it's always better when you hear it.'

The cough is a symptom of 'the virus'. You just have to take the horse out of work till it recovers, and pray that every other horse in the yard doesn't get it. But as the disease is highly contagious, they usually do.

The PA boomed out: 'The trainer states that in the third race, number three will not run.' My dive into the clear waters of financial independence had just belly-flopped. Instead of *income*, I was looking at bills for Des's upkeep, with no prospect of any prize money. Rushmoor won the race, and eventually I stopped feeling sorry for myself and started feeling very stupid.

It became a standing joke with my agent. Whenever anyone inquired about my availability, he took great pleasure in informing the confused producer, especially if he was American, that it probably 'depended how his horse was doing'.

Des now looked likely to miss a race for which Timeform had nominated him as being 'a particularly live candidate', the Ladbroke Christmas Hurdle at Kempton. It was to be a showdown with Browne's Gazette who had pipped Des for the Novice of the Year Award the previous season. Trained by Monica Dickinson and ridden by Dermot Browne, he had won the Waterford Crystal Supreme Novices at Cheltenham. We clung affectionately to the theory that we wuz robbed, but now a deep gloom descended, especially when Ragged Robin caught the virus (Jackie looked after both horses so it was more or less inevitable), and we all went into cold turkey.

A month later Des seemed to be free of the virus and David started working him again. A few rays of light poked through the bleak December sky. Then David announced that he was going to run him at Ascot eleven days before the Ladbroke Hurdle, and though he wouldn't be fully fit, the race might bring him on sufficiently to do himself justice against Browne's Gazette.

The HSS Hire Shops Hurdle was over two miles. Des had to give a stone to Conclusive, Joy Ride, and Northern Trial, and was levels with See You Then, ridden by John Francome. See You Then had come second when favourite for the Triumph Hurdle and was being tipped for the Champion Hurdle. In his only run so far he'd finished a five lengths third to Ra Nova at Newbury.

It was an interesting race. For a start, Des was used to being in front. It was sort of an unwritten law. Thou shalt not take on this horse, he will murder you. Unfortunately John Suthern, riding to Paul Kelleway's instructions, chose to ignore this commandment.

Northern Trial shot off as the tapes went up, and went so fast over the first two Des couldn't get near him. Des was fizzing after his lay-off, and counterattacked down the back. I've rarely seen horses jump hurdles faster. Turning out of Swinley Bottom, they were thirty lengths ahead, but looking way back, you could see John Francome on See You Then giving the impression he knew something we didn't. What he did know, though I'm not quite sure how, was that there was a landmine three strides short of the second last. At least that was the way it looked, as Northern Trial stopped to a crawl, Des went into slow motion, and See You Then and Joy Ride, both apparently avoiding the landmine, swept smoothly past and fought out the finish as Des staggered woodenly to the line five lengths behind them. He was sure to come on for the race, we concluded, and though he now dropped to 12–1 for the Ladbroke Christmas Hurdle, we were confident this was good value, and got stuck in as the ground looked like it would be fast for Boxing Day.

The sound of rain falling heavily on city streets has an unmissable ring to it. You can hear the traffic sluicing down the roads, however hard you try to block it out. Then there is the deadly rattle of raindrops hitting the roof and driving against window panes. It's not just getting completely soaked every time you go out, it's the bloody sound you can't get rid of.

The going wasn't heavy at Kempton. It couldn't be considering how dry it had been; the consistency of the ground was more like porridge, and we knew it wouldn't suit Des. With his perfect action we considered him a 'top of the ground' horse.

Browne's Gazette was the 11–8 favourite. Des, at 10–1, blasted off in front, and though not appearing to like the ground, was still going well three out. Behind him, See You Then seemed to be jumping badly. Turning into the straight, though, there was only one winner. Smoothly changing gear between the last two, Browne's Gazette glided to a very impressive fifteen length win. Des was second, ten lengths ahead of See You Then.

See You Then went on to win the next three Champion Hurdles. So Des hadn't run a bad race, and anyway there were excuses: the ground, the interrupted preparation, and the fact that Browne's Gazette was quite possibly a better horse. But there was something a little worrying about the manner of Des's defeat. When he had been passed by Browne's Gazette he didn't seem to find anything at all. He didn't seem quite the same horse as the season before, and the gloss was going off his reputation a little. Probably we had been spoilt by all the glory, and it was possible he was still not a hundred per cent after his lay-off. His next race would test him, though. We were going for the Irish Sweeps Hurdle at Leopardstown, and Des was carrying the top weight of twelve stone.

David wasn't too happy about that – the Sweeps Hurdle was usually won by some lightweight Irish speedster who had been 'layed out' for the race for about two years – but with the weather cancelling racing in England we had nothing to lose, and he committed the grey for Ireland.

But things were not going well at Ab Kettleby. The Christmas Hurdle was the first race Jimmy had been to that season, as he had spent the previous four months in Saudi Arabia doing a job he intensely disliked. In a way it was a sad return to a part of the world he had once loved. The airless, alcohol-free world of Jeddah compared unfavourably with England in the autumn, and the job he had to do, closing down a branch of his office, was depressing. There were consolations: first, that he might be able to find out what had happened to Grey Mirage, but he couldn't; secondly, that it would bring forward his retirement by a year, which it did.

On the first day of his retirement, 1 January 1985, Des's sixth birthday, Jimmy was on his own. The horses assumed an even bigger part of his life. Ragged Robin was still on the sicklist and then had a leg injury for several weeks which kept him off the course. I went up to keep him company while I finished a script, and inadvertently set a chain of events going which it proved impossible to stop.

It is a complicated thing owning a good horse, perhaps even more so when you have bred it as well. Good horses create such terrible expectations. You expect them to win, and when they do not, you worry and pore over the results, looking for some clue as to why they have not performed up to expectations. Racing is sprinkled with people who have been driven slightly mad by owning great horses. Henry Alper, for example, who owned the great Persian War, was reputed to have rung his trainers no less than three times a day, every day. Good horses, in other words, preoccupy you, and though I always had my work to keep me busy, Jimmy, now retired, did not.

It has to be said he was the first person to suspect that Des had a problem going left-handed. With the furious energy he applied to postmortems, he had proposed the theory after Des's failure at Newbury in his first season. Then when Des was beaten at Cheltenham, the theory resurfaced. He felt not only that his horse did not act left-handed, but also, more significantly, that there must be a reason for it. Now with Leopardstown, a left-handed track, on the horizon, Jimmy started to think about it all again.

One afternoon I found Tesio's wonderful book *Breeding the Racehorse*. Tesio had bred Nearco, one of the most influential horses of all time, and the book had been Jimmy's bible when he started breeding. Leafing through it I came across Tesio's section on horses' eyesight, in which he explains that a horse can see out of the corner of his eye much better than a man. Horses have evolved to run away from predators and what is happening behind them is of considerable interest. Jimmy reread this chapter, and was struck by the line 'That is why we put blinkers on horses who give up as soon as they see another horse closing on them'.

Jimmy mulled this over. Des had, in fact, appeared to 'give up' in his two left-handed races when attacked from behind. Until the previous season's Champion Hurdle, nothing, except Catch Phrase, had got close enough to him to have a go. But when they did get to him, they always beat him. Perhaps he did not like horses coming up behind him, perhaps it panicked him in some way, and perhaps the problem was made worse when they attacked on his left side. Videotapes were promptly produced as evidence.

Jimmy was in no doubt. Des needed blinkers, especially when he went left-handed, but blinkers were conventionally fitted to 'non-triers' to make them concentrate, and if there was one thing Des wasn't, it was a non-trier. I didn't like the idea of even seeing him in blinkers.

Jimmy persisted, and though the idea might have sounded far-fetched, he supported it with an example provided by none other than David. Combs Ditch, the star of David's stable, who'd only narrowly been beaten in that year's King George, had, as long as I could remember anyway, always worn blinkers. He had a quirk, which God knows how David had discovered, that he would only overtake horses on his left side. This was fine at Newbury or Cheltenham because he could make his challenge on the outside, but at Ascot or Kempton it was a nightmare for Colin, who not only had to delay his challenge till the last second, but also come up the inside. If he didn't do this, Combs Ditch wouldn't overtake a parked car. David had provided a copy-book replica of the problem Jimmy thought he had discovered with Des, and Jimmy wanted to ask David to fit Des with blinkers for Leopardstown, but David wasn't keen on the idea and nor, to be honest, was I.

We flew over to Dublin the day before the race, met up with the Elsworths, the Browns, a host of Bullimores and Burridges, and all staggered to bed about two o'clock. We awoke to an enormous photo of Des on the cover of *The Irish Field*.

Well, no, not quite true. We awoke to the sound of David banging on our doors at half-past six saying he and Colin were off to the track and if anybody wanted to come they were leaving in five minutes. I staggered out of bed and climbed into the car which Colin made the mistake of driving. Even at seven o'clock in the morning, David is seriously competitive, and when Colin stopped at a red light guarding an empty crossroad, it infuriated David.

'Go on, Colin, get a move on.'

'The light's red.'

'Go on!' Colin shrugged, and cautiously obliged, only to come on the same problem a few hundred yards further on. 'Come on, Colin, get a move on.' So Colin proceeded to jump every red light between downtown Dublin and Leopardstown racecourse, and by the time we got there David was looking much more cheerful. He was ahead of the morning.

Jackie and Peter Maughan had stayed overnight at the racecourse. The journey had started thirty-eight hours earlier; they had taken the ferry over from Fishguard, and Des had had to stand in a horsebox for over eighteen hours. He seemed keen to get out of his box and stretch his legs, so Colin jumped on him and cantered round the course. David set off round the course himself, prodding the ground with a stick he found, and blowing through his lips like a horse, as he does when he's mulling things over. 'Well you know what I think, Richard,' he said, stopping suddenly. 'Grass is too bloody long.' Leaving me to think about this, David set off cheerfully towards the car yelling at Colin to get a move on or we'd miss breakfast.

Several red lights later we were back in the hotel, with David ordering breakfast in a terrible Irish accent. Three hours after that we were all at the track, where we were given a great welcome by Tony Corcoran, the Clerk of the Course. I went off to join some Irish friends, and the main topic was the grey horse. 'They say he can't win,' someone said. Des was not particularly fancied, it was true, hovering around twelves in the betting. In fact, one of the other English challengers, Prideaux Boy, was preferred at 8–1. But I put this down to the twelve stone – though it was a little odd I suppose, as Des had beaten Prideaux Boy out of sight in their two previous meetings and should have been able to give him nine pounds.

'I think we've got a chance,' I said, and grinned.

'No, that's not what I'm saying,' said this fellow fiendishly. 'They're saying he *can't* win.'

I was still mulling over this cryptic comment when we converged on the saddling box, and the sight which greeted us was not reassuring. Des looked about as lively as a stuffed mule. He didn't try to bite anybody; he didn't even stir as his girths were tightened. David gave me an ominous look.

Des perked up a bit in the parade ring, but as he set off down to the start, the anxieties resurfaced. Des was tanking off with his head in the air, fizzing and popping as if a firework was going off in his head. I stood beside David, Jimmy and the rest of the family at the top of the stand. I looked at Jimmy, and I knew what he wanted to say – 'I wish he was wearing blinkers' – but he didn't say it.

Irish jockeys are not always known to give English jockeys the kindest of welcomes. Colin was obviously going to have his work cut out getting to the rail, but he got away well, and though Des jumped right over the first two, managed to get the rail for the first bend. In the back straight Des's hurdling was fast and furious, and though he never managed to get away from his field, he was still running coming to the second last. But as soon as he jumped that and turned into the final bend, he went in two strides, fizzled out, and trailed in about thirteenth, with the race going to a bottomweight, Hansel Rag, with Bonalma, Another Shot and Fredcoteri filling the minor placings.

We all felt Des had been beaten too quickly for it to be his true

61

form. Colin said that he was always on the wrong leg, and put it down to the weight, but Jimmy was in no doubt what the problem was, and to give him his due, Des had completely packed up when a horse appeared on his right. There followed a rather public 'discussion' between me and Jimmy, observed by a laughing Geoff Lester of *The Sporting Life*, in which he argued for blinkers, and I argued against them . . .

The combination of Des's listless appearance beforehand, and the various 'rumours' suggested another possibility. I asked David whether it might be worth having a dope test, but he didn't think that was it, though he wasn't sure what the problem was.

The truth is usually simpler than you imagine: Des, a notoriously bad traveller – as soon as he got into a horsebox he presumed he was going to arrive at a racecourse in about two hours – had sweated and trembled for the entire time he was in the box, and had refused to eat an oat since leaving Whitsbury, thirty-three hours before. After he got home, it took him several days to recover from the trip.

Dessie's next race, the Oteley Hurdle Race at Sandown, was the only race of his I've ever missed. I was now in deepest Mississippi writing one of the films I had unwisely turned down earlier. David had fallen over on some ice a few weeks earlier and was hobbling around in a cast, freezing his toes off. The conversation continued to revolve around the left-handed issue. Everyone agreed that Dessie could not, for some reason, go left-handed, but David did not go along with Jimmy's blinkers theory. Jimmy's argument was basically there must be some reason for his inability to go left-handed, but David was against the blinkers.

Thankfully there were no left-handed problems that day, because Sandown is right-handed. Des had taken some time to recover from his Irish trip, but was back in good form and had eleven stone five to carry on his favourite track. The other seven runners included the useful Allten Glazed, Flarey Sark, and Mr Moonraker, who were contesting the Schweppes later that month (abandoned as usual). Des showed some of his old spark when he stormed clear of his field from three out, and won by ten lengths from Mr Moonraker. It was at least as good as his performance in the Ladbroke Hurdle and gave David some heart, though not for Cheltenham. He was quoted as saying that 'I suppose we might be fools enough to be tempted to go to Cheltenham again but really he is much better going round the other way.'

I achieved what may well be a first in National Hunt racing in that I listened to the race down the phone in Raleigh, Mississippi, and celebrated in New Orleans. I can recommend it.

We did go to Cheltenham, because there was nowhere else to go, but I think Des's price of 20–1 more or less accurately reflected his chances. David thought he had no chance going left-handed. Privately, he may have felt wider misgivings, as someone I met later was in the market for a point-to-pointer, and asked David if he had anything suitable. David said Desert Orchid might jump fences, though his owners probably would not sell. He also added that he wasn't happy with the horse, and felt he might have lost his way with him. Desert Orchid seemed to be on a downward slope.

Browne's Gazette was hot favourite for the Champion Hurdle, and we certainly had no worse luck than him. Ridden by the man who had once owned him, Dermot Browne, he careered sideways at the start and lost twenty lengths. See You Then was always going well and surged clear on the run in to beat David's other entry, Robin Wonder, who despite starting at 66–1 was by no means unfancied. Stans Pride finished third, Gaye Brief fourth and Browne's Gazette sixth. Des never got into the lead, but chased Northern Trial, who later fell when beaten and was tragically killed, then weakened after a very bad jump at the fifth, and pulled up. He returned with a nasty scrape on his near hind.

By now the contrast between his right-handed form and his left-handed form was so glaring as to be absurd. Right-handed, even in this muddling season, he continued to be in the top half-dozen horses in the country. Left-handed his form was a joke, ooop. Had that been all there was to him, he probably wouldn't have got a Timeform rating at all – if he had, it probably would have included the famous squiggle, indicating an 'unsatisfactory temperament'. We all knew of horses who favoured one direction over another, but it was usually a question of pounds, maybe a stone at the most. In this instance, Des was verging on the brilliant going right-handed and the useless going left.

Jimmy and David continued to discuss this, and the situation was complicated by various misunderstandings about Ragged Robin's well-being and running. David agreed to run Des in the Welsh

Champion Hurdle (left-handed) with blinkers to see if it made any difference. It didn't really solve much, as it was disgustingly wet at Chepstow, conditions which we all thought Des would not like in any case. Chepstow can get unbelievably heavy, especially in the turn after the stand, and had David been there that day, he probably would have pulled him out. With the double asterisk opposite his name in *The Sporting Life* indicating wearing blinkers for the first time, Des lined up against a top class field, including Browne's Gazette, Ra Nova, Stans Pride and Bajan Sunshine.

Des actually looked intrigued by the blinkers and seemed to consider wearing them rather a lark, and stormed into the lead as usual. After the fourth, though, he was struggling in the ground and hating the left-handed bend, and Colin gave him a 'reminder'. Struggling round the bend, the field closed and swallowed him up, and though he jumped another hurdle, he was stone last and Colin wisely pulled him up, while Browne's Gazette got some compensation for the Champion Hurdle by beating Ra Nova and Stans Pride.

Geoff Lester reported afterwards that Desert Orchid, wearing blinkers, 'clearly resented the aids and was never going a yard', but his run here, unsatisfactory as it was, was certainly no worse than the Champion Hurdle. He had stopped dead when turning into the bends on both courses. But even if the blinkers had not stopped Des (and why should blinkers stop a game horse, anyway?), they had clearly not helped him; whatever was wrong with him, that was not it. No more blinkers. David was as gracious and sporting as ever. In spite of the disagreements between him and Jimmy, both men did recognise that the other only had the best interests of the horse at heart.

Because the Chepstow race had taken nothing out of Des, David decided to run him again a week later at Ascot in the Trillium Handicap Hurdle race over two miles. Not surprisingly, perhaps, considering he was carrying twelve stone and giving over a stone to some useful handicappers like Rhythmic Pastimes and Comedy Fair, he went off third favourite at 9–2, with Comedy Fair at 7–4, and Mister Golden at 10–3.

It seemed like the 'normal' Desert Orchid again at Ascot. He led and drew clear from the third. He skipped over the second last, and was still well clear of the hard-ridden Comedy Fair and Rhythmic Pastimes. But now he began to tire very rapidly, and though still three lengths clear at the last, he reached for it, lost his undercarriage, and ploughed into the ground, with his neck twisting over at a sickening, impossible angle.

It seemed he must have broken his neck, and he wasn't getting up. I ran over, but he still hadn't moved. It was a terrible ending to what had turned into a disappointing season. It did occur to me that he was winded, but still he lay there, the seconds ticked by, one minute, two minutes.

Then, just as before, with a great heave, he pulled himself to his feet, and shook himself. He knew the routine by now – fall at the last, have a bit of a lie down, get up – and the whole stand exploded in applause as they saw him get to his feet. *The Sporting Life* recorded that the cheer that greeted this was the biggest of the afternoon. Des almost seemed to have anticipated it. Poor old Comedy Fair had entered the winner's enclosure to an almost silent welcome; all eyes had remained on Desert Orchid. As Dessie stood, his ears pricked acknowledging the cheers of the crowd, the moment made up for all the uncertainty of the season. It was impossible to escape the conclusion that this horse meant a lot to an awful lot of people, and afterwards David said he hoped we realised that we no longer owned this horse, but that everybody did. He was quite right. Des had become public property!

However, ownership has its obligations and we now had to consider the future. Des was going chasing next year, but his hurdles form left something to be desired. He had failed to finish his last three races; his form ran ppf – not encouraging for a horse about to jump fences.

As a confidence booster, David gave him a run on the flat. We toyed between a mile maiden and the Group 3 Mono Sagaro Stakes at Ascot, but plumped for the Ascot race because it didn't require him to go into starting stalls. I had a set of silks made and Brian Rouse was given the ride. Nobody imagined he'd win, but it was a little disappointing seeing him finish second last, and once again he seemed to go out very quickly and not produce anything at the end of the race. Brian Rouse was adamant that he didn't stay a mile and a half, and barely a mile and a quarter, and of course if you accepted that at face value, it would have suggested that he wouldn't stay three miles over fences. But as far as flat racing went, that was it for Desert Orchid, and though occasionally a flat race was mooted as an early season straightener, David always dismissed the idea, by saying that Des was too good for flat racing!

9

Trapped Nerves

DES CAME HOME a couple of weeks later than usual, but within a day of being turned out he was hobbling lame. His leg swelled up with a septic corn. Richard Watson from the Gibson practice, and Jimmy's farrier, John Allington, had a look at his feet and concluded he had probably had corns for some time. A corn on a horse is not like a human corn. It is a bruising in the seat of the foot which is usually caused by the percussive effect of a foot hitting firm ground. When dirt gets into the blood vessels as they dry out, it becomes trapped and infected, so when you remove the front shoes it puts the foot into direct contact with soil, and it gets infected. The problem is, if you don't remove the shoe, then the foot has less chance to recover for the next season.

Richard Watson dug out the poison, and Jimmy and Ruth kept poulticing the foot till the swelling gradually came down and Des became sound again. But he had been so terribly lame for over a week that Richard Watson had described it as touch and go for a while. Des eventually pushed off to Flintham and settled into his summer idyll, mooching around the field nuzzling anyone who might possibly give him a mint, the only sign of any aggression being the odd well-aimed kick at a bullock trying to eat his tail. He was joined by Ragged Robin, but in the meantime that saga had drawn to an unhappy conclusion.

Despite the fact that Ragged had won three novice hurdles, Jimmy had begun to feel that for some reason he was not receiving David's full attention. There had been lapses, mainly in disregarding plans about entering the horse, and in not telling Jimmy when the horse had a problem with a joint. Jimmy became terribly frustrated when he couldn't find out what was happening, and felt that somehow having two horses in the same yard had led to the lines of communication over them becoming entangled. Also, with both horses in the same place, if one horse went down with the virus then they both went down with it. So he thought the problems might be solved if Ragged Robin were moved to Tim Forster.

But Jimmy wasn't actually the main owner of the horse, my brother Johnnie was, and Johnnie, though a fan of Tim Forster's, was also a big fan of David's, and wasn't sure about this. Johnnie was very busy with his work and simply did not have the time to get involved in the rights and the wrongs of it all, though to be fair there had been several occasions when he'd made plans to take time off work, only to find that the horse hadn't been entered for the race in question. The fun of owning horses is partly in the anticipation of races. If you don't know when the horse is going to run it takes some of the fun out of it. But for the time being, despite Jimmy's suggestions that the horse be moved, Johnnie was against it. That was, until Liverpool.

At the beginning of the season Ragged had been aimed at the Haig Whisky Novices Hurdle Final at Liverpool. This was a valuable handicap for which Ragged was set to carry top weight. As so often in racing, though, things had not quite gone to plan, and by the time the race came round, David felt he was being asked to run Ragged against his better judgement. Johnnie, unaware of this, travelled up to Aintree with high hopes. On arriving there he was surprised to find David dismissive of Ragged's chances. I know David felt bad about what happened next. We were all watching the race as Ragged went down to the start, bandaged behind. Colin was riding, and Ragged settled into the pack. Halfway round it was clear he was not going well, and he began to tail off. Then he hit a hurdle hard, and Colin pulled him up.

David and Johnnie walked on to the track, with David shaking his head. 'I knew he was over the top, I shouldn't have run him.' Johnnie looked confused. Hadn't he been laid out for this race? David shook his head in exasperation, saying 'I am *not* having this conversation on the racecourse', and walked off.

It was a small tragedy. David and Johnnie, who have never ceased to like or respect each other, and are good friends today, seemed to have fallen out. After that Johnnie didn't feel he had much option. After one last race at Uttoxeter on his way back to Ab, which no one seemed to want and in which Ragged was unplaced, they decided to send him to Tim Forster the following season.

It wasn't difficult to see both sides of the argument. David had won three races with Ragged and had done so spectacularly with Des that he couldn't understand why the owners were pissed off. At the same time, Johnnie and Jimmy weren't getting much pleasure out of it.

Someone tackled me later and asked me how 'we' could do that? I said that question was part of the problem, as it presumed both horses were owned by the same people. They weren't, and it was that confusion which was at the root of the problem. I also said it was nothing to do with me, which it wasn't, but there was another side to it. People don't do something for no reason at all. Ragged was terribly important to Jimmy, as important as Des really, and he was starting to feel that the confusion over Ragged might somehow taint the gratitude he felt to David for all he had done with Des. So he decided it was probably in everybody's interests to move him. As a result of this, the partnership was slightly rejigged. Midge swopped half of her leg in Des for one leg in Ragged, so Desert Orchid was now owned fifty per cent by me, twenty-five per cent by Simon Bullimore, and twelve and a half per cent each by Midge and Jimmy.

The summer slipped by without further incident, and Des returned to Ab Kettleby for his roadwork. However, Jimmy continued to ponder the left-handed problem. Des was due to go back to David at the beginning of September, and in early August Jimmy rang me to say he'd been riding Des and he wasn't completely happy with his action. He found a small lump on Des's back, and he was tripping over his front feet, usually after giving a slight twitch behind the saddle, and Jimmy thought there might be a problem. Midge had asked around and a friend of hers had recommended a man called George Armatage whom she said was some sort of a back man, and did I object if he had a look at him? I'd heard about 'back people' and didn't really believe in them, but I said if he thought there was a problem, it was fine with me.

About a week later, I got another, very excited call from Jimmy. George Armatage had arrived, and Jimmy said he thought I'd want to hear about this. George Armatage, a shortish, sixty-five-year-old Geordie with a permanent limp, had driven into Jimmy's yard, briefly examined Des's back and immediately dismissed the lump, but said he did have a 'trapped nerve' on the left side of his back, and that it was quite bad. Jimmy nodded, and George promptly disappeared into Des's box, closing the door so no one could see what he was doing. There was the sound of shuffling, a loud slap, then he came out.

'Right, sir,' he said, 'he's straight now. He was in a bad way.'

Still not understanding, Jimmy asked for a little more information. For a start, how long had his back been out?

'About a year and a half, I'd say. Must be some horse to have done what he's done with that.'

Eighteen months would take Des back to his first Champion Hurdle. 'What would that have meant?' asked Jimmy.

'Have you had trouble keeping condition on him?' Armatage asked. It was true, he had.

'That'll be the pain. He'll put condition on now. He'll get too fat unless you watch him.'

George led Jimmy back to the stable. 'Look,' he pointed, 'look at the line of Des's stomach there, watch as it drops. That's him relaxing with the pain gone.'

Sure enough, as Jimmy looked, the line of Des's stomach dropped.

'What else?' asked Jimmy.

'He'll finish his races much better,' said George. 'Won't get so tired.'

'And could it affect his ability to go left-handed?' asked Jimmy.

'Aye, could do,' said George, 'when he's turning left-handed it'll pinch the nerve even more, but it wouldn't affect him so much right-handed. Going right-handed it might even release the pain a little. But you know he's had this problem for some time, so he may never be quite as good going left-handed.'

Jimmy was staring at him. Suddenly this explained everything: the reason why Des ground to a halt going into the second left-hand bend when he was starting to get tired; the reason why it didn't seem to affect him going right-handed.

'So what do we do now?' he asked.

'Just walk him for a week,' said George, 'and he'll be right. No trotting. He's been in a bad way.'

George said goodbye, and ten minutes after he'd arrived, he was gone. I honestly didn't know what to make of this, but if it was true, it certainly explained a lot. I asked a vet I bumped into that day whether what George had been talking about was possible. Absolute rubbish, he said. Impossible. I shrugged and forgot about it, then I got a call from Jimmy the next day.

'Something's happened to Des,' he said. 'He's unrideable. He's so well I can't handle him. Can he go back to David straight-away?'

This I had to see. I was going down to London from Yorkshire, and I dropped in on Ab Kettleby on the way. I could see there had been a change, Des looked dangerously well. He looked completely different. Even Ruth Jackson, a natural sceptic, who had not thought there had been a problem, admitted there must be something in it. The horse was so well now, and so full of beans, that he was proving a real handful out on the roads, and she was worried he'd do himself an injury unless he was allowed to do some faster work.

Jimmy said he'd walk Des for a week, on foot if necessary, and could I get on to David and arrange for him to go back early. So I rang David with the good news, or what I thought was the good news.

I précised the conversation Jimmy had had with George Armatage, telling him how George thought he'd found a problem, and that Des might now go left-handed and might even finish his races better. As I say, I thought David would be pleased, but I soon realised he wasn't. In fact, he was rather upset. He had not heard of George Armatage, was sceptical about back people in general, and was particularly suspicious that George had not let us see what he was doing. He thought that it was a ridiculous suggestion that Des's back had been out for eighteen months, and a slur on his staff for me to suggest it. I realised this conversation was going wrong, and reassured him that it was not intended to be a slur, and that I hoped it might have been good news. I asked if we could send Des back a week early as he was now dangerously well. David said he'd think about it.

The letter arrived a few days later. It was on a single page of plain paper in David's handwriting. It said, basically, that since we had so little faith in him, with the greatest regret, he was no longer prepared to train the horse. He was very fond of the horse, and he personally liked us and would miss us, but that was that.

I later learned that the back issue was not the main problem, though possibly it was the final straw. David had been very upset by the removal of Ragged, and felt that it represented a vote of no confidence in him. He didn't feel able to continue to train Des without the full support of all the owners, and though he could have put either the back issue or Ragged's removal behind him, together they were too much to swallow.

Still under the impression that the back issue was the main problem, I managed to get David later that day. I apologised if I'd upset him, and repeated that I thought he would have been pleased, as George had done something we thought had helped the horse, and I felt I should tell him about it. David said he was sorry, but his mind was made up and we'd have to send Desert Orchid somewhere else. Of course I suppose we could have done, but I certainly didn't want to, so I rang Chris Hill and briefly told him the situation and that the last thing I'd wanted to do was to upset David, but I'd obviously failed completely. He laughed sympathetically, but encouraged us to persevere. Later Jane told me David had been so upset by my first phone call that he'd got up in the middle of the night, written the letter, and posted it at six o'clock. But as far as I was concerned Des was David's horse, David and Rodney had made him, and I simply could not conceive of sending him anywhere else. And though I also thought, still slightly misreading the situation, that David might have been mistaken over the back issue, in retrospect I could hardly blame David for reacting the way he did. I don't know what else I could have done though. Probably just said nothing.

In the meantime we had a serious problem. Des was now so well and behaving so badly that we had to put him into training. I called Colin and explained the situation. Colin immediately said that we had to try to get David to change his mind, but as he knew only too well, David is notoriously inflexible in that department. So we compiled a shortlist of alternatives if the worst came to the worst: Fred Winter, Josh Gifford, and lastly, as a wild card, John Francome, who had recently taken up training.

A day later I tried David one last time. I apologised again, and suggested that we forget the conversation had ever taken place, that we obviously did a lot of things with the horse when we had him home and he didn't need to know about any of it, just put it down to an owner's quirk. David was silent for a few moments. Perhaps my repeated phone calls convinced him that we did have faith in him after all. Perhaps the thought of seeing Des in another yard was too painful – but, anyway, a truce was declared. And we never did discuss the back issue again. Not for a year, at least.

Ruth and her husband Jack drove Des back to Whitsbury, and in a couple of days everything was back to normal. That's the great thing about David, he never sulks. At our usual Sunday conference he told me, without a trace of irony, that Des had never been better and he wasn't surprised we wanted to get rid of him, as he was dangerously well. When I bumped into Rodney at Kempton at Des's first race, the first thing he said to me was: 'What have you done to that horse this summer? He feels like a million dollars.'

I shrugged and said nothing.

10

The Crash of Birch

THAT SEASON DES WAS GOING to jump fences. The transition from hurdles to fences is never smooth at the best of times, and our nerves were already a little frayed by the events of the summer. Now the unwitting object of all this diplomacy and speculation, whom we were all hopelessly fond of, was going to risk his neck over fences.

Desert Orchid himself had no such worries. He appeared to relish the prospect. David was quoted during the summer as saying that he was wasting his time over hurdles, and he had got support for this from Fred Winter. When Fred had tried to buy him, David asked him whether that meant he thought Desert Orchid would jump fences. Fred said he was sure he would. David 'schooled' Des at the end of the previous season with the usual instructions to Colin to take it easy and so on. So Colin rode the grey horse up to the first practice fence and let him have a good look at it.

David stood back, and Colin never knew what hit him. No sooner had he aimed the grey horse at the first fence, then he found himself, about fifteen seconds later, the other side of the fifth fence. Desert Orchid obviously seemed to regard jumping fences as the most enormous lark – he certainly didn't stop and look at the fences and sky them like so many novices do, but really attacked them. His mother had been a brilliant jumper, so this was not entirely surprising, but while it was encouraging, such boldness in a novice can lead to crashing falls.

So David schooled him a great deal in the opening weeks of the new season. Usually he thought schooling caused more problems than it solved, and a gentle introduction to fences at the racetrack was worth hours of jumping at home, but it was pretty clear that

Desert Orchid's introduction to fences was going to be anything but gentle. He had been a brilliant jumper of hurdles, but that brilliance involved almost missing them out, whereas jumping fences involves 'bending the back' and driving off the hocks. If Des duplicated his hurdling technique over fences, there would be one of two results: a broken fence or a broken horse, or possibly both.

Perversely all this schooling led to his first race being over hurdles. He had been fresh when he went back, and the combination of the fun he was having jumping and the extra work he was doing had made him as wild as the wind. David decided an outing over hurdles would get the spunk out of him, and sent him for the Captain Quist at Kempton again.

The presence of Rodney at the track was not then considered the kiss of death it later turned out to be. In fact, it was very nice to see him. If we're talking superstition here, let's talk brown overcoats. For Des's first race, when he had fallen at Kempton, I had not worn the brown overcoat – I didn't own it. In the Champion Hurdle the previous season I dispensed with the overcoat, and Des was pulled up. In the Trillium Hurdle, in which Des had fallen, it had been a warm spring day and I hadn't worn the overcoat. And now today, a warm October day, again I didn't wear the overcoat.

David said Des was fierce as he strutted around the parade ring with his head arched, looking like he was about to explode. He was so convinced he'd win, he would have put five grand on him if he could have got odds against, but Des started at 4–9. Curiously, amongst the big bets laid at the track was one of £1,066–£2,000, and while this didn't make him odds on – he was already odds on – two years later I met the man who had this bet. I was working on a script in Cap d'Antibes when I got talking to a professional backgammon player. He came down to the south of France every season and played backgammon for a living; it was a perfectly reliable source of income, it put his children through school, and so on. In the winter he went back to England and played the horses. My connection with Des emerged, and he said he'd had £2,000 on Des that day. Perhaps surprisingly in view of what happened, he never held it against the horse. He felt it was not quite a pleasure to lose money on a horse like that, but close.

There were six runners, with Wing and a Prayer looking like the only serious rival. The tapes went up and you couldn't see the hooligan for dust. Wing and a Prayer, ridden by Simon Sherwood, went flat out after Des, and thinking he was closing, he was amazed to see the flying grey change gear at the fifth hurdle and zoom off into the distance. Turning into the straight, the race was a procession; Des was twenty-five lengths and motoring. Possibly his schooling over fences now led to his downfall as he steamed up to the second last and disdainfully tried to boot this non-obstacle out of the way – and failed. He went down on his shoulder, Colin came flying over his head, and looking rather surprised, Des continued at his own pace to finish a respectable second to Wing and a Prayer.

His form now read ppff. He was going chasing and had now failed to finish his last *four* hurdle races. We responded to this in typically stoic fashion: we had too much to drink. Half an hour after racing I remembered my dogs in my car and went off to give them a run. Wandering down the finishing straight in the dusk, light spilling out from the grandstands, suddenly in front of me was the object of all this unspoken fear, one steeplechase fence. Well, I thought, that doesn't look so big, I could jump that. So I did. No problem. Feeling considerably better, I wandered back to the bar which was now several more rounds the worse for wear. Only Jane Elsworth was sober.

'Come and look at this,' I said, and led her out of the bar. I repeated the exercise. She considered me. I was clearly seriously nuts, but she was perfectly nice about it.

David, Jane, Kevin Keegan, who part-owned Jamesmead who had just come second in the Cesarewitch, Robert Browse, the Assistant Clerk of the Course and a few others adjourned to a Chinese restaurant in Sunbury. David revealed I'd turned down £70,000 for Des two seasons ago, and when everyone stopped laughing, some sums were done. To realise the sum of £70,000, Desert Orchid would have to win about £300,000, and that was obviously out of the question, especially since he was about to kill himself over fences.

We couldn't postpone his chasing career; in any case, hurdling hardly looked like a safe option any more ... But I don't think any of those connected with the horse could actually be said to have been looking forward to the Woolea Lambskin Novices Chase at Devon & Exeter over two miles and one furlong. Jimmy decided to go to a health farm. Jackie could hardly speak. David wasn't much better, and I found myself anticipating, without any relish, the near nausea I knew would attend that moment in the paddock when it is all about to happen but nothing has happened yet.

Colin, at least, didn't seem too worried, but he didn't have to watch. He seemed more concerned that Charcoal Wally, who had won his first chase at Kempton a couple of weeks earlier, would take him on, and a battle between two front runners would quite likely end up with one, if not both of them, on the floor.

Jackie couldn't watch and stood behind the saddling stalls. I said several prayers, then the tapes went up, and Des set off at an alarming pace towards the first fence. The faster he went, the slower the action seemed to be going; for those few strides before the first fence, time seemed to have stopped. Then he rose, and with ears pricked, jumped it as if he'd been doing it all his life. We celebrated wildly.

Then we realised there were another eleven fences. By now Des was bowling along three lengths in front of Charcoal Wally and, jumping the water neatly, set off round the bend. The next fence was a plain one, then the first ditch. Des came up a stride too early, and with his front feet round his ears, cleared it by miles – it was as good a jump at an open ditch as I'd ever seen. Now the apprehension went into reverse: instead of wanting it to be over, we wanted it to last for ever. Colin had him going at a relaxed pace but he was starting to stretch his field. The fences down the back are all slightly uphill, and he was perfect at them. Rounding the home turn Charcoal Wally was in hot pursuit, but if Des jumped the last three okay he was home and hosed. If . . .

He almost overjumped the second last, but that was the nearest he came to a mistake and, clearing the last easily, he cantered past the line, ears pricked, hard held, to win by twenty-five lengths from an exhausted Charcoal Wally, who had almost fallen at the last. He was a fence clear of the third horse, Pridden Jimmy, and two fences clear of the last, Proper Mommet.

'Made all, jumped well, unchallenged' said *The Sporting Life*. But as Jackie waited for Des to give a 'sample' for a dope test, the course vet said he didn't think much of that and Des would never win another chase. He changed his mind later.

Jimmy, listening down the phone, found out that a health farm was not the ideal place to throw a wild party. As it started to get dark, I jumped the last, just to keep my hand in. A groundsman was leaning on a rake, watching. He nodded, thoughtfully. 'You don't see many people doing that,' he said, and wandered off. During the next few months I kept up this ridiculous ritual and can tell you from personal experience that the fences at Ascot are the toughest.

Considerably fortified by Devon, David now ran Des in the Hurst Park Novices Chase at Ascot. He had only three opponents – Celtic Hamlet, Cocaine and Yacare – and starting at 4–9, we should have been confident. However, I cannot recommend the experience of watching your horse jump down the back at Ascot for the first time. The ground slopes downhill down the back, inviting the horses to speed up towards the ditch. Des had clearly received his invitation, too, and with Colin sawing urgently at his head to restrain him, Des 'guessed' at the ditch, stood right off it, hit it, lurched on touchdown, but recovered and galloped merrily on, ears pricked throughout, to win easily by twelve lengths and a distance from Cocaine and Yacare. He looked magnificent, and Colin was confident enough to look back through his legs at his pursuers on the run in. As Des strolled past the post, BBC commentator Peter O'Sullevan purred, 'What an attractive horse this is.'

He was stronger now, and David liked the way he was shaping up, and said he 'could well win the 1986 King George VI Chase'. He was 'confident he'd get three miles, but would always be better right-handed, so we can forget the Gold Cup.' David entered him for the King George that year, as there weren't any other obvious races for him on the Boxing Day card.

It looked like a clash with the other star novice of the season, Music Be Magic, in his next race at Sandown, the Henry VII Chase, but Music Be Magic went elsewhere, so Des was 4–11 to beat Amrullah, Prudent Match, Taffy Jones and Evening Song. He stood a stride off three fences down the back side, but Colin managed to settle him over the last two and cantered up to win by seven lengths and five from Taffy Jones and Evening Song. According to Geoff Lester, several fellow hacks had not believed the horse bent his back enough to jump fences – but they were warming to the idea.

Des was a model of power and authority in those early races and clearly relished every moment. He was far more entertained by fences than hurdles: he pricked his ears and even started to measure his fences like an old pro. Every time he ran, the same picture seemed to appear in the paper: front legs tucked neatly up under him, ears pricked, looking for the next fence. Not that he didn't make mistakes.

His next test, the first time he'd been over two and a half miles, was the Killiney Novices Chase, again at Ascot. His opponents, receiving between five and eighteen pounds, were Rhythmic Pastimes, Conclusive, Play Boy, Simark and Evening Song, and for the first time that season he went off at odds against at 5–4. He gave everyone their money's worth. He got too close to the third, clobbered it, and went right down on his nose, but Colin somehow clung on, and won by twenty lengths and four from Evening Song and Play Boy. Poor Annie Brown, Colin's wife, had become so nervous by this stage that she couldn't watch, and locked herself in the ladies' loo every time Des ran, sticking her fingers in her ears so she couldn't hear a thing, and only emerging several minutes after the race was over. Meanwhile Jenny Pitman, who *had* been watching, said afterwards that if there was one horse she'd like in her yard apart from Burrough Hill Lad, it was Desert Orchid. It was quite a compliment.

'Orchid looks new N.H. star' ran Roger Mortimer's column in the *Raceform Handicap Book*. We were wondering what to do next. There was no obvious race for him at the Kempton Boxing Day meeting. David decided that the King George came a year too early and the three mile novice chase wasn't worth much. 'Why not put him in the Ladbroke Hurdle?' I suggested. Me and my big mouth.

11

A Bad Dream

O N CHRISTMAS EVE it started to rain, and not just drizzle, it
bucketed down. We were spending Christmas in Nottingham,
and Jimmy sat hunched in front of the Oracle weather service,
occasionally stirring to dial the London weather forecast, and
looking more and more ashen-faced. I wasn't much better. Two
nights running I had had an identical dream. Desert Orchid, rain-
soaked and mud-spattered, was five lengths clear going to the last
hurdle at Kempton. He didn't rise at all, fell, the screens were
raised, and I woke up to the sound of a gunshot. It was odd, as I
had never dreamt about him before.

The dream haunted me, especially since Des had fallen in his
last two races over hurdles, and it kept raining in London, raining
and raining and raining, and even if I'd wanted to ignore it I
couldn't, because as I've said, my father had appointed himself the
speaking weather man. So I called David, and the mood his end
was in strict contrast to the gloom in the Midlands.

'I'm really not happy about this race, David,' I said. 'I've got a
funny feeling.'

I didn't elaborate. David was a cheerful debunker of anything
that didn't make sense to him, and highly suspicious of higher
powers in general. He is, none the less, very clever about people,
and sensitive to unspoken thoughts, and something about my tone
got through to him. He was sympathetic.

'Look,' he said, 'I understand you're worried, and of course we
are taking a risk putting him back over hurdles. But he is really
well at the moment, and I think he'll run a big race.' We agreed
he'd go to the track and we'd walk the course together
beforehand.

Jimmy was now so worried that he had to go to bed early, but I know he didn't sleep, as he came and sat on my bed in the middle of the night and we talked for hours. At least I couldn't dream.

Next day the talking weather forecast had confirmed it was still raining at Kempton. Jimmy didn't want to come: if Des was withdrawn, it would be a wasted trip; if he ran, he'd hate it so much he wouldn't watch. Anyway, Jimmy said, he didn't like racing! But Midge, who did, didn't want to go either. Even Simon Bullimore said he didn't want to go – or for Des to run.

I set off for Kempton with my brother Simon at seven am. Round about Luton we stopped for petrol. The rain swept right in under the garage canopy, and when I got out of the car, I was almost knocked over by the rain.

We arrived at Kempton and I turned up at the weighing room, but David wasn't there. The place was filling up rapidly, so I decided to walk the course. By the time I had got to the last hurdle my trousers were dripping up to my calves. Nearly two inches of rain had fallen in the last twenty-four hours. It was a bog.

'Fancy your chances, today?' asked Geoff Lester as I walked back to the grandstand.

'Not much,' I smiled. 'Have you seen David?'

David was nowhere to be seen. The runners, depleted by defections because of the ground, were entering the paddock for the first race. I saw David flying in through the entrance.

'Hello, Richard, bloody traffic,' he said, sailing past en route to the weighing room.

'Have you got a minute?' I asked.

'Make it thirty seconds,' he said.

The great thing about David is that you can make a plan with him one day, and the next day he's completely forgotten about it.

'Well, the ground's terrible,' I said. 'I've walked the course.' Which was not strictly true, but still. 'I'm sorry,' I said.

David sighed. 'Well he's your horse,' he said.

'Thanks,' I said.

He looked rather tired, then headed off to the weighing room. I stayed where I was.

In the weighing room, Fred Winter was standing by the declarations desk as he walked in. 'Your grey horse could win this today,' he said.

'He's not running,' said David. 'The owners . . .' he gestured. Fred Winter understood. Owners.

About three minutes later I was standing in the same place, blankly watching the horses in the first race being mounted. The PA rang out: 'The trainer states that in the third race number four will not run.' I didn't enjoy that much. The rest of the day passed in a sodden blur. Combs Ditch was narrowly beaten in the King George again. The Ladbroke Christmas Hurdle was won by Aonoch, and in a fair reproduction of my dream, Gaye Brief crashed at the second last, but thankfully did get up and walk away.

The other owners were delighted Des hadn't run, and given the premonitions, and the switch from fences back to hurdles, I didn't see how I could have done anything else. I just hadn't enjoyed it much.

I called David the next day and told him I was sorry to have let him down, and he said he thought Des would definitely have won, though he did admit he hadn't said that before the race. We agreed that the whole thing was over and done with.

'I shall never mention it again,' he concluded cheerfully.

David never stopped mentioning it! Eventually I came to a conclusion which was to have repercussions later. I decided I would never pull a horse out of a race again.

While all this had been going on, Des had been cheerfully waiting in his box to go out on to the track, and an interesting fact emerged. David was weighing his horses at the time and had noted that Des tended to lose about twenty-one kilos every time he ran. Out of curiosity, he weighed Des after Kempton, and though all he'd done was travel to the course, he still lost seventeen kilos.

Nothing kicks you up the backside like racing, and I was consoling myself that whatever the rights and wrongs of Kempton, at least we hadn't risked buggering up Des's fencing technique. Two weeks later he ran in the Thunder & Lightning Novices Chase over two miles at Ascot. His opposition consisted of Charcoal Wally and a horse called Pearlyman. Owing to leg problems, Pearlyman had had an interrupted career, and though he'd won his only chase easily, he was thought to have no chance, and started at 8–1. Well you know what they say about the outsider in a field of three . . .

Des kicked off in front and attacked his fences like a lunatic. Colin was later quoted as saying that what happened next was a result of the horse watching the BBC camera car, which would have been pure Desert Orchid, but much as I hate to disagree with Colin, the BBC didn't broadcast that race so I don't see how it could have been.

He was speeding up to the ditch on the far side, and decided to take off two strides too early. He took off so early, in fact, that he landed before the fence had started! He somehow crashed through the fence and stayed on his feet, but the resulting loss of momentum left Colin on his neck. Colin had just about managed to haul himself back into the saddle, when Charcoal Wally cleared the fence behind him, collided with Des, and knocked Colin off the other side.

Des wondered where Colin had gone, but continued anyway, following Charcoal Wally and Pearlyman until Charcoal Wally fell at the third last, and he and Charcoal Wally fought out a rather half-hearted riderless finish for second place. Des pulled himself up, and was heading for the winner's enclosure when Jackie caught him and led him away. This was obviously something new: in seven previous visits to the course he had won five and come third once. He simply presumed that there was only one place you went after a race – the winner's enclosure! Maybe he'd treat his fences with a little more respect now.

Des then headed for Sandown for a battle with Berlin, who had won his only two chases and was highly thought of. The ground was soft, which perhaps explained why Des was not jumping with his usual fluency – at several fences he lost ground to Berlin. Turning into the bend they were well clear, with Des on the rail and Berlin outside him, but three strides into the bend, Dermot Browne pulled Berlin over, cutting Des up, and practically knocking him over. By the pond, Des had fought back, and everyone presumed he would run on, but he looked tired, and though in the end he was only beaten half a length, and would have won in another fifty yards, it seemed uncharacteristic. Des had been beaten at level weights at his favourite track. Colin was breathing fire, but couldn't object to Dermot Browne as the incident had not happened in the last two furlongs.

We had a meal in the Good Earth at Esher, and David said

Colin was the senior jockey, Dermot Browne was just trying it on, and Colin shouldn't have let him get away with it. Colin had hinted he would gain his retribution elsewhere, but David wouldn't let it go.

'He's too nice,' he said. 'I mean nobody would ever try that out with Richard Rowe. You cut him up, you'd get a smack in the mouth.' I said we all make mistakes, but I thought Colin had every right to think Des would murder Berlin over the last three, but when he pressed the button there was nothing there. I was sure Colin would exact retribution on Dermot Browne in due course. For all I knew he was letting his tyres down as we spoke . . .

David nodded, grinned and had another mouthful of sweet and sour pork. 'Fine,' he said, 'Colin is my best friend. I just thought I'd mention it. Anyway,' he continued, 'it's really your fault. If you hadn't taken him out at Kempton . . .' I laughed.

Heavy snow then descended, and cancelled, amongst other things, the February meeting at Wincanton, and surprise, surprise, the Schweppes at Newbury, the most accident-prone race in history. David hated it when racing was off, and wandered around like a bear with a sore head. He could not stand doing nothing, or seeing other people doing nothing, and even poked his dogs with a stick because it infuriated him to see them asleep.

So, with the gallops frozen over, he took his Cheltenham team down to Studlands Beach. The horses seemed to enjoy the change of scenery, but I'm not sure the same could be said for the work riders. The wind off the Channel turned them blue – or black and blue in Jackie Paris's case. Des is notoriously averse to having his girths tightened and usually kicks and bites at the same time. Jackie was fiddling with a tail bandage while Colin was tacking up Des.

'Wait till I've finished this, Colin,' said Jackie.

'What?' said Colin, tightening the girth. Jackie got both barrels.

David looked forward to Cheltenham, of course, because everyone in National Hunt racing does. It sometimes seems that the whole National Hunt season is really just a glorified warm-up for those three days in March. I never really subscribed to this view, though after George Armatage I wondered if Des might for the first time put up a half decent performance. However, I also wondered if Des mightn't have put his back out again when he blundered into that fence at Ascot.

David also entered Des for the Queen Mother Chase, but in the end ran him in the Arkle Challenge Trophy Chase. Berlin was the ante-post favourite.

When Des walked into the pre-parade ring before the Arkle, he looked lifeless. And when David saddled him, he didn't try to bite anyone and hardly moved when David tightened his girths. Perhaps he was remembering the year before when he'd hurt his leg. He looked so flat that David seriously considered withdrawing him, but decided, since we were there, we might as well have a go.

Des didn't run that badly as a matter of fact, and certainly better than he'd run there before. He led to the top of the hill, but turning down the hill, he fell apart, and under pressure from Colin, found nothing as Oregon Trail and Charcoal Wally swept past and fought a head-to-head battle to the line as Des stayed on in third. Quite what to make of that form we didn't know. At Devon we'd beaten Charcoal Wally twenty-five lengths and now he'd beaten us by eight lengths. Colin did say that for the first time Des felt like a proper horse going round Cheltenham, so if there was something wrong with him, it probably wasn't the original problem.

Two weeks later, at Sandown for the two and a half mile British Aerospace Rapier Novices Chase, his only serious rival seemed to be Clara Mountain from Tim Forster's yard. It was the same Berlin story all over again, only without the rough stuff. Neck and neck over the last three, they touched down at the last together, but Clara Mountain ran on to beat Des by a length and a half on the run in. Tim Forster was pleased he'd won, but not so thrilled at what the handicapper would now do to a horse who'd beaten Desert Orchid at levels. David was philosophical, hoping it would help our handicap, and was gracious in defeat. He never believed in making excuses for beaten horses. But the promise of the early part of the season was not being fulfilled, and David's intention to run him in next year's King George now looked a forlorn hope. Des was also developing a worrying tendency to 'leave' his back legs in a fence.

We tried one last throw of the dice, over two and a half miles in the Contiboard Novices Handicap Chase at Ascot. Des had top weight of eleven stone seven in a field of thirteen. Colin restrained him over the first four fences, then gave him his head, and he went so far ahead the BBC cameraman gave up trying to keep him and his nearest pursuer in the same shot. He jumped well enough to begin with, though he made a mistake at the sixth last and started leaving his back legs in the fences again. There are four fences in this stretch, followed by two in the straight and on TV the foreshortening effect made it difficult to judge if he was maintaining his lead. But at the fourth last no one could be in any doubt. He crashed through it, and Colin did well to stay on board.

Repington and Just Alick jumped past him over the second last, and he was out on his legs, ears pinned back, struggling. At the last he again left his back legs in the fence, and as he struggled to the line, he was overtaken by Garfunkel and The Catchpool. For the first time in a race over fences which he'd finished, he was out of the first four and out of the winner's enclosure.

We celebrated, because we were pleased he had survived his season in one piece. David and Colin both thought Des was now 'over the top', that mentally he'd blown a fuse, the pressure of racing had got to him, his efforts were being dissipated in nervous energy. Anyway, it didn't matter. Even if Des wasn't over the top, his owners were. Six weeks earlier, Ragged Robin had been killed in a chase at Worcester.

12

The Shadow of Death

It's one of the ironies of racing that the best loved horses, the chasers and hurdlers who come back year after year, are also subjected to the greatest risk. The insurance rates tell their own story. If you want to insure your horse against being killed, you will find that flat racing is insured at five per cent of value, the same as a horse out at grass. Hurdling is rated at seven and a half per cent and steeplechasing at a whacking twelve and a half per cent – and this despite the fact that chasers are by and large older, more physically mature, and more experienced.

The attrition rate is heartbreaking, and I know of plenty of owners who only have flat horses as they cannot stand the thought that their horses may not only get beaten, but also killed. The danger is always there, and whenever a horse gets killed, however tough the face is dealing with the disaster, you can be sure somebody will be questioning whether it's all worth it. Going home with an empty horsebox is a heartbreaking, sickening journey.

But sport is about risk, and that is perhaps why National Hunt racing is more sporting than flat racing. The rewards are small, the risks are high, and it touches us more deeply. It can be a very emotional business, but that, of course, is why we do it: if it didn't affect us, it would hardly be worth all the effort and struggle.

Ragged Robin was sent back to Tim Forster at the same time that Des went back to David. He first turned out in a two and a half mile handicap hurdle at Worcester, and coming from a seemingly hopeless position at the final bend, won going away. That was the last hurdle race he ran in, as it was decided he should go chasing that year, the same season as Des, but a year younger.

Ragged Robin was a very game little horse, and though he

lacked the speed and charisma of his brother, he almost made up for it with sheer application. He first ran at Hereford; he did not jump particularly well and would have finished second but for Welsh Oak falling at the last. This was a mixed blessing. Ragged had now lost his novice status, and in spite of his sketchy jumping, all concerned were inclined to keep him going over fences rather than return him to hurdles, as the following season he would be in handicap company.

It is a near statistical certainty that novices will fall sooner or later, and it usually teaches them to respect their fences. So it was not too alarming when Ragged fell at the drop fence at Sandown. Next time out, at Cheltenham, he fell again; he simply did not get high enough. Tim Forster decided he was asking too much of him and took him to Worcester, a much easier course with softer fences, and an established course for novices.

I was in Ireland at the time and called Johnnie after the race to see how it had gone. He was crying. Ragged had been in the middle of the field when he had jumped a fence too low, and had broken his shoulder on landing. Johnnie, Jimmy and Midge had been halfway across the course going to the stricken horse when they heard the crack of the vet's gun. It was a desperately sad ending for such a brave little horse, and a heartbreaking closing chapter to an unhappy episode. There are so many hopes and fears tied up with owning a horse: some you can articulate, some you can't, but you feel them all when the horse is killed. Johnnie, though he loves racing, and still came to see Des, was no longer interested in owning a horse.

There is a strange rider to this tale, and though it has nothing to do with Desert Orchid, I might as well tell it. When Ragged ran at Worcester first time out I was still in my fence-jumping phase, and I fancied the Worcester fences. I jumped a couple as I walked my dogs after racing, when I came to the first fence in the back straight, the fence opposite the stand. I cleared it easily, but for some reason fell on landing – well not exactly fell, more like twisted on landing. It was the first time I had ever 'fallen', so I decided to try it again. Exactly the same thing happened: I fell on landing, not heavily, but I fell all the same. I decided to forget it before I hurt myself, but I didn't forget the incident. It was at that very fence that Ragged Robin was killed.

13

Going Home

T HREE WEEKS AFTER THE Contiboard Chase at Ascot I drove the horsebox down to Whitsbury to take Des home for the summer. David had sent him over to Peter Coates's farm to rough him off, but in the intervening period the weight had dropped off. David apologised profusely.

On getting him home, Jimmy immediately called George Armatage. George is a difficult character to get hold of, and it was a week before he turned up. Though Jimmy had been feeding him, Des still hadn't put on much weight.

George took one look at Des and disappeared into his box and there was the usual banging and slapping. After a few moments George appeared, saying he was all right now. It hadn't been the same problem, the 'trapped nerve', but it had been another problem in his back. Jimmy asked him how long he thought it had been out.

'Oh, three or four months,' he said. 'Must be off now,' he said, and disappeared. A bill for thirty pounds arrived about three months later. Almost immediately, Des seemed relaxed – and though Jimmy cut down his food, within three days he had started to put on weight.

After talking to Jimmy, I gave George a call; I still had not met him. I had to try several times before I found him in, but when I did, I thanked him, and explained that we would like him, if possible, to go down to David's next season if I could square it with David.

George saw no reason why not, as he regularly went to Michael Stoute's and Barry Hills's yards, among others. I didn't know this, but without going into detail, I said David had expressed reservations about letting him into Dessie's box unattended, and didn't necessarily believe in his treatment. George's response to this questioning of his skill was blunt. I shelved plans to take him down. I, or rather Desert Orchid, was plainly sandwiched between two forthright people.

About this time I sent a mare to be trained by Mary Reveley in Yorkshire. We talked about this and that (mainly about Desert Orchid, as she was a fan), and the subject of backs came up. Not only had she heard of George Armatage, but he regularly did all her horses. In fact, she said that she 'could not train without him'. She then told me a lot about George, whom she always called Mister Armatage. Apart from Michael Stoute and Barry Hills, he went to Jimmy FitzGerald and others, and was also regularly flown over to France and Ireland. He had fixed Gold Cup winners and Derby winners, and one of his most famous patients had been Shergar. I asked her whether it bothered her that he wouldn't let anyone see what he was doing, and Mary laughed and said you just had to get used to the idea, he wouldn't let anyone see what he was doing, not even his wife! It had bothered Mary's son and co-trainer Keith to begin with, but after he had seen the results he'd come round to him. She'd had horses sent to her who'd scarcely beaten another horse in their lives, but after George had fixed them they'd gone and won three in a row.

Mary is a brilliant trainer in her own right, and a great fan of David's, and that made her recommendation of George Armatage all the more valid. I decided to call David again towards the end of the summer. He was his usual affable self, but stuck fast on the issue that he wouldn't let anyone go into Dessie's box without either him or a member of his staff being present. He didn't know George – he could be giving the horses anything – and it was his licence on the line. He had a perfectly good point, and he was the horse's trainer, so that was that.

So it was back to Des's normal routine. Jimmy and his vet worked away at his corns for six weeks, then he spent two months out in the field at Flintham before returning to Ab Kettleby. Jimmy and Ruth did most of the roadwork, but it was tinged with sadness as they could not help missing Ragged, who had become as much of a part of the scene as Des. Midge had been racing all her life, and had seen several favourites killed over the years, but that didn't compare with the hollow feeling she got when she saw Ragged's box, or picked up the headcollar with his name on it.

Towards the end of the summer Des began to show all the right signs, prancing round the roads, baulking at the farm traffic. With his fat turning to muscle again, we all hoped we were sending him back to David in good shape for another season.

PART THREE

Hitting the Front

14

Dreams of Glory

I CALLED DAVID A COUPLE OF WEEKS later and he reminded me that he still wanted to run Des in the King George. I said it was okay with me, but I don't think Timeform would have been too happy about the idea.

They wrote: 'While he was clearly one of the best of his generation, he was clearly not the best.' The handicapper agreed. He considered Des had been twenty-three pounds better over hurdles than he was over fences. So for his first race, the Holsten Export Lager Handicap Chase over two and a half miles at Sandown, he was set to receive no less than twenty-five pounds from Very Promising, who had gone on to be as good over fences as he was over hurdles.

Des was also carrying more condition than usual, which made it ironic that he won the Best Turned Out Award for the first time. I always felt sorry for Jackie, because greys usually need more cleaning up, but never gleam as much as chestnuts or bays. Des was probably fatter than last year because David hadn't schooled him as much, as he now became so overheated at the mere sight of a schooling fence that David only dared give him one school a few days before he raced so he could get his eye in.

Des looked wonderful and cantered down to the start with his ears pricked as if they were spring-loaded. In retrospect, on ten stone three, by far the lightest weight he ever carried, he was a stone cold certainty that day, receiving twenty-five pounds from Very Promising, and only giving three pounds to the Queen Mother's chaser, The Argonaut.

He jumped round in the lead, and Very Promising and The Argonaut closed right up to him coming to the last. Touching down a length in front, Colin pressed the button and he shot up the hill, winning by four lengths and three from The Argonaut and Very Promising. It was an encouraging contrast to his performances against Berlin and Clara Mountain the previous season, and the press took note.

'Des delights the faithful' ran Rolfe Johnson's story in the *Daily Express*: this was the first abbreviation of Desert Orchid that appeared in print. For a brief period, Rolfe had been David's secretary when Chris Hill went to work for Chris Bell, David's former assistant, in Malton. Now Chris was back at Whitsbury and Rolfe wrote: 'David Elsworth has always insisted "Des" would stay three miles. Here, over two and a half miles, finishing with his ears pricked having beaten off the heroic challenges of Very Promising and The Argonaut, the flying grey looked likely to vindicate his trainer's words.'

Rolfe's was a lone voice: no one else thought Des had a hope of staying three miles. Hacks started to shake their heads sadly about David, poor chap, plainly whacko, oh dear, and it became a chorus. He may be a good horse, but he *won't stay three miles*. David stuck to his guns. His conviction was supported by a scepticism about the traditional theories that dominated thinking about distances. He thought there was a great deal of rubbish written on the subject, and did as much as anyone else to debunk these theories effectively.

Curiously, one of the things that now was being deemed to count *against* Des in the stamina stakes was that he was a brilliant two mile hurdler and chaser, which suggested that he could not be as good over three miles. It was also felt that he had failed to stay two and a half miles on three occasions the previous season, that there was speed on both sides of his pedigree, and being a front runner wouldn't help.

On the other hand, he had stayed twenty-one furlongs as a four-year-old, so he should be able to stay twenty-four furlongs over fences three years later; he was good over two miles over fences, apparently not quite as good as he was over hurdles, but he might be as good when put over three miles; he had only failed to 'stay' the previous season because he might have had something wrong with him; there was some stamina in his pedigree; and being a front runner had nothing to do with it, he had shown that he was capable of settling in front – in fact that was the only place he could settle! Of course everyone had forgotten the first reason, overlooked the second, had never known about the third, weren't interested in the fourth, and the fifth hadn't occurred to them. This left them with David's assurances, delivered with his usual one-liners and wry, self-deprecating confidence. As he put it to me, he thought it was a lot of fuss about nothing. He knew Des stayed two and a half miles, and looking at Kempton, it was only 'two throws of a cricket ball' further.

Des was already a *cause célèbre* among jump fans, so this debate took on added prominence. You couldn't ignore him in a race. He was becoming whiter and whiter and, in the way front runners tend to, always pricked his ears, which made him photograph well. His big black eyes set against a white face on a big head also gave him more expression than bays or chestnuts. He was compact, bouncy, jaunty and well put together. Most of all there was his exuberance and enthusiasm for racing and above all for jumping – he attacked his fences and clearly regarded the whole thing as the most enormous lark. Then again, besides being a flashy bugger, he loved an argument. David often said that when he woke up on a dark winter's morning, this was the kind of horse that he wanted to get out of bed to train.

His next race, the valuable H & T Walker Goddess Chase at Ascot, was anticipated with interest. It was a handicap over two and a half miles confined to the previous season's novices, and Des, with eleven stone six (seven of those were a penalty for winning at Sandown) was not even top weight. That honour went to Charcoal Wally. It was widely felt that he would have to win, and win well, to have a chance in the King George. David was confident he was in good form.

I watched the race with David. David, like most trainers, prefers to watch races on TV; I prefer to watch it 'live'. On this occasion we compromised. From the owners' enclosure you can see the TV in the steward's box.

The two and a half mile start is in Swinley Bottom, the furthest point of the course from the stand, and David clearly had the advantage watching on TV. But the first surprise was that Des wasn't leading. Brendan Powell on Charcoal Wally had taken Des on, and led all the way past the stands, and was still leading as they headed down the back straight. It was clear, also, that Des seemed hurried at his fences and wasn't jumping with his usual fluency. Charcoal Wally was still in the lead as they went past Swinley Bottom, and Des then clouted the eleventh and lost ground. He hadn't made up the ground at the twelfth, but David murmured, 'He'll stay on, watch him, he'll stay on.'

Charcoal Wally was going backwards now, but it wasn't Des who was taking over. It was Berlin, ridden by Dermot Browne. Colin shook Des up, and gave him a couple of slaps, and he did start to run on. David was more animated: 'Watch him, he'll stay on!' Des was at Berlin's heels now and slugging away, but his ears were back and he looked to be in trouble. The crowd roared as they approached the second last, but Des was a length and a half down. Two other horses, Church Warden and Amber Rambler, were looming up outside him. Another roar went up as all four horses were in the air together over the fence, but Berlin slipped past him and Church Warden had also gone past. Berlin cleared the last with Church Warden right behind him and sprinted for the line, but Church Warden shot past to win by a length and a half. Dessie came off the worst with Amber Rambler in a duel for third place, four lengths behind. Fourth.

David looked at me, for the first time there was some doubt in his eyes, 'Well, he did stay on, didn't he?' It was a question, not a statement.

'Yes,' I agreed. 'He did.' There were lots of things to like about the performance: at the weights he'd come out top horse, he'd jumped satisfactorily, he had stayed on, but then again, it is possible to confuse positive thinking with muddled thinking. Because one thing seemed certain – it was not a King George-winning performance.

David congratulated the winner, while pointing out we were giving him thirteen pounds, and refused to dismiss the 'possibility' of running him in the King George. But he was disappointed. We all were. We adjourned to the bar for a postmortem, and though he had been beaten by good horses, we wondered whether Des was really good enough to run in the King George; I suppose we dreaded the answer that he wasn't. David had been so confident beforehand that Des was in great shape, and we looked for excuses, but didn't really come up with any. I made a remark which David has never let me forget: 'We usually win the warm-ups, but never seem to win the big ones.' This was true at the time.

David said he was sure he'd find the answer and a week later called me. 'I think the H & T just came too soon after the Sandown race, which must have taken more out of him than I thought. I'm going to give him a month off.'

The two mile *versus* three mile bandwagon rolled on to the Frogmore Handicap Chase at Ascot, over two miles, and Timeform neatly broke the tension by cheerfully putting its foot in it. First, with the comment 'Sure to win more races in all but the very best company' (swiftly removed subsequently), and second, their ratings in which they gleefully estimated that Des would come last of the eight runners in this particular contest.

It was a glorious December day, just ten days before the King George, and Des looked very well. He was carrying eleven stone five, and to begin with it was the same old team, Charcoal Wally and Desert Orchid slugging it out up front and swopping the lead every two fences. Brendan Powell, riding Charcoal Wally, always figured this was the way to beat the grey horse.

Then turning into the straight, Annette's Delight and Little Bay shot past the pair of them, and it looked like the H & T Walker all over again. Colin got to work, though, and Des had caught them again by the second last. They were in the air together; then Des simply found another gear and shot forward. By the last he was ten lengths clear, and by the line he was easing down, as the others fought out a frantic dogfight for second place twelve lengths behind him. With a twinkle in his eye David told the press that if they thought he was good at two miles, wait till they saw him at three, and declared him a definite runner for the King George.

There was a complication, however. Combs Ditch, so narrowly beaten in the two previous years, had recovered from a leg wound sustained in the summer, and was trying to make it third time lucky. Colin Brown rode both horses.

Colin remained as cheerful about the whole thing as you could expect, but he was suffering. It was an impossible decision to make: his head told him one thing, and his heart another. 'Brown's dilemma' and 'Now Brown faces big problem' ran the racing headlines. He was forced to desert either the horse on whom he had come a close second in the last two years and whom he knew stayed and handled soft ground, or the horse which he already admitted was the best he'd ever ridden, but who everyone kept telling him was a specialist two-miler and could only handle fast ground. David sympathised, and said he could delay the decision until an hour before the race, but left it up to him. In the meantime, he needed a jockey to ride whichever horse Colin rejected. David had been impressed by a jockey's riding of a horse of his at Newton Abbot the previous March. The horse was called Nord Hinder. The jockey was called Simon Sherwood.

Simon Sherwood, commonly known as Sharkey, had not exactly come up the hard way, though I doubt there is an easy way to come up. (Simon spat blood when Brough Scott said on TV that Simon was a rich man in his own right and 'didn't need to ride'.) He had ridden since the age dot on his family's farm in Essex, and progressed through Pony Club to hunting and after a successful point-to-point career, he had originally burst on to the jumping scene, if that is the right word, with a winning ride on Lakin at Fakenham in 1982, as Mr S. E. H. Sherwood. He was working as an assistant to Harry Thomson Jones, and later worked for Gavin Pritchard-Gordon. After two successive seasons as champion amateur, Mr Simon Edward Harlakanden Sherwood in due course became plain S. Sherwood and turned professional. He was an immediate hit. He had a balanced, quiet, almost lazy style, but he was also tough. Perhaps most impressive of all was that capacity to think under pressure which marks all great sportsmen. That was one thing in his favour. The other was that he was available.

To be honest, I always thought Colin would reject Des and take the ride on Combs Ditch, because I don't think he really had much choice. Any other jockey would have done the same. If Combs Ditch won without Colin on his back, then Colin would have looked like an idiot, whereas if Des won there would be another day because we made it clear to Colin that if he did abandon Des, the ride would still be his next time.

Simon, a great friend of Colin's, would also have chosen Combs Ditch if given the choice. Combs Ditch was a proven stayer and encouraging reports on his fitness had been drifting out of Whitsbury. Desert Orchid, on the other hand, he considered a much less certain conveyance. He had this image of a hairy thing that used to tear off out of control, and was slightly anxious that he would fall in a heap after two and a half miles.

It wasn't just a question of the distance, either. Timeform had now raised Des to his old hurdle rating of 165, but he still had nearly a stone to find with Combs Ditch. David never put any pressure on Colin, although he did confide to me that he'd slightly prefer him to ride Combs Ditch, as 'Comber' was a tricky ride, with all sorts of quirks, and Colin knew him very well, while Des was more straightforward.

'Anyone could ride him,' he said. 'I could.' Though he did add that he thought Simon would suit him.

If Colin had been reading the hacks' pre-race summaries, he'd certainly be in no doubt who to ride. Various comments included: 'David Elsworth and Colin Brown believe he will stay three miles but I doubt he will do so at this level and it will be surprising if Brown prefers to ride him'; 'I will only believe Desert Orchid can win a top three mile chase when I see it'; 'Although the popular front-running grey came from behind to beat Charcoal Wally at Ascot (2 m), I shall be amazed if he has the necessary stamina here'; and 'though his trainer is confident about him staying this trip, it would seem unlikely bearing in mind his previous racecourse evidence and his free running style. Any give in the ground would further lessen his chance.'

On Christmas Eve, it started raining, as usual, and continued on Christmas Day, turning the good ground into soggy, stamina-sapping mud, exactly the ground Des was supposed not to like.

But the hack who wrote that 'the trainer was confident' had never written a truer word, as down at Whitsbury D. Elsworth and R. Boult were busy producing a videotape that surely would have become a classic had it not been removed by burglars. Alan Argeband, an old friend of David's, turned up on Christmas Day with his Christmas present, a video camera, and proceeded to film David and Rodney.

Fade in, David, microphone in one hand, large whisky and soda in the other. There is the persistent sound of electronic ping-pong from next door and the clattering of plates in the kitchen.

David: 'So, here we have young Rodney Boult [several standard insults, etc]. Now, Mr Boult, what do you think will win the King George tomorrow?'

Rodney laughs. 'Well I know what *you* think!'

David: 'No, well all right, do you think Desert Orchid will win it?'

Rodney squirms and screws up his face and looks in some pain. 'I just can't see it, I'm sorry, I'd like him to win it, I'd *love* him to win it, but I just can't see it. He's just too good over two miles. I'm sorry.'

David is nodding solemnly at all this. Rodney explodes with laughter. David: 'Now ask me.'

Rodney: 'Well we all *know* what you think!'

David: 'Yes but ask me. Go on.'

Rodney laughs again. 'All right, David, who do you . . . What am I supposed to be asking you?'

David: 'Come on Rodney, get it together.'

Rodney: 'Well, what is it?'

David: 'Who's going to win the King George?'

Rodney: 'All right, who's going to win the King George tomorrow, David – sorry, Mr Elsworth?'

David turns with a big grin to the camera: 'Desert Orchid. Desert Orchid will win the *King* George VI Chase tomorrow. A certainty.'

Hold on David's grinning face, while Rodney laughs and the sound of electronic ping-pong continues offscreen, followed by a crash from the kitchen.

We were conducting a semi-serious knees-up of our own, but not necessarily for the same reason. Jimmy was cheerfully convinced he had no chance at all and was looking forward to a race for a change. Midge was thrilled just to have a *runner* in the King George.

Simon Bullimore at home in Essex with his family was cheerful because he almost always is cheerful. My brothers were cheerful because it was the perfect way out of Christmas. And I was cheerful because I'd finished a script two days before.

I hadn't talked to David for a week, so I rang him up on Boxing Day morning. He said he'd never had Des so well. He said he was dangerous.

'You really think he has a chance?'

'He'll win it, boy. Definitely.'

To understand the task that lay ahead of Des that day, you have to understand that the King George VI Chase is generally considered at least the second top staying chase of the season, and in some quarters the top chase. Statistically, the winner of the King George is more likely to be the top chaser at the end of the season than even the winner of the Gold Cup. The past winners read like a *Who's Who* of racing greats, and today's field included the twelve-year-old Wayward Lad, who had won the race an incredible three times, and who was one of the best horses never to have won a Gold Cup; Forgive 'N Forget, the 1985 Gold Cup winner, the top chaser in training and in deadly form; Combs Ditch, who had run a very close second two years before; and Bolands Cross, who was being hailed as the new star of jump racing. There were nine runners in all, the others being Beau Ranger, Cybrandian, Door Latch and Von Trappe. Desert Orchid was taking them all on at level weights. Despite David's confidence, it seemed an impossible task, and we set off cheerfully for Kempton Park.

15

King for a Day

As I walked on to the course I could already see cars getting stuck in the mud. It wasn't really wet; the high tide mark stopped around my ankles. I couldn't see Des liking it, but after last year I was saying nothing. Besides, there was a holiday mood in the air. All that energy locked up over Christmas was unleashed in a frenzy of competition. Here was adventure. It was also the first year Rank had sponsored the meeting and the course was littered with advertisements for Butlins, which served as a reminder that the British do not necessarily require a civilised climate in order to enjoy themselves outdoors.

I bumped into Colin, who told me he had chosen Combs Ditch, and I wished him luck. He wished us luck too, and meant it. My heart went out to him, he was probably under more pressure than any man there. His loyalties were completely divided and that's enough to take the fun out of anything. He never complained, but remained as cheerful and friendly as always.

Crowding round the pre-parade ring before the race, we considered the opposition. Given their reputations, it was a relief to see that they were, after all, only horses.

Des appeared jig-jogging with Jackie beside him, and she managed a tight smile. Then David appeared carrying the saddle and weightcloth. He saddled Combs Ditch first, while Des continued to jog around the rapidly emptying pre-parade ring. Combs Ditch was sent on his way into the paddock and David gestured Jackie into the box.

She walked Des in and spun him round. He remained peering out at the crowds, shivering in excitement, and David blew through his lips as he tacked up the grey. 'Bloody awful day,' he said, then with a big grin, 'but it's about to get better.' As he tightened the girths he told Jackie to hold tight, and when he reached for a couple more holes, Des exploded, laying his ears back, trying to take a chunk out of Jackie's shoulder, kicking the back of the box. 'Save it for later, Des,' he grunted, and as we walked behind Des into the paddock, David put his arm around my shoulder and said, 'I've never had him better, boy. Never.'

The Queen Mother was standing in the paddock wearing what looked like an orchid on her lapel. As we were a little late into the paddock, the jockeys were already waiting. Simon Sherwood was standing apparently absorbed in some detail on the numberboard, but when he saw us he grinned out of the side of his mouth. He tipped his cap.

'Ah . . . er.' David seemed to have temporarily forgotten his name.

'Simon,' Simon said.

'Simon,' said David, 'this is . . .', he turned to us. David trying to remember names is like most people trying to remember the names of the Kings and Queens of England in the right order. He frowned.

'These are the Burridges,' he ad-libbed brilliantly, 'and the Bullimores.' We all shook hands.

'Thanks for the ride,' Simon said.

'Now,' said David, putting his arm around Simon's shoulder, 'these buggers are going to let you go, they don't think he'll stay – but I'm telling you he will stay, and you've got to ride him as if he'll stay every yard.'

Simon nodded calmly. 'Colin said to try to give him a couple of breathers.'

'Never mind what Colin said, that bugger's chosen the wrong horse,' then he paused for a moment, and frowned, 'though as a matter of fact, yes, see if you can give him a couple of breathers round the bends.'

The bell sounded for the jockeys to mount, and to a chorus of good lucks, David and Simon walked off towards the grey horse, who by now was sweating freely.

David legged Simon up – it was the first time Simon had ever sat on the horse – and repeated, 'Ride him as if he'll stay, Simon. Remember.' He wagged his finger at him. 'Be lucky.' As Jackie

spun Des back on to the track round the paddock, David walked
off to talk to Colin Brown and the Torys, the owners of Combs
Ditch.

We walked out of the paddock with Jim and Anne Tory, all
wishing each other luck. It really is a unique experience standing
in the paddock before a big jumping race. There is no enmity at
all, or none that I have ever witnessed, just camaraderie. Perhaps it
is the mix of relief and anxiety which descends on everybody when
they realise that there is no longer anything they can do. I don't
know. All everybody wants is for all the horses and jockeys to
come back safely, and there is a feeling that you somehow increase
your own luck by wishing everybody else luck.

I detached myself from the Torys and walked up the ramp to
catch the end of the parade. I wanted to see the horses canter
down. Bolands Cross caught my eye, but Des was perfect – at least
he started out perfectly, but suddenly he realised he had a new
jockey on his back and he carted Simon for several hundred yards
before Simon managed to pull him up in front of the first fence.

I dug a couple of fifty pound notes out of my pocket and
headed for the bookies. Des was to start at 16–1, but all I could
see were fourteens. I headed for the boards, then suddenly
wondered what the hell I was doing. If Des won the race, if he
actually won it, I wouldn't care if I'd *backed* him. What I needed
was a consolation if he *didn't* win. I put one of the notes on
Bolands Cross at 5–1.

I walked back to the stand and joined Rachel and my brothers
John, Simon and Hugo on the lawn opposite the winning post.
Nobody said a thing as the last few moments before the off
crawled past. I stared at the ground and said a small prayer. The
starter called them together. 'And they're under starter's orders.'
Time had stopped. 'And they're off.' I raised my shaking
binoculars, and stared out across the drizzly, colourless acres of
Kempton Park.

Simon managed to lob the grey horse out on the rail, and
running to the first, immediately opened up a lead. Then at the
second, the first ditch, he put in an extraordinary leap and even
Simon, though his expression was masked by the usual complement
of goggles, helmet, etc, appeared a little surprised. Ears pricked,
Des set off confidently round the corner, with Simon balanced

perfectly over his withers, and coming to the third was about fifteen lengths clear.

Behind him, Colin, who now had no doubts where his loyalties lay, yelled at the other jockeys, 'Don't let him go!' Combs Ditch had to settle in behind the others, so for him to move up on Desert Orchid he had to get the other jockeys to move up first. They were in no hurry, though; there was a long way to go, and they all thought the grey horse would stop dead after two and a half miles in that ground.

Up front, Dessie was bowling along easily, looking at the crowd, thoroughly enjoying himself. He got a little close to the sixth, but was still ten lengths in the lead turning into the straight. At the second fence in the home straight, the second last next time round, he put in one of the best jumps he's ever done. He stood off outside the wings and sailed over. Watching from the stands, it occurred to me he was jumping better than he'd ever jumped – perhaps he actually preferred jumping at three mile pace. For the first time, there was a little twitch of expectation, and my binoculars started to shake a bit more.

Away round the bend they went with one full circuit to go. Des sailed over the water and the next plain fence, then put another big leap in at the ditch, and turned into the back straight. Seven more fences to go, Simon was ten lengths clear, and he hadn't moved. He was giving Des a breather, 'a good blow'.

Over two more fences and the first signs of consternation appeared in the chasing pack. Forgive 'N Forget was being shaken up by Mark Dwyer, and Door Latch and Bolands Cross were under pressure. Combs Ditch and Wayward Lad were further back, and didn't look like they'd make it. Over the fifteenth, five out, Des seemed relaxed, and Simon still hadn't moved. But now they were going into unknown territory, and you could sense the crowd focusing on Des, trying to see some sign that he was weakening. Behind him you could sense Mark Dwyer praying for some sign that he *was* weakening.

Now the sixteenth, the fourth last, the last before entering the home straight. Des got close to it, and hit it, hard. There was a gasp from the crowd, but Des kept running. Turning into the straight for the first time, Simon's brain was still working. Hold on, hold on, don't ask any questions yet.

Now the old grey ears were going back, and now behind him Forgive 'N Forget was closing, and there was a great roar from the crowd as the favourite started to close. Simon *still* had not moved, and glancing round, he saw the yellow colours of Forgive 'N Forget. Mark Dwyer was riding his horse hard and Simon registered that he didn't seem quite close enough. He set his horse at the third last, and landed running.

My brother Simon yelled beside me with that deep, strangled, hoarse quality born of great emotion, 'Come on Des!' Around him the crowd echoed back like a great chorus and the stand exploded in sound. Des had his ears flat back and Simon was going for him, not reaching for his stick, just riding him out hands and heels. Behind Forgive 'N Forget, the 'top chaser in the land', as Graham Goode was bellowing into his TV mike, was beaten. Simon kicked and got another fantastic leap at the second last. This horse wasn't tired, he was running on, he was the *only* horse running on.

The stand exploded with a great deafening roar. Somewhere in a box David was screaming himself hoarse. 'Come on, Des, go, go!' In front of his TV set at Whitsbury Rodney was bouncing up and down riding a finish on the sofa as he screamed at the TV set till he was blue in the face. Peter Maughan was screaming, Jackie was screaming, Des was coming up the last fence in the King George, a good fifteen lengths clear – and cleared it! The noise around doubled in volume and I realised it was me, shouting, screaming. Johnnie, Rachel, Simon, Hugo, all screamed at the tops of their voices, as Simon flattened into the horse's neck and scooted for the line, flashbulbs popping all around him. As he passed the line fifteen lengths clear of Bolands Cross, he gave the old grey horse a great slap on the chest.

Chaos. Sheer pandemonium. We went completely berserk, doing a kind of impromptu watusi which eventually ended in us cannoning into a woman in a fur coat and practically knocking her over. Her only comment to her companion as she inspected this evidently deranged rabble was the faintly disgusted 'I presume they backed the winner'.

We set off for the winner's enclosure like a loose scrum, the girls tucking in behind us. I was so wildly excited that I put on my glasses, and it was a good three minutes before I realised that one of the lenses had fallen out.

We swarmed up to Simon as Jackie led him into the winner's enclosure. 'Smashing,' Simon grinned. 'I'd take him out hunting any day. Didn't he jump!'

Des swanned into the winner's enclosure as if he'd been waiting for this moment all his life, and stood head up, ears pricked, surveying the crowd. This was more like it. He milked it for all it was worth.

Jimmy was in tears, patting his horse, patting Simon Sherwood; Midge was in tears; Simon Bullimore was grinning from ear to ear and spluttering 'Fantastic, fantastic, wasn't that the most fantastic thing you've ever seen!' My mum was laughing and patting Des; Pony was patting him; Johnnie was cradling his eleven-month-old daughter Amy. But I looked around, and there was someone missing – David.

I hadn't seen what had happened to Combs Ditch, but halfway up the straight, Colin had felt him get distressed, pulled him up, and jumped off. David had set off down the course to supervise the administration of oxygen to him; it was a recurring problem. So at the moment of his greatest training triumph, David was hundreds of yards away from the winner's enclosure.

Jane stood in for him as the prizes were handed out by the Queen Mother. Yes, that definitely was an orchid on her lapel. Jimmy received the trophy; not only had he bred the horse, but he had also suffered intensely on his path to glory, and would no doubt start to suffer again once the euphoria had died off. But those few moments were, without any doubt, the happiest moments of his life – of all our lives, really. That's what horse racing does. A race like that gives you such a pure, indivisible shot of exhilaration that it wipes everything else off the board. Simon Sherwood, already changed into his colours for the next race, got an enormous cheer when he received a magnum of champagne from the Queen Mum, and she looked pretty chuffed about the whole thing, too. And last but not least, Jackie Paris received her prize, a two week holiday for two from Rank. So while we went off to celebrate, she went off to wash the sweat and mud off her charge and put him in his stable. Eventually David arrived, his face creased into smiles, but tinged with anxiety about Combs Ditch.

'Well done, David,' I said. 'You're a genius.'

'Aw, shucks,' he said, grinning. Selected highlights of our party were invited up to have a drink with the Queen Mother, and for once David didn't turn down the glass of champagne, which he doesn't like, in favour of the whisky and soda, which he does.

Much later Colin joined us in the Rank box to which we had been invited by Angus Crichton-Miller, the Rank Public Relations Officer. They rather recklessly asked us all in and we immediately lowered the tone of the place. Colin could not have been more gracious or sporting on what must have been one of the most disappointing days of his life, and we'd all paid tribute to him in the winner's enclosure. David's tribute, as always, was the best. 'We all feel sorry for Colin. He has been a great influence on Desert Orchid's career and has been the main contributor to the horse's confidence.' Colin, for his part, didn't begrudge us our celebrations for a moment.

Later, as we were about to leave, Monica Dickinson, the trainer of the great Wayward Lad, congratulated me. I thanked her, and said we still had a good way to go before we got anywhere near his record. 'Perhaps you have,' she said, 'but I think you've got the right horse to have a go.'

We got back to the course and I picked up the trophy from Michael Webster and everybody everywhere was congratulating me. Somehow we got home, and the events of that night remain something of a blur. I do remember being with the rest of my family and doing a lot of shouting at a race we'd recorded on video.

At some stage I must have gone to bed, because I woke up the next day and there was an unfamiliar shape outlined on the table against the dull December sky. On closer examination, it turned out to be the King George VI cup. It hadn't been a dream.

16

Staying On

DAVID HAD COME SO CLOSE to winning the King George two years running that he must have thought his day would never come. So to pull off a win like that was good enough, but to be sure it was going to happen beforehand made it that much sweeter.

Everyone wandered around on a high for days, and the day after New Year's Day, Des's official eighth birthday, a stack of birthday cards arrived addressed to Desert Orchid, c/o David Elsworth, Whitsbury.

But the gods were about to exact their retribution. The day after the King George, Simon had a crashing fall at Kempton on Drive On Jimmy, and ended up in hospital with severe concussion and crushed vertebrae. Then Des coughed, so his next race, the Victor Chandler Chase, was off. Then a big freeze came, and everything was off, so the horses went to the beach. A racing yard never stays still for very long, especially one run by D. Elsworth, and with all thoughts of racing put on hold for the time being, at least there was a certain videotape to watch.

The weather relented just in time for the early February meeting at Sandown, and Des was entered for the Gainsborough, a three mile and 122 yards limited handicap. Colin was back on board but it was going to be tough: not only would Sandown's uphill finish test Des's stamina, not only would he be giving his Kempton rival, Bolands Cross, ten pounds, but also at Kempton they had let the grey horse go and they wouldn't make that mistake again. He had arrived in the big league, and the pressure was on. Colin had to show that the King George victory was no fluke.

All the other jockeys decided to wind Colin up by taking Des on on the way down to the start. Richard Rowe on Catch Phrase shot up Dessie's inside and Des took off, overshooting the inspection fence by several hundred yards. When Colin finally pulled him up and persuaded him to have a look at the first fence, Des looked puzzled. He had run eight times at Sandown, and never started here before.

John Oaksey, who'd been as thrilled as anyone when Des won the King George, talked on TV about the pressures facing Colin, and didn't envy him the downhill run to the first fence. But Colin rode the race to perfection.

Des looked dwarfed by the much bigger Charter Party, Stearsby, Catch Phrase and Bolands Cross. Colin was able to control things from the front. Again Des looked happier at three mile pace, and though there were none of the extravagant Kempton leaps, he was jumping well, occasionally putting in a short stride and popping one. Colin was riding him cleverly.

He disputed the lead with Bolands Cross over the railway fences but went on going into the bend and bounded up the finishing straight on the first circuit, looking full of himself. Going down the back straight for the second time, he was still going well within himself, as Stearsby and Bolands Cross started to hustle a little. Then Bolands Cross dropped his hind legs in the water, and Stearsby became the challenger as they went into the bend with Des a length up.

Both Bolands Cross and Stearsby closed again at the pond, but Colin had been waiting in front. Touching down at the pond, he shot clear, and good horses though they were, the race was over, they were struggling behind him. Charter Party fell at the second last, and to an incredible roar from the crowd, Des put in another great leap at the last, and strode on to win by ten lengths. At the weights this had been almost a better performance than the King George.

Jane Elsworth said she'd never heard anything like the reception he got afterwards. The racing scribes wanted to know why we weren't running Des in the Gold Cup – some of these people were the same people who'd said Des had no chance of staying three miles! The reason was simple: we had not entered him. The demands of the Gold Cup were quite different from the King George: Kempton rewarded brilliance and fast jumping, while

Cheltenham suited the slogger, it was a more punishing course, especially when wet, and none of us considered Des was ready for it. We'd all come to the conclusion he didn't like Cheltenham anyway.

With an eye on the weather, David entered him for the PZ Mower Chase at Thurles, but when the Wincanton meeting was given the go-ahead, David ran Des in the Jim Ford Challenge Cup Chase. The Jim Ford was a traditional trial for the Gold Cup, and it was also a conditions race, which meant that Des, who had shot up in the weights after the King George, would not have to give lumps of weight to his rivals.

There is a board in the bar at Wincanton which features the names of the winners of the two principal races run there every year, the Kingwell Hurdle and the Jim Ford. Neatly inscribed in the last entry of the Kingwell, three years earlier, was the name Desert Orchid. As the meeting had been lost to the weather for the last two years, Des was attempting a unique double: winning the Kingwell Hurdle over two miles and the Jim Ford Chase over three miles one furlong in 'successive' meetings. Three horses were trying to stop him: West Tip, the previous year's Grand National winner, Fire Drill and Mr Moonraker.

It was raining heavily, and Des didn't appear to think much of that. Was the King George winner expected to get wet?! As the crowd waited outside his saddling box with dripping cameras, there followed an undignified round of shoving and pulling, but finally Peter and Jackie managed to persuade the old fool to walk into the parade ring.

He made a complete cock-up at the fourteenth fence, but then ran on to win very impressively by twelve lengths and a distance from Mr Moonraker and Fire Drill. He seemed to be getting better and better, but from running on his 'home' track over three miles, Des next had to run on his 'away' course in the two mile Queen Mother Champion Chase at the Cheltenham Festival. He was due to clash with two brilliant Cheltenham specialists, Pearlyman and Very Promising. Pearlyman had come on stones since they'd last met at Ascot, and would never again start as the outsider in a three horse race. Though Des had beaten Very Promising easily at Sandown, he was receiving twenty-five pounds that day, and was now re-opposing at levels. More significantly, while some horses were pounds worse off at Cheltenham, the opposite was also true – horses who liked Cheltenham appeared pounds better there than anywhere else. It's difficult to say why exactly, but perhaps it's because the course is rather shapeless. If you asked a hundred people to draw a map of the course from memory, I don't suppose any two drawings would look the same. It's not like most courses, straights then bends; it's always turning or jinking or going up and down, as well as having the long uphill finish which most people associate with the place.

It takes a great horse to win there, but it often struck me as an odd place to hold a Championship, like running the Olympic Games over an obstacle course. It also doesn't tend to suit front runners. It's bad luck on horses who don't act at the place, but it was still a big thrill to be there. The atmosphere was electric, and Des had become a star – he was one of the big boys. His form figures looked good, too – 141111.

There were a couple of other things to feel good about too. We felt the problems that had stopped him going round left-hand bends were solved. He might be a few pounds worse off, but not several stone. The other thing was the horse himself. In contrast to the previous year's Arkle, he looked magnificent. He bounded down to the start, looking at everything. He was getting the hang of the place now – this was his fourth year here – and seemed to assume that everyone had come to see him; there were enough people who *had* come to see him to encourage him in this illusion.

Colin lined him on the outside, and he was bouncing off the ground. He jumped the first a little right, and drifted towards the stand; the same thing happened at the next. There's a long run to the next in the straight, and Des had drifted so far away from the other horses he appeared to be taking no notice of them. What he was taking notice of was the grandstand. With his ears pricked and his head turned to one side, he wasn't looking where he was going, but was becoming more and more interested in these people. He was responsive enough as Colin shook the reins at him, and three strides off it, Des saw it for the first time, his ears flicked back, and looking a bit surprised, he jumped it well enough and set off round the bend.

He jumped right again at the cross fence, but kept the lead and jumped beautifully all the way down the back. He negotiated the

17 King for a day. Jimmy receives the King George trophy from the Queen Mother. Note the orchid on her lapel.

18 Another successful day. Richard Burridge and Colin Brown after Des proves the King George was no fluke and wins the Gainsborough Chase at Sandown carrying top weight.

19 Bravest horse of the year. Des is out on his feet at the last after clawing back the lead from Gold Bearer to whom he was giving thirty-six pounds in the Peregrine Handicap Chase at Ascot in April 1987.

20 Fat city. Desert Orchid on his holidays at Flintham in the summer of 1987, not looking much like the champion of anything.

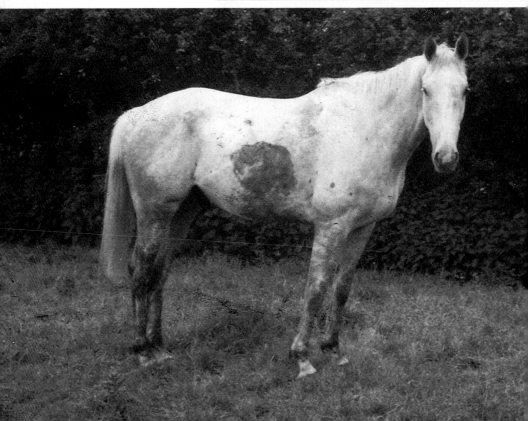

21 Colin Brown's last ride on Des. Janice leads them into the second spot after the Queen Mother Chase at Cheltenham, March 1988.

22 The Chivas Regal Chase, Liverpool. Desert Orchid wins for the first time left-handed with his new regular pilot, Simon Sherwood.

23 Moments before the Whitbread, April 1988. From left: Simon Sherwood, Midge Burridge (in black hat), David Elsworth, Dessie, Richard Burridge (in dark glasses), Janice Coyle, Peter Maughan, travelling head lad. David Elsworth is about to win his first Trainers' Championship.

24 An incandescent performance in an almost perfect race – fine weather, no
fallers and a great finish. Desert Orchid sails over his favourite fence, the ditch at
Sandown, and shrugging off his corns, goes on to win the 1988 Whitbread Gold
Cup over three miles and five furlongs.

25 Desert Orchid comes up to Yorkshire to do his roadwork for the first time. From left: Trevor Lowe on Des, Clare Pears on Peacework (Desert Orchid's oldest half-sister), Richard Burridge on Trailing Rose, and Carol Milburn on Made For Life.

26 Janice Coyle looking nervous before Des's first race of the season at Wincanton.

27 Desert Orchid soaks up the applause after one of the most exciting races ever run at Ascot, the Victor Chandler Chase 1989. Simon Sherwood is about to receive his kiss from Janice.

28   Before (left), during (below) and after (right) the 1989 Gold Cup. One of the most emotional horse races of all time.

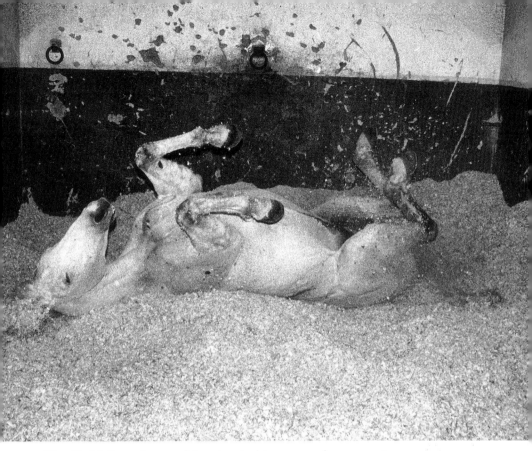

29 The Gold Cup victor celebrating in his own style.
30 Desert Orchid looks in better shape than the owner and trainer the next day.

31 The highs and lows of racing, and a contrast to the year before. Anxious faces after Des falls in the Martell Chase at Liverpool.

32 Three weeks after Liverpool he is back at Cheltenham to receive a second Bravest Horse of the Year Award and an award for the greatest contributor to National Hunt racing from Piper Heidsieck. For once Rodney Boult is allowed on the racecourse!

bends, too, but hung to the right. Coming down the hill he was still in the lead, though his ears were flicking back. Again drifting right at the second last, Very Promising and Pearlyman went by on the inside rail. Coming to the last he drifted right and jumped it two lengths behind Pearlyman and Very Promising and, still drifting right, he stayed on magnificently, though always three lengths behind Pearlyman and Very Promising, who fought out the finish of the Festival, with Pearlyman prevailing by a neck.

Des finished twenty-five lengths in front of the next horse, Townley Stone, and hadn't been far short of his best. Certainly if you totalled the lengths he'd lost by drifting and jumping right, they'd have considerably outnumbered the lengths he was beaten by, but then we knew that before we started. The main thing was that for the first time he really seemed to enjoy himself there, and I think that was the best race he ever ran at Cheltenham. It gave us some hope for the future, and though he was clearly several pounds worse there than anywhere else, he had now run thirty-seven times right-handed and only seven times left-handed, so he could just have been more used to going right-handed.

The fact that he had now run forty-four times in four and a half seasons was itself a reason for his enormous popularity. He turned up on the racecourse much more often than most horses, and this despite the usual interruptions – the cough, the weather, the ground. David and Rodney deserved the credit for this. Jimmy deserved some credit, too, for making sure he had a complete break in the summer.

I don't know anyone better at keeping a horse sweet than David, but the great thing about David was that he never lost his nerve, or let the horse's success get on top of him. He never ducked a race because of the opposition. He announced Des was going for a race, and he went for it, never mind who else was running. Some trainers might not have had the nerve or style to play with such a straight bat and would have protected the horse – not David. He had discovered that Des was a tough horse who thrived on racing, so that was what he did, he raced him. Naturally if you ran a horse as often as he ran Des he was bound to get beaten sometimes, but there was no disgrace in that. A horse is measured by his best performances, and while it would have been easy to duck the Queen Mother Chase because none of us thought we could beat Pearlyman, our horse was well, so we ran him, and he was beaten by two brilliant horses, and good luck to them.

We were surprised, however, by David's next suggestion. After the King George, David had been quoted as saying 'I just wish they would give him nine stone seven in the Whitbread. Then you would see how far he would stay, but as it is I suppose I'll have to be content with winning this again next year!' Now David was suggesting Des run in the Whitbread, not off nine stone seven pounds, but off twelve stone! But the Whitbread was six weeks away, and in the meantime David thought that the horse would need another race to keep him ticking over.

He sent him to Ascot three weeks later for the two and a half mile Peregrine Handicap Chase, in which he was set to carry no less than twelve stone four, and his six opponents were on ten stone, including, incredibly, Clara Mountain, who taking into account Luke Harvey's four-pound claim, was now thirty-six pounds better off with us than the year before, when he'd beaten Des at level weights.

It was a cold, windy day, and the three-quarters of an inch of rain which had fallen the day before had turned the ground stodgy. Giving weight away on that ground was that much harder. Luckily nobody had told Desert Orchid that the others were carrying two and a half stone less as he strutted around at the start.

It turned out to be Colin's favourite race. They set off at a sensible pace, but Des's jumping carried him a few lengths into the lead down the home straight. Then down the back he opened up and went ten lengths clear. He was jumping unspectacularly but accurately in the soft ground. Turning past Swinley Bottom, the field started to close, and Gold Bearer came out of the pack. Des was still going as well as anything, about two lengths clear of Gold Bearer, whose rider, Guy Landau, was claiming four – so Des was giving him thirty-six pounds.

Then Des made a mistake at the thirteenth, the last ditch. Perhaps he slipped on take off, but he screwed badly, pitched on landing, and Gold Bearer suddenly went four lengths clear. In that desperate ground, giving away thirty-six pounds, it looked like it was all over. But Colin jumped the next well and set off in pursuit. It still looked impossible, and with any other horse it probably would have been impossible, but rounding the bend into the home straight he'd fought back to within a length and a half. Then as they straightened out, the wind hit both horses, almost knocking them backwards.

Des struggled on, now both horses were desperately tired, but he was running on. How deep he had to reach inside himself that day it's hard to know, but it was raw courage that took him back to Gold Bearer, and now it was Guy Landau who was in trouble.

They were in the air together at the second last, and Des fought his way through the headwind into the lead. Colin felt his horse getting more and more tired, and as he came to the last a length and a half up, he could not see a stride on the horse. Des somehow climbed over it, probably the slowest jump he ever made, and out on his feet, struggled on to the line, and with the crowd screaming him home, won by a couple of lengths. You'd think he was completely exhausted, but right on the line he pricked his ears, and they stayed pricked till some of the following horses overtook him after the post, then they went back again. Desert Orchid might know where the finishing post was, but he hated to be overtaken, even after the race was over.

It was a magnificent, battling victory. Afterwards when I was watching the replay of the race, I noticed he'd been changing his legs. David admitted they had had some worries with his corns. I said it was odd he seemed to have had corns at this time of year for the last two seasons. David looked thoughtful; he just hoped the ground wouldn't be too fast for the Whitbread.

But the ground was firm. Immediately after the Peregrine Chase, Des was lame, then in the weeks leading up to the Whitbread, the corns erupted again. David said his blacksmith Paul Henderson had cut out the corns, and David's vet, Jan Puzio, said everything was okay. His shoes had been replaced and he hadn't missed a day's work.

There was no point worrying about it. The papers were full of it, with the headline in *The Sporting Life* 'Desert Orchid to join greats'. But Des did have a hell of a lot on his plate, quite apart from the problems underneath his plates. On twelve stone he had to give thirteen pounds to Door Latch, twenty-five pounds to the previous year's winner Plundering, twenty-six pounds to his old rival Ihaventalight, and thirty-two pounds to Lean Ar Aghaidh who had just come third in the Grand National. And, of course, the further the distance, the more the weight counted. But if the feet were all right, we thought he could do it.

It was a warm April day and Des looked edgy. Even more ominously, I left off my overcoat. Des was relaxed at the start and looked good on the run to the first fence. He jumped it well, but as he landed on his near fore, the foot he always landed on, and the foot with the corns, his ears flashed back and stayed back. Coming to the ditch, he untypically put in a short one and his ears flashed further back on landing. Outside him, Lean Ar Aghaidh was jumping brilliantly, but Des continued to run into the bottom of every fence. Jumping the first of the railway fences Des did something I'd never seen him do before, he deliberately landed on his right leg. It was getting painful to watch. There was something wrong.

Going into the bend, he was still running, and when he hit the softer ground approaching the pond he picked up the bit again and jumped the pond properly, but on landing his ears flashed back. On TV John Oaksey, who knew nothing about the corns, commented on his bad jumping and suggested his feet might be hurting.

Again he put in short ones going to the fences in the straight, then down the backside it got even worse, he was falling further and further back, and distinctly audible on TV you could hear Oaksey murmur, 'Pull him up.' Des was last, and struggling, his feet must have been really hurting, but he was so game he wasn't giving up. Colin popped him over the water and started to pick up a few stragglers, but at the next, the first railway fence, Des almost stopped, slipped and almost fell. To his great credit, Colin, who knew him so well, pulled him up.

Lean Ar Aghaidh went on to win in great style as Colin rode Des back across the track. He wasn't lame, and actually got a round of applause as he cantered past the stand, which I don't imagine happens too often to well-backed horses who have just pulled up. The crowd wasn't applauding him for that race, of course, but for the whole season.

David was embarrassed about the corn, and was given some stick in the press for not revealing it beforehand. You couldn't really blame him, because the advice he received was that everything was fine. When Des did come home, though, his feet were in a bad way. Richard Watson and John Allington went to work on them, and after weeks of treatment, they slowly began to heal, and eventually, by the middle of June, Des was well enough to go out to grass at Flintham.

It had been an unbelievable season. In October he'd just been a promising two mile novice chaser. Now, in May, he was about the top three mile chaser in the country, and possibly the world.

17

Spoiling for a Fight

THERE WERE MORE GARLANDS TO COME. After Ascot Geoff Lester told me that Des had won the Bravest Horse of the Year Award presented by Piper Heidsieck, and we were asked to Cheltenham to receive it. He was commended as 'the best, bravest and most popular chaser in training'. The day was also an eye-opener. The view through the glass walls of the room we had lunch in was staggering. I began to see why people made such a fuss about Cheltenham.

Two weeks after the Whitbread, I got a phone call from my father. He was in tears. 'Have you seen Ceefax?' he asked. 'Des has won the National Hunt Horse of the Year Award. I can't believe it.' The horse he had bred from a mare whom he had been advised to shoot, the scraggy grey he had been advised was 'useless', the muddy horse he could see at that moment grazing outside his window, had become a champion. Unbelievable.

Two months later we were invited to Goodwood House to receive the award. On my way down from my house in Yorkshire I dropped in at Flintham to congratulate the old boy. I leant over the gate and a white head paused in mid-munch, a pair of white ears pricked quizzically. I climbed over the gate and Des wandered amiably towards me, tripping over his feet, belly swinging from side to side, his measured amble interrupted only by laying his ears back and throwing his head at his companion, to remind her he still did not expect to be overtaken, even in a field.

As he nuzzled my jacket searching for mints, it was difficult to recognise that this sloppy old fool caked in mud could be the champion of anything. But there was still something there, something which you forgot when you hadn't seen him for a few weeks. Tail whisking to fend off the flies, occasionally raising his head to consider something in the distance, there was something exceptional about this horse, something magical, even in a field; it had to do with that eye that seemed to take everything in, to know what everything was and to demand to find out about anything he didn't. At the same time youthful and wise, he was a horse who always made you smile and sometimes laugh out loud when you spent time with him.

For instance, if you stopped giving him peppermints, he'd usually clamp his teeth on the sleeve of your jacket and stand looking at you, implicitly proposing the swop of your sleeve for another peppermint. It was easy to get out of this blackmail by simply sticking a finger behind his teeth and tickling his tongue. He'd let go of your sleeve, look at you in surprise for a moment, then promptly clamp his teeth back on it again. Now and again something in the distance would suddenly catch his attention, his ears would prick, and he would stand staring at it for minutes on end. Then just as suddenly he'd lose interest, consider you again, and clamp his teeth back on your sleeve. This mixture of inquisitive detachment and naked self-interest was somehow very endearing.

It seemed somewhat incongruous that the black-tie crowd gathered in the hallowed halls of Goodwood House were there to honour a muddy old horse no doubt at that moment snoring away while the owls hooted above him. The trophy was a wonderful bronze of a horse being ridden into the winner's enclosure, and below it was a plaque detailing the previous winners. The first name on the plaque was Arkle: that was followed by Mill House. Not bad. The plaque was sprinkled with the names of most of the great horses of the last twenty years, and I suppose it was also an achievement of sorts that apart from Red Rum, Desert Orchid was the only champion who'd won neither the Champion Hurdle nor the Cheltenham Gold Cup. However, that was the last I saw of the award because Jimmy promptly snaffled it – he claimed more people would see it at his house!

Later that summer the roadwork started to get difficult. The countryside was changing, the harvests were coming earlier, and small tractors and trailers were being replaced by giant grain wagons and combines that completely filled the narrow lanes around Ab Kettleby. Coming across one of these monsters Des baulked and backed off. Traffic stopped behind him and one comedian sounded his horn. Des let him have it with both back legs, fortunately missing the bumper or he would have broken a leg, but carving two neat grooves across the bonnet. Jimmy told the driver he was lucky to have his car kicked by Desert Orchid, as it probably added to its value. The driver unfortunately took a less sympathetic view.

As he got fitter, Des became increasingly cranky. One rainy day, P. J. Swarbrick, the girl who rode him these days, was looking for a work sheet, and used the Bravest Horse of the Year sheet. Des came to a puddle, and stopped, and P. J. was eventually forced to go round another way. If Piper Heidsieck had seen the Bravest Horse of the Year refusing to go through a two inch puddle, they might have had second thoughts.

I drove Des down to Kempton in early September and we swopped him into David's horsebox in the carpark. David inspected Des critically. All trainers close their eyes in silent prayer every time they send their stars off for a 'holiday' with their owners. No doubt they could all tell stories of horses returning as fat as elephants or as thin as bicycles or having been kicked or run over or tangled in wire. Thoroughbreds do appear to be the most accident-prone and feckless of species, and one you would suspect would be in danger of extinction if left to their own devices. Not only do they like to kick and bite each other, but they can also fall over, impale themselves on fence posts, tangle themselves in wire, get colic, and contract a string of injuries ranging from splints, cracked heels, mud fever, ringworm, pricked feet – you name it. Somewhere in the course of 300 years of breeding self-preservation seems to have been eliminated from the genetic pool, and even in a box they are capable of sustaining the most unlikely injuries. But if worrying about these things made any difference, then Des couldn't have been in better hands. Nobody could conceivably have worried more than Jimmy.

David agreed Des looked fine. We had a drink and he told me Jackie had quit. She'd gone to work in the butchers in Fordingbridge. I rang Jackie that night and said how sorry we all were; she was apologetic, but said she'd been thinking of leaving for some time and knew that she wouldn't be brave enough to quit after Des had come back, so she thought she'd better do it while he was away. I wished her luck but it was a sad day, as Jackie had looked after all our horses, Desert Orchid, Ragged Robin and Made For Life.

David had not told me whom he would be getting to look after the horse, in fact he was curiously evasive about it. A couple of weeks later, he told me he had given him to 'Janice'. I did know vaguely who Janice was – a small, pretty girl who always seemed to be laughing and bossing people about – and I sort of began to understand why David had been evasive, because though she has the most innocent of faces with big soulful eyes, and though she always looks about sixteen, and though she was only four foot eleven, or more accurately, as she insists, four foot eleven and a *half*, she had everyone in David's yard wrapped round her finger. I suspect they knew she would be getting Des, but David wanted to inject a little suspense just to show her who was boss around there.

In fact, Janice wasn't particularly enthusiastic about taking on Des as he had a reputation for being a cranky old bugger who liked to mess about and hold things up. Rodney was equally unenthusiastic, pleading with David not to give the grey horse to *her*, the female fireball, as 'She'll give me hell'.

Janice was David's longest serving 'lad'. She went straight from the racing school in Goodwood to David's yard at Lucknam Park, and when David moved to Whitsbury, she went with him. Her first ride, age seven, had been on a donkey on Blackpool beach, and she rapidly progressed to gymkhanas and flapping races on ponies. When she was nine, she used to rig up a saddle on the back of the sofa out of bailer twine, using the handle of her mum's eggwhisk as one stirrup and the potato masher for the other, and rode finishes on the back of the sofa while her family tried to watch TV. She claims she was always being 'sent shopping' at school because she was so 'disruptive', always chatting away and giggling. When she started going racing with a friend who was a permit holder, nobody seemed to object. Her mum even stopped bothering to write sick notes. Whether that had anything to do with it, or whether she was just naturally talented, she subsequently became an accomplished horsewoman, and was now one of David's best work riders. Of course, like all work riders, she dreamed of riding winners: David had given her a few chances, and she had won the Florence Nagle Girls Apprentice Handicap at Kempton and later won two more races.

Janice has become well known since, and has had reams of material written about her. Pretty, elfin, winsome – all of them accurate enough in their own way, but the word I'd use to describe her, if I had to use one word, is bossy!

She and Desert Orchid were very alike in this respect. Just as Des was acquiring this fluffy, cuddly, isn't-he-cute image, so Janice began to acquire an adorable, giggly, butter-wouldn't-melt-in-her-mouth sort of reputation. But just as Des in reality could be a crabby, bossy, dangerous beast who liked to have things exactly his own way, so Janice could be a tempestuous, furiously self-assertive ball of fire. They were well matched.

There was another good reason for her to take over Des. She lived in a bungalow only yards away from his box. So as Jackie went to work at David Pirie's butcher shop in Fordingbridge, Janice took over the role of 'doing' the grey horse.

By this time, David dismissed the business of training Desert Orchid, saying that the horse did three-quarters of the work and Rodney did the rest. In one sense he was right. He just needed to keep Des ticking over, whereas his skills were called into play training the young horses and the horses with problems. That was in private. In public he was increasingly identified as 'the trainer of Desert Orchid' and he wouldn't have been human if he and Chris Hill weren't occasionally forced to point out that he did train other horses, about a hundred of them. It was just ironic that the horse he was most famous for actually occupied less of his time than any of the others.

The Terry Biddlecombe Challenge Trophy Chase at Wincanton was an obvious choice for the first race of the season, a conditions race over two miles five furlongs. Everyone else apparently agreed, and only two rivals turned out: Britannicus, who would have received no less than sixty-three more pounds in a handicap, and Sugar Bee, the Maryland Hunt Cup winner whom Tim Forster was running to get a handicap mark for the Grand National.

We all enjoyed meeting at Wincanton again. Courtesy of his incredible winning sequence the season before, we had got into the superstitious habit of wearing the same clothes at every race. With Des's defeat in the Whitbread, we could abandon our superstitions and wear some new clothes for a change. But I kept my brown overcoat on, just in case . . .

Starting at 1–7, Des jumped spectacularly and won by a fence, prompting my brother Simon to suggest that David was going to be hauled in front of the stewards for 'schooling' Des in public. It was an easy introduction to the world of Desert Orchid for Janice, though several of the less expert paddock judges seemed to think Des had grown. Janice, three inches shorter than Jackie, made him look much bigger. Afterwards David hinted he was reconsidering his summer plan to put Des in the Gold Cup and said he preferred the Champion Chase. He didn't have much enthusiasm for either, though, adding that 'if there was a decent chase anywhere else around at Festival time I wouldn't let him near the place.'

For the next race United Racecourses came up with the goods. They were so keen to attract him that they initiated the Boxing Day Trial Chase, and the Kempton Clerk of the Course, Michael Webster, claimed the race conditions were written with 'David steering the pen'. It was a two and a half mile chase which attracted only two rivals, Bishops Yarn and Galway Blaze. Though they were both brilliant horses – Galway Blaze had won the Hennessey – they decided they couldn't beat the grey horse and so settled for a race for second. Des was well clear and easing down at the finish as Galway Blaze and Bishops Yarn fought a furious finish to the line about a hundred yards behind him.

David needed more serious opposition to stop the grey becoming complacent. 'Dessie needs a bloomin' race' ran a headline. We headed for the two mile Tingle Creek Handicap Chase at Sandown at the end of November. We thought this might attract Pearlyman, as we were itching to have a go at him on a right-handed track, but Pearlyman didn't make it.

'Desert Orchid for seventh Sandown win' was the general tone of things beforehand, but arriving at the course we heard an unpleasant rumour that Des could not beat Long Engagement at the weights. However the rumour had not reached the ring, and a deluge of money went on Des: £60,000 in big bets alone, with one brave fellow putting £22,000–£20,000 on him.

The omens continued to be unfavourable. Though Des had won his races easily so far, we were not altogether happy with him. As we watched from our normal place in the stand, our feelings were mixed. He uncharacteristically 'put down' at the downhill fence but then put on a great display of jumping at speed with Far Bridge. Then Far Bridge started getting away from his fences half a length quicker; whether this was because Des had two stone of dead weight on his back I don't know, but it meant that he had to catch up between each fence.

He pricked his ears coming to the pond fence, and the Sandown crowd roared as he went half a length up. You didn't have to look very hard, though, to see a horse closing on him – Long Engagement ridden by Richard Dunwoody. Dessie laid his ears back as Colin tried to steal two lengths off the bend, but Long Engagement would not be shaken off, and the horses bumped, jumped the second last upsides, and Long Engagement went three lengths up: Des couldn't peg him back.

David had got his 'competitive' race, and Janice got her first taste of the Desert Orchid factor when she led Des into second spot only to find she was getting more applause than the winner. Colin was emphatic that Dessie had 'blown up' and the race was just what he wanted.

The only problem had been that Des hadn't seemed to be so happy when taken on. It looked like it might be a problem on Boxing Day, as a horse called Beau Ranger was also running in the King George.

Two seasons before Beau Ranger had beaten Wayward Lad at Liverpool, but the following season he hadn't won a race and the owners took him away from Jackie Thorne and sent him to Martin Pipe. In the meantime, Beau Ranger had come down considerably in the handicap, and won the Mackeson off ten stone two. A few weeks later he beat Forgive 'N Forget by twenty lengths at Haydock, and though he was getting a lot of weight that day, he was clearly a contender. He was also a front runner, and his jockey, Peter Scudamore, had made it clear he wasn't going to make life easy for Desert Orchid. Des was now the target in every race, and Peter had decided that the only way to beat him was to take him on.

We discussed this problem several times before the King George. The evidence from the Tingle Creek did indeed suggest Des was not quite as effective when not allowed to dominate. Almost all his experience, both at home and on the track, was of being in front. Rodney had never known a horse who liked to lead so much. So on the presumption that he seemed to derive some benefit from being in front, we weren't about to surrender the advantage to Beau Ranger tamely. On the other hand, there was a danger both horses would cut each other's throats, and to complicate things further, there was another front runner in the race in the shape of Cybrandian.

At that stage the race looked like it would be between Desert Orchid and Beau Ranger. Forgive 'N Forget wasn't running, Bolands Cross didn't seem quite as good as he had been, and Castle Andrea, Castle Warden and Golden Friend looked outclassed. The only other runner, apart from Cybrandian, was Nupsala, a French chaser whom nobody seemed to know anything about. So if it was a two horse race, Desert Orchid might just as well establish his superiority over Beau Ranger early.

Colin seemed happy enough to wrestle with this problem, and had a better Christmas than the year before: at least he didn't have to worry about which horse he was going to ride. Then ten days before the race, Des pulled out lame, and David found a corn in his near fore. He had only ever had corns in April, and this was not good news: it not only threatened his appearance in the King George, but also his campaign for the rest of the season.

The corn was 'dug out' and the foot poulticed, but Des had missed some work. David told me he might have to pull out of the King George but swore me to secrecy. If it got out Des was on the sicklist it could only encourage more horses to take him on. However, with David continuing to sound gloomy in private, I thought it only fair to tell my fellow owners.

Then, shock horror, five days before the race, Forgive 'N Forget was announced as a runner because Jimmy FitzGerald had heard that Desert Orchid had corns. David dismissed this 'rumour', and wondered 'where it had come from', though through the kitchen window he could see the blacksmith working away. Privately, to me, he wondered where *exactly* this 'rumour' had come from. Jimmy took it upon himself to uncover the mole, and a day later he had the culprit. Midge had apparently mentioned the corn in her aerobics class in Melton Mowbray! Of course from there it was easy to understand how this nugget of information had wound its way to Jimmy FitzGerald's living room in Malton. Was it? I could hear Midge laughing in the background.

'Will you shut up, Midge,' exploded Jimmy, 'we've probably just lost the King George as a result of your bloody aerobics class!' Midge, by now, was helpless.

Two days later it was good news. It had been touch and go, but Des was now fit and raring to go, and we all converged on Kempton with Jimmy still muttering murderously about exercise fads.

Des did look a little on edge in the paddock beforehand, and Forgive 'N Forget looked magnificent. We didn't think much of Nupsala, though: a big, slope-backed horse with his front toes turned out, he looked rather awkward even at the walk. Forget him, we thought.

Des perked up going down to the start and the usual buzz settled over the crowd. Everyone knew the opening fences were likely to be entertaining.

That was an understatement. The tapes went up and the three front runners looked as if they'd been shot out of a catapult. They hurled themselves at the first fence and, still accelerating, went flat out for the ditch. All three stood way off it, and hurtled into the bend, as the Channel Four commentator Graham Goode gasped 'the pace is *extraordinarily* hot!' Des, Beau Ranger and Cybrandian had pulled fifteen lengths in almost as many seconds, and skidding round the bend, hurtled towards the third.

There was no margin for error, but it was Des who made the mistake. He clobbered it, went down half a length, and Beau Ranger had won the opening round. Racing archivist Michael Tanner clicked his stopwatch on the first half-mile, and recorded the extraordinary fact that three chasers, carrying eleven stone ten and jumping three fences, had actually covered the first half-mile of a three mile chase *faster* than the top three-year-olds, carrying nine stone, had covered the first half mile of that year's 2,000 Guineas!

Colin was later criticised for not dropping off this blistering pace, but that is what he now did, settling down half a length behind Beau Ranger, with Cybrandian a half length behind him. The first half mile had been run on one breath, and now the crowd decided it was safe to breathe again and look back to see what was happening behind. Forgive 'N Forget led the chasing pack about fifteen lengths behind and the field was stretched out behind him, with Castle Andrea almost a fence behind.

The leaders turned into the straight. Beau Ranger's ears were pricked. Desert Orchid's were not. The pace was slowing. Turning away from the stands Colin looked like he was giving Des a breather, but on TV John Francome said Beau Ranger seemed the happier of these two going at this pace. They jumped the water and set out on the second circuit. Cybrandian was falling off the pace now and behind him the field was getting strung out.

Jumping the ditch, the pace began to take its toll, and Bolands Cross took a crashing fall. At the seventh last, Cybrandian also took a heavy fall. But as they continued down the back, Des looked strong again: he was coming back. The crowd began to buzz. Jumping the sixth last he moved upsides Beau Ranger, and at the next jumped into the lead. There was an enormous roar from the crowd. Beau Ranger was struggling now, out on his legs, as the tougher grey horse opened up a lead approaching the fourth last. But two other horses were ranging up behind him, Forgive 'N Forget, and, incredibly, check your racecard, Nupsala.

Des was still fighting, running the rail like a greyhound, ears flat back, with Colin riding away for all he was worth. Nupsala and Forgive 'N Forget were on his shoulder now, and Nupsala was cantering. Des launched himself at the third last and a great leap just about kept him in front, but beside him Nupsala was pulling double. Again Des fought back, but touching down at the second last, André Pommier eased Nupsala forward, and went five lengths clear, while behind him Des was gone, out on his feet, exhausted by his battle with Beau Ranger. Forgive 'N Forget also passed him and set off after Nupsala. Just one more fence to go. Nupsala popped it, and strode away as Forgive 'N Forget, also exhausted and out on his feet, was driven into the fence by Mark Dwyer. He hardly rose and took a terrible fall, burying Mark, while behind him Des measured a stride and climbed over. Way ahead Nupsala sailed on and won the King George, while Des plodded doggedly on to take second, with Golden Friend third, and Beau Ranger fourth, twenty lengths ahead of Castle Warden, the only other finisher.

Beaten by the French. François Doumen, the trainer of Nupsala, couldn't have been more charming about the whole thing, but the implication was damning. Up till now, British and Irish steeple-chasing had been regarded as the best. French steeplechasing had been regarded well, if not as a joke, then certainly as idiosyncratic – ex-flat horses competing over event-type obstacles. Now we were faced with the distinct possibility they simply didn't bother with our races because the prize money was so low.

Afterwards I asked François Doumen whether he'd consider the Whitbread. It occurred to me that Nupsala might get top weight and let us in with eleven stone seven. François looked intrigued.

'The Whitbread? And when is that?'

'End of April,' I said. 'The ground is usually fast.'

'Good, good,' said François, looking interested. 'And what is the distance?'

'Three miles five,' I chirped up. 'Should suit your horse.'

'Yes, yes,' he said, looking even more interested. 'And how much is this Whitbread worth?'

'About £30,000,' I said, thinking he'd be impressed. Now a cloud crossed François's face. He frowned.

'£30,000? Oh no, no. We have a race worth £40,000 every week at Auteuil.' So much for English racing.

Poor old Colin got some of the blame for the 'cut-throat' tactics that were presumed to have exhausted Des in the first mile of the race. The King George really was a desperately unlucky race for him. Beaten twice on Combs Ditch, then choosing the wrong horse, and now this. I just thought it was bad luck. If he had let Beau Ranger go, and Beau Ranger had won, then he *would* have been vilified. In the circumstances he did fine. Once Beau Ranger had gone, Colin accepted it, gave Des a breather, then attacked down the back straight. And he had beaten Beau Ranger. He just hadn't won. As Rodney put it, 'Well, by the end, we beat Beau Ranger. But, in the end, Beau Ranger beat us.'

18

࿇

A Chapter Closes

WE THOUGHT DES WOULD NEED a holiday, but a week later he was trying to cart Rodney on the gallops. With 1988 two weeks old and Des now officially nine, he showed no signs of growing up as Janice chased him round his box, finally caught him and loaded him on a horsebox bound for Ascot. 'Tough horse,' said David.

The Victor Chandler Chase had first appeared on the racing calendar in 1987, but had been lost to the frost. It was an enterprising shot at filling a gaping hole – a valuable mid-season two mile handicap on a right-handed track. Two mile chases invariably produced wonderful spectacles, but there was little encouragement for them from the race planners, especially at this time of year. For some reason, probably due to the legacy of point-to-points, three mile chases were considered the real thing and two-milers also rans, so it was encouraging for independent bookmaker Victor Chandler to be rewarded with a great turnout for his race. Pearlyman was top rated at twelve stone, with Des on eleven stone eleven; Long Engagement, having shot up the handicap, was now on ten stone nine, with Panto Prince on ten stone five, and Townley Stone and Clay Hill on ten stone. Pearlyman had come right back to his best over Christmas, winning the Castleford Chase at Wetherby by five lengths from Little Bay, but the horse we feared most was Panto Prince, a big, black horse whose ungainly action had not prevented him from becoming an electrifying two-miler. Giving him twenty pounds could be tricky, as could giving twenty-five pounds to Townley Stone.

It was a murky day as we turned off the M4 towards Windsor, but crossing the Thames, the mist seemed to lift and the sun burst

131

through. Halfway into Windsor Great Park, a thick fog descended like a blanket and visibility was down to fifteen yards. So much for one of the great jumping spectacles of the season. You couldn't see a thing.

Racing was put back half an hour, then another half an hour. Everybody with video recorders groaned, knowing they would be returning to ping-pong highlights, or something. The fog had not lifted, but the stewards decided to rescramble the card and put racing back another half an hour. Miraculously, the fog did start to lift, the runners for the first race went down to the start, and the runners for the Victor Chandler appeared in the pre-parade ring. Des looked magnificent, looming out of the fog. Then the fog descended again so brutally that even the black Panto Prince disappeared six strides into the return leg of the pre-parade ring. Racing was abandoned.

For anybody who doubts the grip on the imagination that racing holds on the committed, they should have been there that day. People milled about, suffering the terrible unscratchable itch of an energy that had nowhere to go. The England/Ireland Rugby International was starting, and a betting frenzy broke out; every bet conceivable was thrown at TV screens. It was a funny day, but it was also a great shame. Our last chance of taking on Pearlyman on a right-handed course had gone. Two weeks later we were back to three miles again at Sandown in the Gainsborough Chase, now sponsored by Lee Cooper Jeans.

One of David's favourite sayings is that a trainer's worst enemy is the owner's best friend. Just as the trainer has established an 'understanding' with an owner, up pops some 'friend' with a theory that the owner's horse will not like Folkestone because the grass is too long, or that stable jockey Joe Schmo has ridden twenty-three consecutive losers at Newbury so he shouldn't be trusted at Haydock which is quite like Newbury, or that the horse in question doesn't like overtaking chestnuts on a left-hand bend so that should be taken into account in future. This overlooks the point that an owner doesn't have any friends! If he's got a bad horse, his friends have lost all their money backing it, and if he's got a good horse, he becomes so boring on the subject no one will go near him.

Before the Gainsborough I suddenly found I had some friends

telling me they thought it was crazy that David was also planning to run Rhyme 'N' Reason in the same race. It was true that the Gainsborough had been established all season as a target for Des as it was about the only valuable handicap that really suited him: it was over three miles at Sandown, and it was a limited handicap with a top weight of twelve stone and a bottom weight of ten stone seven. But David was now planning to run one of his own horses against Des, despite the fact that there was a good race for Rhyme 'N' Reason the following Wednesday at Ascot.

That year Rhyme 'N' Reason had been transferred to David's yard from David Murray-Smith's by owner Juliet Reed. Murray-Smith had won the Irish Grand National with the horse three seasons earlier but things had not gone well since, so Juliet decided to send him to David. Like Beau Ranger, his handicap had fallen, and David had won two good handicaps with him, notably the Mildmay Cazalet over three miles five at Sandown.

I had been down at Whitsbury six weeks earlier. David was musing 'Good horse, this. Haven't quite worked him out, but when I do, watch out. He'll beat you in the Gold Cup.' I wasn't particularly worried about Rhyme 'N' Reason at Sandown though, because I was reasonably hopeful we'd beat him, and the reason he was running him was straightforward enough: Juliet Reed was going to the West Indies that Sunday and wanted to see her horse run. David had tried but failed to change her mind. Perhaps in this instance it was a case of a trainer's worst enemy being the owner's travel agent . . .

So Des had to give twenty-one pounds to Rhyme 'N' Reason, Darkorjon, the Queen Mother's horse, Sunyboy, Foyle Fisherman and Allten Glazed, as well as fifteen pounds to Run and Skip and seventeen pounds to Charter Party. The family was out in force, congregating in the Eclipse Bar with Jimmy in agonies as usual, chain-smoking and cursing the weather. Eventually I bumped into David.

'Horse is well, Richard,' he said. 'But mind you, he'll have to be to beat my other horse.'

'Well you know what worries me about Rhyme 'N' Reason?' I said, smiling.

'What's that?' said David.

'You're his trainer,' I said. I realised it was a stupid thing to say as soon as I'd said it, but I had meant it as a compliment. David exploded.

'Are you saying I'm trying to get Des beaten?'

'No, of course not,' I protested, appalled.

'I love that horse, you understand, I love him, I'd never try to beat him.' He stormed off. I thought David was just in a funny mood, so when I next saw him – in the saddling box – I apologised and that was that. But he continued to be in a strange mood.

Des seemed quiet in the saddling box but looked good in the paddock, though a little wound up. He had attracted the usual bumper crowd and Brough Scott started with an apology: 'It gets boring to keep saying he's the most popular horse in training.'

With David and Peter busy with Rhyme 'N' Reason, I legged Colin up, and Colin was a little worried about the ground. It was heavy, and Des had never won on heavy going before. I squeezed out of the parade ring just in time to see Des cantering down to the start. He looked rather free.

Before the race John Oaksey and John Francome were discussing the Colin Brown and Peter Scudamore tussle in the King George, and as the Gainsborough started, it looked a bit like the same story all over again. Peter on Run and Skip went five lengths clear. Colin outjumped him at the second and pulled alongside. At the third Run and Skip outjumped Des, but cannoned into him, and the same thing happened at the fourth. Colin took a pull, came back inside, and Des went half a length up and his ears pricked for the first time.

Turning into the bend, Peter tried to tighten Des up against the rail – this was getting rough – but Des went on by a length. Des cruised past the stands, but after the bend Peter Scudamore kicked on and barged into Des again. Des clobbered the downhill fence. With Peter again squeezing him up on the rail – this *was* getting rough – Des's ears flattened against his head.

His ears pricked again as he headed over the water, and he was clear going into the turn, but now Charter Party loomed ominously up on his shoulder. Going to the pond Des was still leading but he seemed to be getting stuck in the soft ground. He outjumped Charter Party at the pond fence, but Charter Party came back, and they jumped the second last together. Colin asked for a big one at the last, almost overjumped and lost momentum. Charter Party sped away and halfway up the run in Colin accepted defeat, only to be overtaken by Rhyme 'N' Reason right on the line and beaten a neck into third.

Des was led, for the first time in his life, into third place at Sandown. Although he'd been beaten, it had been a good performance. He'd failed by eight lengths and a neck to give the future Gold Cup winner, Charter Party, seventeen pounds and the future Grand National winner, Rhyme 'N' Reason, twenty-one pounds.

David still seemed to be in a funny mood. Eventually I took Jane to one side and asked her what was wrong. She gave me a tight, harassed look. 'Read the papers tomorrow,' she said.

The Cavvies Clown story broke the next day, and cast a cloud over David's whole season. Cavvies Clown had been tested positive for steroids in three races, and David was being investigated by the Jockey Club. Cavvies Clown had been given a course of steroids to help him earlier in the season. After waiting for the prescribed period to pass before it was officially safe to race again, David sent him to Ascot where he won, but was tested positive for steroids. Cavvies Clown won again and was tested again but proved negative, and then mysteriously was tested positive in his two subsequent races. Somehow the steroids had hung around in the horse's system for much longer than they should have, and David was in trouble. The Jockey Club, notoriously keen to impress everyone with their rectitude, took a dim view of this, and David didn't help his cause by losing his temper with the Jockey Club security man.

As the inquiry was delayed again and again, the rumour became stronger that he might lose his licence, which would mean the dismantling of everything he had worked for over the years, and while few of David's owners initially were aware how serious this was, we all considered the affair blown up out of all proportion. David was certainly not a 'needle man' – rather the opposite, he only checked horses' blood if he had to – and even took exception to scoping horses, because he did not like jamming tubes down their throats.

So while this should have been a wonderful time for David – he was in the running for the trainers' championship – it took the fun out of everything. Months later, Cavvies Clown was disqualified from all three races, and David was fined £17,500 – a record fine and itself pretty vindictive.

But life went on, and David again entered Des in the Jim Ford at Wincanton. The race traditionally attracted a small, select field, and this year was a lulu. Besides Des, and the previous year's Sun Alliance winner, Kildimo (he looked a future Gold Cup horse at the time), the third runner was Burrough Hill Lad, making a comeback after two years off the track with a leg injury. Burrough Hill Lad was the outstanding chaser of the first part of the Eighties. He had won three Gainsborough Chases, a Gold Cup and a King George and, before his enforced retirement, his main problem was getting a race, as no one would take him on. A big, black, old-fashioned type, he was Jenny Pitman's pride and joy. His victory in the 1984 Hennessey was the handicap performance of the Eighties, and had prompted the handicapper, Christopher Mordaunt, to give him his highest rating since Arkle and Flyingbolt. Jenny was confident he was fit enough to do himself justice and, for once, Des took second place in the celebrity stakes.

David was anxious for Des to have an easy race, and Colin set off at a respectable pace with Kildimo and Burrough Hill Lad settling in a few lengths behind. As Des galloped over the island fences, he looked like his tail was on fire as the low winter sun shone through the fine grey hairs. Down the back for the second time, Colin stepped up the pace. Going over the ditch for the last time, Kildimo was still going easily and Burrough Hill Lad moved up to within half a length. An uncomfortable, but familiar, trickle of apprehension ran down the back of my neck. Into the straight, and all three horses started to wind up together. They were in the air together at the third last and still accelerating. Burrough Hill Lad hit the second last and his chance was gone, but Kildimo was still running. They took off and landed together, Graham Bradley summoned unthought-of speed out of his horse, and on the run in the staying chaser out-sprinted the two-miler and won by a length and a half.

A three horse race is inevitably a tactical affair, and Colin blamed himself, saying maybe he should have stretched the others more. But he had been trying to give Des an easy race, and who would have backed Kildimo to beat Desert Orchid at level weights in a sprint over three fences? One person who did not blame Colin was Rodney Boult, though his presence on the track suddenly explained the defeat! This was the fourth time he had been to see Des, and

Des had never won. We decided Rodney was a jinx, and warned him off. David was a little disappointed, but thought it was possible Des hadn't quite come to himself yet.

Now Cheltenham was approaching, and this year Des had been entered in both the Queen Mother Champion Chase and the Gold Cup. David was not particularly confident about either; he thought both Cavvies Clown and Rhyme 'N' Reason could beat Des in the Gold Cup, and he didn't think the grey horse could beat Pearlyman in the two-miler. So we pretty much wrote off Cheltenham and looked beyond it. If he ran in the two-miler, he might have a couple more races left in him. If he ran in the Gold Cup, a much tougher race, that might be the end of his season. Both suppositions depended on the ground, so we decided if it was heavy, he'd go for the two-miler, and if it was fast, he'd go for the Gold Cup.

I was going to America to work on a script, so to monitor the Good Lord's decision about the weather, I parked my Jeep, which leaks like a sieve, at Gatwick. If the floor was wet when I returned, it had rained; if not, it had stayed dry. Arriving back on the Saturday before Cheltenham the floor of my Jeep was bone dry. I enthusiastically rang my bookie, and put a hundred quid each way on Des for the Gold Cup at 25–1. There was a pause, the sound of the phone being shuffled around, then a new voice on the phone – the manager.

'Hello, Mr Burridge,' he said. 'Does this mean you'll be running Desert Orchid in the Gold Cup?'

'What do you think?' I said.

Rarely has anyone with inside knowledge placed such an ill-advised bet, as it then started to tank down, all weekend. By Sunday night the going at Cheltenham was heavy.

David was becoming gloomy about Des's chances, but more and more bullish about Cavvies Clown. He said he was happy to leave the decision to us. I rang Colin and we talked for half an hour. Colin knew Des didn't run to within a stone of his form at Cheltenham, and the rain would make things worse. On the book we had eleven pounds in hand of Charter Party, but Charter Party was a Cheltenham specialist, and Des was not. The thought stuck that Des might finish an exhausted fifth or sixth and leave the rest of his season in the mud at Prestbury Park. The Almighty had made the decision: it was the Champion Chase.

Feeling like an idiot about the bet I'd struck, I rang David to tell him. 'Good,' he said.

It was business as usual with Pearlyman and Very Promising on a damp, cold, breath hanging in the air Cheltenham day. Julian Wilson murmured one of those wonderful racing euphemisms about 'searching ground', and Des went off fourth favourite at 9–1.

Our only chance was to make this a test of stamina. Colin let Des blast off, as usual jumping to his right, most obviously on the cross fence. Halfway down the back straight they were twenty lengths clear and jumping beautifully. Colin gave him a breather, then hustled him into the bend. No sooner had our hopes started to rise than they collapsed. Halfway round the bend Des's ears were back, and the rest of the field was swallowing him up. He plugged on down the hill running on guts and stamina. Pearlyman, meanwhile, was cruising, and round the final bend shot into an unassailable lead. Once he'd straightened out, Des did start to get a little power down, and though he looked tired, slogged on to overtake Very Promising on the run in, pricking his ears in his self-congratulatory way one stride past the finishing post, though Pearlyman was five lengths ahead of him.

It was Pearlyman's second successive win in the Queen Mother Chase, and it was a wonderful performance. Des was simply not good enough to get near him at Cheltenham, but we were proud to come second. Very Promising was also a brilliant two-miler, and would have been a worthy winner of the race in any other year.

It had been an unlucky day for Colin, though, as Sir Blake, owned like Rhyme 'N' Reason by Juliet Reed and John Moreton, had fallen at the last in the Sun Alliance Hurdle when he looked to be winning, and Colin was subdued in the bar afterwards. I didn't read anything in particular into it, and was certainly not prepared for the call I got the next day.

At eleven o'clock on the morning of the Gold Cup, Colin called to say he was retiring. It was a sad day, made worse by seeing Forgive 'N Forget put down after breaking a hind leg after jumping the fourth last in the Gold Cup.

Colin had been such a big part of the fun we'd had with Des over the years. He'd won seventeen out of forty-four races on him and his friendly, articulate presence had contributed to the horse's popularity. He nominated the highlight of his career as 'just being able to ride Desert Orchid'. David paid him the tribute: 'Whoever rides for me, I will never get anybody more loyal or with more integrity than Colin. He has been a great help, and we've had some marvellous times together. I shall miss him but, whatever he does, I know he will do well.' Colin retired to run The Ibex at Chaddleworth, and renamed one of the bars 'The Orchid Bar'.

People asked whether we regretted not running Des in the Gold Cup that year, but the only lingering regret I did have was for Colin. If he had won, it would have been a fantastic end to his career, but in the end – and I think he agrees – a gallant fighting second in the Queen Mother Chase was a better note to finish on than an exhausted third or fourth in the Gold Cup. The bookies certainly did not think he would have won the Gold Cup, with Des quoted at 25–1 before he was taken out, and I think they were right. Charter Party was on a high and was a Cheltenham specialist, as well as being a mudlark. Today I am inclined to form the same opinion I had then: that Des was not ready for the race, and that he would probably have trailed in a tired third or fourth. As things worked out, there was a bonus. Des was still a fresh horse after Cheltenham, and so we could think about running him at Liverpool.

It was not difficult to decide who'd get the ride on the grey horse. After the Gold Cup, in which Simon Sherwood rode Cavvies Clown into second place, David casually mentioned that if Simon had nothing else to ride at Liverpool, the ride was his. Simon, equally casually, replied, 'All right'.

Simon, in the intervening fifteen months, had gone from strength to strength. He was now, more than ever, perfect for Des, but their partnership nearly got off to a shaky start. David's confidence about Liverpool was waning. The owners always felt that Aintree would suit Des, because although it was left-handed, it was not shapeless and undulating like Cheltenham, but flat and tight, and the fences were grouped together in straight lines, one group on the back straight and another in the home straight, with none of the fences jumped on the turn. We hoped Des could jump the fences fast in the straight, then take breathers round the bend, as he did at Sandown, Kempton and Ascot. Though all those courses are very different, the fences are in a straight line and are punctuated by bends. Des had learnt to take breathers round the bends, and to conserve his efforts for the business end of the race.

David wasn't so sure, though. He wanted to run Des in the £5,000 Alanbrooke Memorial Chase at Sandown in two days' time, and that would have precluded Des running at Liverpool. David thought that while Des would win the Sandown chase, he had no chance at Liverpool. I hadn't realised David was so against Liverpool, so I called him, and he confirmed his plans to run at Sandown. I spent about ten minutes trying to change his mind, which as anyone knows is completely impossible! So we just sort of vetoed Sandown. David accepted this and, by the time I arrived at Liverpool nine days later, was feeling more positive about the whole thing, and had even gone so far as to have three £25 doubles and a £50 treble about his three runners at the meeting: Desert Orchid in the Chivas Regal, Sir Blake in the Mumm Novices Hurdle, and Rhyme 'N' Reason in the National.

It was a great feeling arriving at Liverpool. I had always loved the place: it is one of the few sporting venues that not only matches the expectations generated by TV, but also exceeds them. As we gathered in the bar before racing, I was also struck by a possible symmetry. Des's form went 1122322 and I thought it might be appropriate if he ended with another couple of 1s to balance it out.

Dessie had apparently borne the journey well, which was reassuring as he had not been away overnight since the Irish Sweeps Hurdle three years earlier. For security reasons his top door had been closed overnight and he wasn't able to keep an eye on the goings-on outside. Janice looked tight-lipped as she walked him round before the pre-parade ring, and Des rewarded her by trying to bite a large chunk out of her. With his coat gleaming he looked as hard as marble, and better than he had looked all season.

He had four opponents: Beau Ranger, his nemesis from Kempton; Kildimo, who'd beaten him at Wincanton; Weather The Storm, whom he'd beaten at Cheltenham; and Contradeal, a talented but highly strung horse, who'd come third in the Hennessey. They were all carrying eleven stone five, except Weather The Storm who had eleven stone thirteen.

Des tried to cart Simon down to the start. Simon had not yet been down to Whitsbury to learn the 'trick' of controlling him from Rodney, and looked relieved when he managed to pull him up. While Des stood around looking interested, Peter Scudamore jumped off Beau Ranger and it soon became clear he'd lost a plate. Martin Pipe had indicated he didn't want his horse reshod at the start, so Beau Ranger was out. I regret to say that none of us was sporting enough to accept Richard Pitman's view that this was 'a great shame'. Meanwhile Contradeal was boiling over and decided to have some kicking practice on the plastic rails, smashing them completely.

Finally the tapes went up and the grey horse lobbed down to the first fence as if he was not entirely convinced the race had actually started. He popped the first two, then came to the water. He stood miles off it, landing just as far the other side. Simon didn't move a muscle, and Des gracefully accepted the suggestion that he should now turn left. He set off round the bend with his ears pricked, Simon sitting perfectly balanced and not moving. Neither appeared to have the slightest doubt they were going to win.

Ten lengths in the lead going round the first bend, ears pricked throughout, Simon had Des popping round, nothing dramatic, just enjoying himself. Six out he accelerated. Suddenly the opposition was struggling behind him. Ten lengths in the lead Simon glanced back. At the second last he glanced back again. He had outspeeded Kildimo round the left-hand bend, and was too far ahead for Graham Bradley to do anything about it. At the last Des's saddle slipped, the only moment of anxiety throughout the entire race, and Simon rode him out to win by eight lengths.

Des had won for the first time going left-handed, and had won easily. As he pulled up, Simon patted him and crumpled his ears. Janice patted her heart as if she'd just recovered from a heart attack. Dessie baulked before going into the winner's enclosure, but then wandered in looking pleased with himself. Simon said that Des had not been happy going left-handed, but in every other respect he seemed better and stronger than he had been the last time he rode him. David was grinning – it had been only the second winner at Liverpool of his entire career.

The press celebrated Des's first left-handed victory and started to talk about next year's Gold Cup, but Des's win was eclipsed

two days later when Rhyme 'N' Reason won the National in great
style, cracking a leg in the process, which made his victory all the
more gallant. He returned to the traditional Grand National
winner's reception at Whitsbury the next day; Des was thoroughly
put out as a result, and sulked all day. He was used to being the
star of Whitsbury.

Janice proceeded to make it a memorable week by winning the
seven furlong Florence Nagle girls race at Kempton for the second
year running on Hymn of Harlech, owned by Simon Bullimore's
brother Tim. A week later the grey horse worked with Hymn of
Harlech over six furlongs. Rodney was riding Des and Janice was
on Hymn of Harlech, so Des was giving Hymn of Harlech about
two and a half stone. Des 'won' the gallop by three lengths. He
was clearly as well as ever, and David had no hesitation in aiming
him for the Whitbread.

With the disappointment over the corns the previous year,
everybody was extra attentive. David, despite seeming sure to lose
the three Cavvies Clown races, had a chance of winning the trainers' championship, and it hinged on the Whitbread. Josh Gifford,
his closest pursuer, had a runner in the race, Golden Minstrel.
Therefore, if either of them won, they'd also win the championship.

Des's corns duly appeared ten days before Sandown, but his
attendants were ready. Laser treatment was applied twice a day,
and the foot, his near fore, was constantly poulticed by Janice. On
the Wednesday before the race, he was lame again, so the shoes
stayed off and he was boxed up to gallops so he wouldn't have to
go on the roads. Paul Henderson, the Whitsbury farrier, made up
special racing plates which spread the weight round the foot; he
included a cushioning rubber pad between shoe and foot to try to
offset the effects of the firm ground.

'Desert Orchid is Whitbread Toast – corns and all!' ran the
Sporting Life headline (later destined to be a tea towel). John Oaksey
wrote in *The Daily Telegraph*: 'the question most of us want to see
answered is whether, going his favourite way round, Desert Orchid
can last home well enough to hold a Gold Cup winner. If the
answer turns out to be "no" then I dread Saturday, but if it is
"yes" they had better tie the roof down at Sandown.' It was a race
which lived up to its advance billing.

It was a perfect spring day: fresh, sunny, and full of the promise of the summer ahead – one of those days which it makes it worth living through the English winter for. The flat racing crowd had come out of hibernation, and tweed and wool gave way to cotton and silk. The Whitbread was, as usual, the only jump race on the card, and the contrast between these tough, battle-hardened old pros with the brat pack of highly strung two-year-olds and Classic hopefuls emphasised the glamour of jump racing. The mix of elements got richer the closer you looked: David's chances of winning the trainers' championship; the doubts in the press about whether the grey would stay three miles five furlongs; our own doubts about his corns on the firm ground; and the competitive-looking field of twelve runners.

Des looked outstanding in the paddock, fresh, hard and purposeful. Janice's mother had made her a jumper in my colours, with a triptych of grey horse's heads knitted on the chest, and she wore it as she strode round, alternately admonishing and soothing Des, occasionally responding to comments from the crowd round the rails – Janice was becoming famous herself.

Simon Sherwood was as nonchalant as ever about the whole thing, laughing and talking out of the side of his mouth, and David's instructions were reassuringly reminiscent of the first King George. 'Ride him as if he'll stay – because he will.'

Des was applauded as he went down to the start, and milled about, nodding in his familiar way, waiting to get going. There was frantic activity in the ring with attention focusing on four horses: Des, on eleven stone eleven, drifted from 5–1 to 6–1; Kildimo, on eleven stone twelve, went out to 13–2 and came in to 6–1; Strands of Gold, on ten stone, came in from 7–1 to 6–1; and the favourite was Aquilifer, on ten stone three, who went off at 11–2.

The crowd buzzed as the starter called the horses in, and Simon made no attempt to get on the inside, but lined up right on the outside. The tapes went up.

I had the same hopes before the race that I'd had at Liverpool: that the symmetry of his form would be completed with another '1'. But I had never dreamt it would be such a perfect race, or that Des would dominate it in such a magnificent, incandescent fashion.

He soared over the first fence and cleared the first ditch by miles, and set off up the straight with his ears pricked, giving no indication of any problems with corns. Down the back straight he put in an exhibition, jumping three lengths ahead of the field. (Graham Goode murmured he was 'spreadeagling his field'.) Coming back over the pond fence Des's ears were pricked, looking at the crowd, and he skipped over the ditch – a fence he never failed to jump brilliantly – and strode confidently up the hill.

He went wide at the top bend, as if he thought he'd already won, allowing Run and Skip, who had by now seen enough of Des's backside to last him a lifetime, to come upsides, and the grey horse's ears flickered back for the first time. Des kept the lead, and at the sixteenth, John Oaksey gasped audibly on the TV as Des took off a stride too early and reached for the fence. Simon was controlling it beautifully, with that instinctive feeling for the horse he seemed to have.

Going into the bend, Run and Skip, in receipt of eighteen pounds, was now driven into the lead by Phillip Hobbs, and from the stand it didn't look too good for a few moments. Simon gave Des a breather and let him gather himself for the final hill. Coming to the pond fence he came back on the bit, hit the front, pricked his ears, and leapt over it. The crowd started to roar.

Coming to the second last, Run and Skip was beaten, but Strands of Gold and Kildimo were challenging. Over the second last and the roar got louder. Strands of Gold was beaten and it was the two top weights going for the last fence. Jimmy Frost, the rider of Kildimo, said later that he thought he would 'win five minutes'; Simon looked over at him thoughtfully.

They came to the last and jumped it perfectly, both in the air together. Two strides out of the fence, Simon hadn't moved. Jimmy Frost had his stick out. Des was going on half a length, and almost as a grudging concession to the fact that this was the finish of the Whitbread, Simon began to ride him out, but he never looked like he would go for his whip. Ears flat against his head, Des lengthened, and the crowd went completely wild. Simon gave the grey horse a great pat on the neck as he passed the post two and a half lengths in front of Kildimo, and there was a moment – a moment that stretched for ever – of sheer delirious joy, as the wall of sound built and built. On TV Graham Goode was yelling 'I have never, *ever*, heard a crowd warm to a horse like they've warmed to Desert Orchid. This was a spectacular performance, a superb jumping exhibition, by the most popular horse in training, that's number two, Desert Orchid . . .'

Ears pricking, Des was pulling up, after what John Oaksey later called an almost perfect steeplechase: no fallers, no injuries, perfect jumping ground and, for the vast majority of the crowd, the perfect result. Simon ruffled Janice's hair, and Janice was crying with joy as she led him down the path towards the winner's enclosure. Simon Elsworth, David's son, and Peter Maughan walked beside him, clearing the path packed with people, all applauding the grey who appeared to be nodding in appreciation. David shed the odd tear, too. He had won the trainers' championship, and it was wonderful that Des had clinched it for him. Perhaps he could see back to that November day in 1982 when Des had first pulled up in his yard. He had come a long way since then. We had all come a long way.

Everybody belted for the winner's enclosure and it was soon fifty deep. All the owners, Bullimores, Burridges, all those who'd followed him through the good times and bad were there and somehow managed to get into the enclosure, with one exception – me. I was pushing my way through the crowd towards them. Halfway down the steps, my path was well and truly blocked by a woman. I tried to squeeze through on one side, she cut me off; I tried to squeeze through on the other, again she cut me off. 'You're not getting past,' she insisted. Des was about to enter the enclosure. The crowd surged and an opening appeared to one side of the woman. I squeezed through, and she was outraged. 'Bloody rude flat people!' she exploded.

Des was pausing now in the entrance, looking around; the applause died, then redoubled, and he strode in with the press and photographers closing like a wave behind him. All the flat jockeys had come out of the weighing room to applaud him, and Peter Maughan, in all his years of racing, had never seen anything like it. The owners of Strands of Gold congratulated us, saying it was a pleasure to come third to Des, and they really seemed to mean it. The scenes that followed were recorded for the nation by Channel Four.

Janice pats Des and murmurs 'Good boy, good boy', but he

nods furiously, as if wanting to dispense with all that nonsense. Jane Elsworth ruffles Janice's hair as she giggles. The whole family, especially a wonderfully over-excited Jimmy, pat the horse and grin and embrace each other as Brough Scott yells over the noise of the crowd, 'I have David Elsworth with me here and Janice Coyle.' David gives a rumpled smile and Janice giggles.

David pays compliments to his blacksmith and vet and actually says he's 'over the moon', an expression I've never heard him use before. Brough Scott says, 'Janice ...' Janice coos 'Oooo' and turns away, helplessly patting the horse's neck. 'Tears coming down the face?'

'Yes,' admits Janice, 'it's been a fantastic last couple of weeks.'

'How worried were you about his feet? I saw you walking him round on the grass beforehand.'

'Oh, it was just a precaution, we were quite worried earlier on in the week.'

The camera tilts down to a shot of Desert Orchid's legs, while in the background Jimmy chimes in 'How about your corns, my darleeeng?'

'He's got some cushioned pads that the blacksmith thought would be a good idea,' adds Janice.

'You're a good horse,' adds Jimmy.

'And Mr Burridge ... And Richard, you're writing a book aren't you?'

'Well, I think I'm going to have to,' I burble happily. 'This horse is becoming a legend.'

Des nods his head up and down. Brough grins.

'If a horse could ever talk, I really think . . .'

'But you can talk, you brute . . .' Jimmy contributes gleefully into the horse's nose.

Brough laughs. 'We'll give you a pat from Channel Four.' Janice starts chatting on about breaking Wayward Lad's record, and Brough is laughing at the comedy of it all. The crowd cheers again.

'He really does seem to know he's here, doesn't he? He seems to know he's done it.'

Jimmy interprets. 'You've won, my pretty.'

Brough turns to Janice. 'You rode a winner yourself on the flat, do you ever think you'll get a ride on him one day?'

'Ooo, no,' coos Janice. 'My winner a year's enough for me.'

David enters the frame, poses for photographs, and Des is finally led away, everyone applauds, and Brough says to camera, 'And as the cheers ring out, let's take the starting price for Desert Orchid's Whitbread.'

Afterwards we get presented with trophies by the Queen Mother, who recognises Amy and compliments Johnnie on how much she's grown. I yak away like an idiot. Grins are plastered across everybody's face. Brough concludes that Desert Orchid is the pride of England, and Channel Four goes into a commercial for Whitbread beer.

Golden days.

Dog Days

WE WORE THAT VIDEOTAPE out that summer. It just got better and better.

Des came home two weeks later and again Jimmy, Richard Watson and John Allington went to work on his corns. In the end they decided to leave his front shoes on for the summer, but we could be grateful that all in all Desert Orchid had been remarkably injury free. His tendons were miraculous: they were so clean he scarcely looked like he'd had one race, let alone forty-eight over hurdles and fences, as well as hundreds of miles galloping to prepare for those races. The fact that he always carried big weights and that most of his races were run on fast ground made it more extraordinary. At nine, his legs were as good as if he'd been in a field all his life. He was well put together, of course, and beautifully balanced. This was what made him such a wonderful jumper, but it also evened out the pressure on his legs. However, it was David's brilliant use of the Whitsbury gallops that deserved most of the credit, as well as his sheer professionalism – he never ducked a race, but he never risked Des unnecessarily either.

The long rest in the summer probably helped too, but it was mainly a mental rest, a change from the routines of training. Around July each year, though, he began to look as if he'd had enough of hanging around in a field, and was ready for something different. This year, for the first time, following two weeks on the horsewalker at Ab Kettleby, he was due to come up to me in Yorkshire to do his roadwork.

Even though Jimmy had managed to get away without any major disasters, the increase in agricultural traffic in the narrow roads round his house had taken the fun out of it. The roads and tracks over the Yorkshire Moors, on the other hand, were ideal: they were quiet; they were steep, which helped to build up muscle; and they were spectacular, which took the boredom out of walking and trotting a couple of hours each day.

I had three other horses there, my mares Made For Life and Trailing Rose and my brother's horse Peacework. At fifteen stone I was too heavy to ride Des, but I could ride one of my poor old mares without anyone giving me a bad time; I did need help with the other horses though.

Trevor Lowe was a great friend of Colin's, and helped him out with his livery yard. He took his holidays and came up to Yorkshire, despite the fact that he was allergic to horses. He was very attached to Des, and didn't seem to resent the constant sneezing that went with the grooming. Clare Pears and Carol Milburn also came over every morning to ride out. Clare was working for trainer Charlie Booth, and had ridden work all over the world. She was an extremely able horsewoman with a wealth of experience that came from spending her life in racing stables; she was always very relaxed and never seemed to take anything too seriously. Carol had spent her working life looking after horses in Yorkshire, and was also a very good horsewoman. They made a good team, and I was looking forward to having Des to stay. Courtesy of the prize money he'd won, Desert Orchid had effectively built his own stables, and Dick Atkinson, who'd built my house, finished them a few weeks before he was due to come up.

Living in a remote spot, I only managed to get all the hay, shavings, food, etc, delivered after I learnt to drop Desert Orchid's name unashamedly. Predictions that it would take weeks to deliver were instantly revised when I mentioned they were for Desert Orchid! Castle Howard-based vet Edmund Collins agreed to make the hour and a half return trip to sort out any problems, and John Haykin came out to shoe the old boy, usually accompanied by his wife Mary, who was a big fan of the horse.

Life settled into an easy routine. Riding out every morning across the moors, as grouse exploded out of the heather, the horses seemed to enjoy the change. There were days it was so windy we felt as if we were about to be blown to Norway, or so foggy we could almost get lost on my front drive, but by and large it was wonderful. God knows how many exhausted ramblers we rode past, who neither knew nor cared about Desert Orchid's existence as they plodded past, nearing the end of the coast-to-coast walk dreaming of hot baths and cups of tea. Most cars just trundled past, although occasionally one braked, backed up, and the occupants leant out – that's not . . . is it?

Word gradually began to leak out. The peace of the Yorkshire Moors started to be interrupted by the arrival of journalists and TV crews, and I suspect David must have wondered what the hell was going on with all these bulletins issuing forth from North Yorkshire.

After the press came the visitors, and my neighbours became increasingly confused by the number of people asking directions to my house. Luckily my house is almost impossible to find even if you *have* got directions to it, and the pressure was somewhat relieved by the appearance halfway through the summer of a grey hunter in a field on the other side of the dale. People would circle this field indefinitely, convinced that this was Desert Orchid, but never getting near enough to prove or disprove the theory.

Des took it all in his stride. He put in the occasional buck to keep his riders on their toes, but he seemed to enjoy the change of scenery. When I was out with my dogs on the moors, I could see his white face staring at us a quarter of a mile away, as curious as ever. Admirers who came to visit him would cluster round, breathlessly murmuring that they couldn't believe that they were really standing next to Desert Orchid. He was a star now and seemed to realise it.

George Armatage had remained elusive throughout Des's stay, although he wasn't far away in Northumberland, but he turned up ten days before Des was due to go back to David and, fighting his way through the local pony club, happily pronounced Des 'straight'. This was the first time I had met George, or Mister Armatage as you irresistibly called him. He was a figure of considerable authority, with a touch of genius, by which I suppose I mean that he was able to work some magic with horses that I didn't understand at all and that according to most vets was impossible. He played the part well. Short, slight, lame and with fiendishly twinkling eyes, he radiated a kind of intense, wary intelligence. He was also fearlessly blunt, and I could see how people could be intimidated by him.

Made For Life had a 'thoroughpin', which George clicked back, Peacework's back was out and Trailing Rose's shoulder needed to be put right. Immediately after George had seen to them, the horses all seemed to walk out better. The treatment had taken five minutes, and only required that they walk for two days, which is what they were doing anyway. The 'problems' were so slight that ordinarily it wouldn't have occurred to you that there was anything wrong, but the difference it made was significant. I always felt bad we were never able to give George more public credit for all he did for us, but he couldn't care less. If it got out he was treating Desert Orchid his workload would have become worse. As it was, he left home at five o'clock most mornings, and his wife Nancy hardly saw him. He was the sixth generation of Armatages who had been practising this remarkable art, and he was teaching his grandson. He was always as ready to tackle 'ordinary' horses and hunters as racehorses. I liked him enormously.

The summer was soon over, and Martyn Jenkins ('Jinks'), David's horsebox driver, drove up to get Des. We stayed up discussing the upcoming season. Jinks almost always drove Des to his races, and admitted he had mixed feelings about them. Although he went racing almost every day of his life, watching this horse made him nervous. It was the same for Peter Maughan, and Janice was already so nervous that she had to rely on video recordings for any accurate idea of what had happened in a race.

The next day the perfect weather we had been having broke, and it was a filthy, foggy day for Des's return. After a week had gone by, I hadn't heard from David, so I called him up. 'Well, Richard,' he said, 'he's well, but he's bloody fat. We may be struggling to give him any prep races before the King George.'

I murmured something about him doing ten miles' walking every day and his legs being hard enough to get on with some work, and hung up, wondering where I'd gone wrong. When I heard from David again he was being interviewed on TV a couple of weeks later.

'And how's the grey horse?' asked Julian Wilson.

'Well,' said David, scratching his head, 'he's so bloody well I could run him next week.' I never dared ask what had happened in those intervening two weeks.

So Des was back in his familiar Whitsbury routine, with Rodney swinging out of the gate on him, calling out 'And who can lay up with me today, boys?' Nobody could. By now Des had practically worn a groove in the road up to the gallops, and knew the routine backwards: get mucked out, have a roll, go out at eight, do two or three canters up the short one, or go a mile up the all-weather, always in the lead, walk back, have a pick of grass, perhaps a roll in the sandpit, then have breakfast. He was as keen as ever, bouncing around on his toes, flashing his tail or laying back his ears if anybody tried to overtake him. He resented any patting or cuddling – it was a serious business this training. But on the way back from the gallops Rodney, walking by his side, could let go of the reins and Des would make his own way home.

Everyone was pleased to see him back, and again David picked the Terry Biddlecombe Chase at Wincanton for a pipe-opener. The Sunday before, Simon Sherwood came down for Des's annual 'school', and was accompanied to the fences by a useful flat handicapper, Imperial Brush, who as far as anyone knew was not planning to jump fences that season.

'Right, Simon, you jump the fences, and Paul [Paul Holley, riding Imperial Brush], you take your horse along the outside of the fences.'

Simon thought this was slightly eccentric, one horse jumping and one horse running along outside, but not wanting to look like an idiot, he acted as if it was the most natural thing in the world. Des and Imperial Brush lined up together, and in a dizzying blur of action, Simon jumped the five fences as fast as he ever jumped fences in his life, and then looked ahead for Imperial Brush. Then he looked back. Imperial Brush was about ten lengths *behind*.

By now Des was showing all the right signs as he turned into a biting and kicking machine. Janice tried to sneak up on him on the morning of the race, but Des knew what was going on: he'd missed first lot, the horsebox was parked outside, and it looked like it had his name on it. He probably just liked to make it clear he knew what was about to happen, and he wasn't going to be fooled into walking into the horsebox as if he didn't know what it meant.

But if he did know what was about to happen, we certainly didn't. Despite all the planning and dreaming that went on all summer, what happened next was perhaps one of the most extraordinary sequences of races ever seen on a British racecourse. Once I had said to David rather hopefully, 'One year he'll win everything.' I don't suppose I ever thought it would come true.

PART FOUR

At Full Stretch

20

Unbeatable

A MEXICAN WAVE OF RAISED CAMERAS greeted Des as he walked round the Wincanton parade ring, leaving a line of goofy grins in his wake, while the more regular racegoers attempted to remain stoically indifferent to the grey's cult status. Who were these lunatics jumping about and yelling 'Dessie!'? Shouldn't they be in school? The approach roads to Wincanton which normally seemed to have been laid out by somebody with a sense of humour, now became almost impassable. Glancing into cars on the way to the course, you were more likely to see *Jackie* or *Pony Club Monthly* than the *Racing Post* or *The Sporting Life*.

Des was acquiring a quasi-mystical reputation: people wrote with heartbreaking tales of sick children and dying relatives in the hope that seeing the old horse might help. And in the crazy way these things work, occasionally it did seem to.

Quite what effect this had on those whose job it was to treat him as a racehorse was difficult to say. Janice always looked as dangerous as a trembler switch before racing anyway, alternately laughing and frowning, while Peter Maughan had long since assumed a cool, professional, friendly mask. Jane Elsworth was in charge of damage control and affected a reassuring detachment: sometimes she giggled helplessly at some absurd turn of events or display of affection, sometimes her eyes narrowed furiously, but she was a placating, softening influence, searching out owners in need of special attention, of whom Jimmy was usually the most obvious. Despite the fact that he had always dreamt of breeding a championship racehorse, it was difficult to say just what actual pleasure he got out of it. He worried between races and was a nervous wreck on race days. He worried when the horse came home; he worried when the horse was at Flintham. The only time he didn't worry was in the first eight weeks or so of training when the care of the horse lay with somebody else and there were no races on the immediate horizon. But that golden period was now drawing to a close with Des's first race. Midge enjoyed it all enormously, though the colour started to drain from her cheeks as the race approached. Simon Bullimore remained as remorselessly cheerful as ever – weren't all horses like Desert Orchid?

Even David was jittery at Wincanton. At the end of the season he usually had to hold our hands, but with the whole season before him, it was sometimes the other way round. Des was jittery too – that was the charm that underpinned all this hype. He was desperately excited, trembling in the saddling box.

Simon's record on Des was now three wins from three rides, and he hadn't picked up his whip. All his equipment seemed superfluous, as in the assumption that he would be in the lead from start to finish, he didn't even put his goggles down. Des started at 2–7 (the commentator suggested beforehand that if you wanted to get rich you'd have to be as brave as the horse) and he sailed round Wincanton, winning effortlessly by fifteen lengths from Bishops Yarn and Golden Friend.

My brother Simon made his usual crack about Dessie schooling in public, and David looked relieved. His next race was to be the Boxing Day Trial Chase at Kempton, but then the ground was too firm, and David pulled him out. Simon Sherwood went to ride for his brother Oliver at Worcester instead. We were all in Oliver Sherwood's debt that season. Though he, and John Jenkins, retained Simon, he never appeared to resent the reshuffling caused by his brother's occasional defection, and seemed to enjoy the whole thing as much as we did.

David was worried by the ground, not because Dessie disliked it, but because there was that much more risk of damage to legs or joints. There was no point leaving his season at Kempton in mid-November. By the end of the month David had no reservations about running him in the two mile Tingle Creek at Sandown.

Simon was rather gloomy about the Tingle Creek. He had never ridden the grey over two miles and didn't think he could be as good as he was over three. And since Des's handicap rating was based on his three mile form, it would be tough to concede eighteen pounds to Panto Prince, twenty pounds to Jim Thorpe, and especially twenty-two pounds to Vodkatini, a brilliant specialist two-miler with only one chink in his armour, admittedly rather a major one, that he sometimes refused to race.

Simon's reservations were private but some of the press voiced more public doubts. Many of the people who were telling the world two years earlier that Desert Orchid was a two-miler, pure and simple, and would never stay three miles, were now advising us that he was a three-miler, and would not have 'the speed' to win over two miles. We knew this was not true, as only the very best of David's flat horses could beat Des over six furlongs at home, but two-milers did need to be able to get away from their fences quickly, and Des, with his considerable weight disadvantage, might find this difficult, as he had found the year before in the Tingle Creek.

Des was returning, as Brough Scott put it, to 'the scene of his greatest triumph', the previous year's Whitbread, and both horse and jockey could be forgiven for being a little disorientated. The two mile start was in the same spot as the three mile five start, and this time Des had to go round only once, rather than twice. Then Vodkatini whipped round at the start and refused to race – shades of Beau Ranger at Liverpool, with Des's main opponent out before the start.

Des led throughout, and jumping magnificently, stretched his rivals down the back straight. Approaching the pond fence, Dessie pricked his ears. Didn't they have to go round again? Then Simon pressed the button, and suddenly they went three lengths clear. Panto Prince and Jim Thorpe tried to close, but Des was five lengths clear going to the last, and sailing over it, Simon changed his hands and shook the reins, and stormed on to win by twelve lengths. 'An amazing performance this,' raved Graham Goode. 'Desert Orchid, twelve stone, twelve lengths clear, his twenty-third victory and it will never be easier.'

Simon got his regular kiss from Janice and was shaking his head with admiration afterwards. He thought that to come back from a Whitbread and win a two mile chase so easily off top weight was amazing. He never picked up his stick, he explained, because the horse was always doing his best, and he didn't need to bully him. And though there was later reason to think neither Jim

Thorpe nor Panto Prince were at their best that day, Dessie's victory was hailed as one of the greatest handicap performances of the decade, on a par with Burrough Hill Lad's victory in the 1984 Hennessey. Dominic Gardiner-Hill in the *Racing Post* went so far as to call it the best race of his career. Not bad for a horse who wasn't 'effective' at two miles.

Now the madness started to build. The fact that he had won the Whitbread and Tingle Creek in successive appearances at Sandown seemed to demonstrate an unprecedented versatility. Strands of Gold, to whom he had given twenty-five pounds in the previous season's Whitbread, had just won the Hennessey, and John Francome offered to 'plait shavings if he [Desert Orchid] didn't win the Gold Cup'.

From David's point of view, the Tingle Creek was a good trial for the King George four weeks later, and Rodney started to feel he was showing all the right signs. The same could not be said for Simon. A fall a week after the Tingle Creek led to a haematoma on his groin, and after several blood transfusions, and the sight of his lower abdomen going black, it was touch and go whether he'd make it. Simon spent the days leading up to Christmas with the physiotherapist, but eventually reported fit the day before.

A fax from François Doumen's stable confirming Nupsala's entry had gone astray and Nupsala was out. It seemed part of the strange run of luck we were having, following Beau Ranger's lost plate and Vodkatini's refusal to race. Des was now a red-hot favourite, and really, if there ever was a horse for a race, it was Desert Orchid for the King George – three miles at level weights round Kempton was perfect.

But you know what it's like when something is peddled as a certainty – you start to worry. And when rumours began to circulate that someone might try to get at the horse, I worried more. Des was a very hot odds-on 1–2 favourite, and it was a classic nobbling situation. Of course the chances of this happening in a trainer's yard are infinitely slighter than if the horse is stabled overnight at the racecourse, because David's staff would probably have noticed someone hanging about, but there were always so many people hanging about Desert Orchid these days. There had also been a rash of mysteriously beaten hot favourites in England and Ireland the previous year, most of them with the same symptoms: listlessness before the start, never going at any stage during the race, and usually being pulled up, then showing signs of dehydration afterwards and urinating frequently. The Jockey Club forensic people never found anything, but you can't test for something you don't know exists. It only takes a bright lab assistant somewhere with an overdraft to come up with something new and the nobblers are in business.

David said he'd get a lad to sleep in the feed room, which seemed rather hard cheese on the lad on Christmas night. In the event, I was doing nothing on Christmas day, and David suggested I join them for Christmas dinner. So I piled my dogs into my old Citroën and drove to Whitsbury. After a few rounds of David's hospitality I was obviously not going anywhere. I had an inspired idea. Who stood to gain most if Des won the King George? Me. Instead of hauling some poor lad out of a warm house on Christmas night and getting him to sleep in a freezing feed room, I'd park my car outside the stable and sleep in it. I'd often slept in it when doing field trials with my dogs, so I borrowed a duvet from Jane, put the seats back and went straight to sleep. The only problem was that I was woken up by the stable lads going to work at half-past five.

In retrospect this did look eccentric, and I slept so soundly that someone probably could have come and swopped Desert Orchid for a Friesian cow and I would have heard nothing. But show me a man who's never done anything eccentric and I'll show you a man who's never had a drink – or owned a racehorse for that matter.

Rodney was very confident beforehand. It was remarkable how Des always seemed to come to himself at Christmas. We got to Kempton and there was a power cut. Everybody stumbled around in the gloom for about two hours with no PA or TVs or Tote, and no lights in the bar. It lent an eerie unreality to the day. There was an enormous cheer as the lights came on shortly before the second race. Meanwhile, Simon Elsworth stood outside Des's box and never left him alone for a moment.

When he walked out into the pre-parade ring Des looked mean, chewing on his bit. Jimmy's nerves were getting worse, if anything. He hated it when Des was a certainty. He also hated it when he wasn't, but that's another story.

Simon Sherwood looked fit enough as he walked into the parade ring, but there was always that moment when he looked puzzled, as he looked down at his colours, grey and blue – that rang a slight bell – then looked up and a compact grey horse pranced his way across his line of vision. Oh yes, right, Desert Orchid, of course.

If he was relaxed, the same could not be said for Lucy, his girlfriend. Annie Brown was there with Colin, and she commiserated. She was relieved she no longer had to spend Desert Orchid's races in the lavatory, but unfortunately the baton of anxiety had merely been passed on to Lucy; Lucy now couldn't bear to watch. There seemed to be a case here for setting up a support group – the society for the distressed partners of Desert Orchid's jockeys.

Kildimo – whose owners had chosen to have lunch with Mrs Thatcher instead of coming to Kempton – was taking on the grey horse, as were Vodkatini, Charter Party and Cavvies Clown. Simon's biggest worry was getting down to the start, and, sure enough, Des carted him; with Simon's damaged stomach muscles screaming in protest, he just managed to pull up before the first fence, where I suspect the presence of several cameramen had as much to do with Des's decision to pull up as the presence of the fence. Having taken his usual photocall, he wandered back to the start and looked dangerous. Whatever pressure anyone else was under, it certainly wasn't getting to Desert Orchid.

The starter called them in, and there was a big cheer as Vodkatini consented to race. For the first circuit Des bowled along in front, a picture of relaxed, controlled power, while Vodkatini fought for his head behind him, and Charter Party, Kildimo and little Cavvies Clown followed in single file. The crowd was quiet, sensing that the race hadn't really started yet. Simon gave Des a breather coming into the straight, and tried to do so again turning out of the straight, but the old horse didn't want to take a breather, thank you, and Simon shouted at him to behave himself. Coming to the water, Des was so relaxed he started examining the crowd, actually hanging away from the rail to get a better look. Simon shouted at him again; at the last moment Des saw the water jump, but made a cock-up of it and Vodkatini overtook him. Des's ears went back, and stayed back as Vodkatini outjumped him over the next two. Simon managed to keep the rail, though, and accelerated into the bend. All the horses were jumping well under pressure, but at the fifth last Des stood off a mile, and Simon sneaked a look round, still a length up, but the others were closing. Another good jump at the fourth last allowed him to keep his advantage, but the pace quickened behind him and Vodkatini and Kildimo ranged alongside. Simon was still not moving, still holding Des together.

The crowd roared as three were in the air at the third last. Now Simon crouched lower in that drive position and all three horses were flat out for the second last – if one of them got it wrong here they'd still be cartwheeling. They flew the second last, but suddenly Vodkatini had come to the end of his rope, and Kildimo was never going to get there. Then came those final agonising moments before the last fence, when you don't like to tempt fate by shouting too loudly – you didn't like to tempt fate by breathing – but Des cleared it beautifully, and Simon was flat out for the line. They passed the post to an explosion of flashbulbs, Simon punched the air and slapped the grey's neck.

The crowd exploded. Kildimo was second, Vodkatini third, and Cavvies Clown fourth. Simon was grinning as he dismounted, murmuring that he 'buzzed a bit for the first mile'.

Desert Orchid had won his second King George, and he was down to 3–1 for the Gold Cup, with a run. We had not discussed running Des in the Gold Cup, but one person was in no doubt – Simon Sherwood. His only problem was that his brother Oliver might claim him for his horse The West Awake, if The West Awake recovered from a leg problem in time for the race.

Three weeks after the King George, David had no hesitation in putting Des back to two miles in the Victor Chandler Chase. For the first time the race looked like it would be spared by the weather.

We'd got this far before. The first half of the season was straightforward, with all roads leading to Kempton. The second half of the season was more difficult, with only the Gainsborough and the Jim Ford as 'natural' objectives. The second half of the season was always harder.

The Victor Chandler Chase was a normal handicap – top weight twelve stone, bottom weight ten stone – but the race closed early, and Vodkatini, who was taking Des on yet again, was set to receive twenty-three pounds for the nine lengths he'd been beaten in the King George. Vodkatini was a better two-miler than three-miler, and this looked very tough. David was more worried about Panto Prince, whom we had beaten in the Tingle Creek. He had won since, and there was reason to think there had been something wrong with him at Sandown. He'd come back with a sore under his saddle.

It was a sunny January day. Despite being the top chaser in training, Des somehow conspired to be the underdog – people muttered that we were asking too much of him at the weights. As the tapes went up, Brendan Powell on Panto Prince employed his usual tactics of harrying the grey horse and not letting him settle. Coming up to the second, Des accelerated as if it were a hurdle, but jumped it beautifully, though Panto Prince, carrying twenty-two pounds less, got away more quickly.

Des had the rail and accelerated into the bend, going a length up, but Panto Prince wasn't letting him go. Down the back they were stride for stride, and they were going so fast at the ditch that Des took off a stride too early and landing steep, pitched, and for a few moments his nose was on the ground. Simon picked him up, but Panto Prince had gone three lengths up. Behind them Vodkatini took off from the same place as Des, but landed in the fence and took a crashing fall.

Two out Simon started to close. Long Engagement on ten stone also started to run on, and the three horses rounded the turn into the straight line abreast. Dessie went a little wide and Panto Prince took a two length lead. The bell announcing the arrival of the horses into the straight rang like a bell summoning the seconds out of the ring, and there was an enormous roar from the crowd.

Both horses cleared the second last, and the roar died a little as Panto Prince was quicker away and went three lengths up. Simon, for the first time, looked in trouble, and took out his stick – and Des slowly began to peg Panto Prince back. The roar started to build and build and build. It was so loud it made the hairs on the back of my neck stand up.

Des is level with Panto Prince as they take the last and land running. The roar grows. But again Panto Prince goes a length and a half up. The roar dies, then starts to build again, as again Des fights back. Panto Prince is on the rail, but Des is going for him, closing the gap, leaning on him, as Simon flashes his stick. Every stride he's gaining, but only by inches.

'Desert Orchid's fighting back though, Dessie's fighting back like a tiger!' yells Peter O'Sullevan, his reserve cracking under the strain, as Simon throws everything he's got at his horse. The line is only yards away now, Panto Prince is still ahead and not stopping. Simon puts down his stick as Des drifts towards Panto Prince, both horses are flat out, Des giving his rival twenty-two pounds, but still he's closing the gap, inch by inch; he's still fighting back. The crowd is going berserk, the black head of Panto Prince is stretching for the line, with Des going for him, leaning on him, as they come to the line . . .

'It's a photo!' shouts Peter O'Sullevan above the crowd, then a moment later, 'Dessie's won it; he's won it. Desert Orchid has won it by a fraction I would say!'

The screams of the crowd segue into applause, and some people say they think it's one of the best races they've ever seen at Ascot, topping even the famous King George and Queen Elizabeth Stakes battle between Grundy and Bustino. Simon is apologetic about using his stick, and says he did it more to encourage himself than the horse, but his unbeaten record is still intact.

As the crowd greeted Des's entry into the winner's enclosure, Richard Pitman, reviewing the finish, points out there could be an objection or a Stewards' Inquiry, as the horses had got very close.

Panto Prince's connections accepted defeat very gracefully, but possibly they did have grounds for an objection. Rodney, watching on TV, certainly thought they did, as he knew the old horse and had seen him do the same thing on the gallops: if a horse tried to overtake him, Des leant on him, intimidating him, and Rodney was sure this was what Des had done in the last hundred yards. I suspect David knew, too, but these days whenever anything happened we thought it better not to advertise, David just grinned and said, 'Put in the book.'

A sense of disbelief greeted his win here: it wasn't just the victories over a variety of distances and ground conditions, it was the *way* he achieved them. There was such a frenzy of anticipation in the press before his runs these days, but Des was managing not only to live up to his advance billing, but actually to surpass it. There was always some wrinkle, some drama to keep the legend alive. Brough Scott wrote a very perceptive piece about Dessie in *The Sunday Times*:

> It's not just what he does, it's the way he does it. Great achievement though it was to revert to two miles and give twenty-two pounds to a specialist like Panto Prince, statisticians could claim that great horses like Arkle would have done it with a leg tied up. So Desert Orchid's brilliance has a touch of vulnerability, too. Defeat is possible. If you watch and love him as the whole nation now seems to, you have to take your heart along in the binocular case.

The clamour for a decision over the Gold Cup continued, but David was keen to savour this victory first. 'That's the hardest race he has had so far. Three times I thought he was beaten. He's a true professional, though, and never gives up.'

There was also the question of Simon's availability for the Gold Cup, as he had set up such an understanding with the horse it seemed unthinkable that Des would go for his toughest race without him. If Simon was claimed for The West Awake, we would be that much less enthusiastic about running him. Des was also entered for the Champion Chase, and with Pearlyman on the sicklist, it looked wide open.

The ripples from his Victor Chandler Chase win kept spreading, and we all found ourselves caught up in it. There were so many owners, and relations of owners, and relations of relations, but somehow this horse was big enough to sustain us all. My brother Johnnie's clients in Hong Kong seemed more interested in Desert Orchid than in the futures market. My brother Simon's advertising colleagues were more inclined to watch the video of the Victor Chandler Chase than their latest commercial. My mum Anne became a celebrity in Wetherby; she was also on the Hunter Improvement Society committee, and all *they* wanted to talk about was Desert Orchid.

Simon Bullimore became the toast of Essex, and his family achieved the status of minor royalty. My youngest brother Hugo, a designer and carpenter, made a cutout of Des jumping the last at Whitbread, and was swamped with orders. My sister Frances became the star of Haileybury, my uncle Phillip and his wife Audrey became the toast of Worthing. Midge's family, her sister Jan and her brother-in-law Peter, found themselves spokesmen for the grey horse every time they went out to dinner, and her brother Godfrey found the discussions in his chambers revolving round Ascot and Cheltenham.

For Midge and Jimmy it never stopped, there was only one thing people were ever interested in, and that was Desert Orchid. There was a downside to this, too. Midge overheard one disgruntled Leicestershire stalwart declare, 'If I hear the name Desert Orchid once more, I'm going to be sick!'

For Simon Burridge and me Desert Orchid's fame imposed another chore. So many people now lined the walkways trying to pat him before a race that we agreed with David that it might be a good idea to walk behind him out to the course in case anybody tried to get at him. Simon had almost as big an affinity for a camera as the grey horse, and enjoyed it, especially as the crowd kept shouting 'Good luck, Simon!' – to Simon Sherwood. Quite how this squared with his avowed declaration that he was in fact 'at a meeting' all day was his problem, but he seemed up to the challenge. In fact, people who formerly would have regarded spending a working day at a race meeting as verging on an impeachable offence, now seemed to regard it as an honour that someone they knew had something to do with Desert Orchid. The whole office was glued to the TV on race days.

The one person whom this success did not really affect, though, was Jimmy, as his horse had been consuming all his nervous energies for so long that it couldn't get any worse. Monty Court commented in *The Sporting Life* on Jimmy's appearance in the paddock before Desert Orchid's next race, the Racecall Gainsborough Chase at Sandown. In a piece entitled 'The Agony and the Ecstasy', he wrote:

The two faces of Desert Orchid were very much in evidence at Sandown last weekend . . . As Desert Orchid strutted arrogantly out of the parade ring and towards the course, haunted James Burridge, with the pallor of a man who has just received terrible news, turned from the buzzing crowds and walked slowly away from the grandstands. Condemned men have had more spring in their step on their way to the gallows.

David and Jane, meanwhile, had gone to Australia, their trip courtesy of David's three wins at the Grand National meeting of the previous year. David took time out from sunning himself on the Great Barrier Reef to try to dial up the 0898 race commentary of the race sponsors, Racecall, to hear what was happening. I had just come back from a working trip to Australia and could have told him it was impossible.

The drama started even before the race, as Des reared up entering the parade ring and twisted a plate off. With the cheers of the crowds frozen in their throats, Janice led him back to be reshod. There were puzzled examinations of the card as the announcer declared that there would be a delay as 'Number One' was being reshod. Number One? Oh, Desert Orchid.

The dreaded corns had also made a reappearance the week before, and on the same foot that was about to be replated. But we felt we were being protected then by some divine authority, and regarded these problems as added spice to the victory that somehow or other we sensed awaited Des.

Peter Maughan legged Simon Sherwood up and Simon looked confident, saying he wouldn't go crazy, but concluding that as nothing was likely to take him on, he might as well make it. By now Desert Orchid was *the* target in any race, and realising it was up to the others to figure out how to beat him, Simon could afford to be relaxed. Des's reputation was intimidating the other jockeys, and Simon rode him in such a confident manner that he seemed to suggest that it didn't matter to him if the others settled in behind or took him on, they weren't going to beat him, so they needn't bother to get worked up over it.

Tony Fairbairn of Racecall gave Janice the Best Turned Out Award, and Des cantered to the start to the applause of the crowd. Simon had been down to Whitsbury and learned the 'knack' of cantering him from Rodney, and didn't get carted this time. That visit to Whitsbury had marked Simon's only ride on Des at home apart from his schooling visit. He had been well and truly run off with, and on dismounting, told David that he'd be happy to come down and ride out in future, just as long as he didn't have to ride *that* horse again. Rodney was laughing in the background.

Simon gave a pretty good indication as to his riding tactics when he didn't put his goggles down, and set off two lengths in the lead, measuring his fences, and despite starting at two mile pace, appeared to be enjoying himself. At the ditch in front of the stands, Pegwell Bay, the brilliant dual Mackeson and AF Budge Chase winner to whom Des was giving eighteen pounds, ranged up alongside, but Des went on again, though Simon had to boot him round the bend. The drop down in distance, this time accompanied by a roar from the crowd, had perhaps convinced Desert Orchid he'd already won.

Pegwell Bay then took it up after the downhill fence, and taking half a length out of Des at the next, went three up. Des's ears went back, and at the last ditch, Pegwell Bay went five clear. Simon didn't move, and coming out of the island fences, Des ranged up on Pegwell Bay's quarters. As they straightened out of the bend, with both horses going well, Pegwell Bay was still half a length up. Simon was sitting quietly though, and shaking Des up after the second last, ranged alongside Carl Llewellyn on Pegwell Bay as the crowd started to yell. Des touched down just in the lead at the last, but Pegwell Bay got away quicker and went half a length up. Now Simon went to work, flattening himself against his horse's neck, never looking like he'd go for his whip. For a few strides the result seemed to be in doubt, but halfway up the run in, Des surged forward and as the roar from the crowd almost drowned out commentator Graham Goode, Des won very cleverly indeed by three-quarters of a length.

Both Graham Goode and John Oaksey indicated that they would take early retirement if this kind of thing kept happening, and Des got three cheers in the winner's enclosure. Simon gasped that this must be the best chaser of the last twenty years, and the applause went on and on. The other jockeys came out of the weighing room to applaud him, and once again, it was not just his victory, but the manner of it. Labour MP Robin Cook said he 'identified with him'. As the cry for 'horses away' went up, the crowd shouted 'shut up', and Janice, giggling helplessly, led him round for several more minutes as every attempt to clear the winner's enclosure was greeted with boos.

Simon was adamant that Des should run in the Gold Cup, and he was free to ride him. Jimmy and Midge and Simon thought he should run. Janice thought he should run. David was still in Australia, so that just left me.

I still wasn't sure. The Gold Cup was a hard race, and recent winners had not exactly blossomed after it. No race is likely to improve a horse's health, but it didn't seem like much of a reward for all of the things Des had accomplished to run him in a tough race round a course he didn't like. He didn't know it was the Gold Cup. Well, maybe he didn't.

Against that was the fact that the Gold Cup was run on the New Course (as opposed to the Old Course over which he had previously run), and that might suit him better: the bends weren't as tight, and there were two fences in the finishing straight rather than one, which would allow him to recover from the effect of the left-handed bend leading into it. On his return from Australia, David thought we should go for the Gold Cup, but decided to leave the final decision until we saw what the ground was going to be like. Whatever happened, the Gainsborough had been his last chase before Cheltenham. There was one bit of bad news, though. Courtesy of his successes at Sandown, Des was proposed for the freedom of Esher. He was turned down.

Then we were offered half a million pounds for our horse. Perhaps David thought we would be tempted, as he turned down the offer without consulting us. . .

The decision to run, when it came, was almost an accident. Simon had been offered the ride on Barnbrook Again in the Champion Chase, and wanted to know what we'd decided. I said I'd give him a decision that evening and called the other owners, then called David. It was the Gold Cup.

I told Geoff Lester of *The Sporting Life* that if it did come up soft, Des was the best equipped to deal with it, and that 'some of the others won't find it so easy to jump out of soft ground with twelve stone on their backs', adding a phrase that would come back to haunt me that he would run 'come hell or high water'.

All hell broke loose at Whitsbury as the press descended en masse. Chris Hill must have felt more like a theatrical agent than a racing secretary as he struggled to slot in one interview after the other.

A week before the Gold Cup I added to Chris's woes by agreeing to do an interview with Julian Wilson in Desert Orchid's box. This was partially as I had got caught up in a ridiculous franchise wrangle in Yorkshire between Yorkshire TV and Tyne Tees TV, both of whom insisted I was in their area. As I couldn't get Yorkshire TV to save my life, I didn't see how this could be so, but eventually I was so fed up with arbitrating on which TV company could interview me that I rather feebly agreed to do both. I never saw the Yorkshire TV interview, for obvious reasons, but the Tyne Tees one was done very well by Doug Moscrop, the only slight blot being the fact that as they filmed the outside of my house, the Yorkshire TV crew could be seen pulling up and decamping outside it. This did not quite gel with the image they were portraying. 'Richard Burridge, who lives alone on the Moors with his two dogs Woody and Cracker' should probably have been amended to 'Richard Burridge, who lives alone on the Moors with several journalists and TV crews', and I couldn't quite face doing another interview in my house so we went down to Whitsbury.

Julian was a little cautious about the idea of doing an interview inside a box, murmuring that he wouldn't care to do this with a two-year-old at Newmarket, but proceeded, with his clipboard as a first line of defence should the grey decide to launch an attack. I managed to keep Des's attention with a packet of mints for about five minutes, and then he suddenly eyed Julian's clipboard with interest, and stepping forward, gripped it with his teeth. Julian had to wrestle the clipboard out of his mouth before he could continue . . .

Des seemed so incredibly well, so relaxed, and so full of himself that my anxieties about Cheltenham seemed misplaced. He had proved that he was by some way the best chaser in training, and that should have been enough to compensate for his dislike of Prestbury Park.

The ground was drying out, and the forecast for the Gold Cup was good. Although we became increasingly nervous as the day approached, it seemed I could take some consolation that the bravado with which I had declared Desert Orchid would run 'come hell or high water' would not be tested.

A Day at the Races

I DARE SAY THERE ARE eight million versions of what happened that day, but I will just tell mine.

I dreamt that I woke up on an overcast morning in Leamington Spa where I had been staying with some friends, Jill and Simon Arrowsmith. I made myself a cup of coffee and turned on the TV. They were running a report from Cheltenham, but there was obviously something wrong with the set. It looked like it was snowing. After fiddling with the controls for five minutes, it turned out the problem was not with the TV. It *was* snowing.

In the dream I set off for Cheltenham. I didn't have a map, but I didn't need one. I just headed into the bad weather. At Stratford it started raining, big flat raindrops splatting on the windscreen. At Evesham I doubled the wiper speed. The raindrops were starring now, the visibility was dropping – snow. I couldn't see a thing. Luckily, getting to Cheltenham is easy. Whenever you come to a sign telling you to go one way to the course, you go the other way.

I pulled into the carpark at about ten, ridiculously early, and as it turned out, not a good idea at all. The snow had stopped, but it was raining hard, an icy wind slanting the rain vertically across the course. Through the misty side window I could see snow covering the hills. In the dream, I flashed back to all those hours in front of the Oracle weather forecast, all those reservations. And now this. I couldn't help laughing. This dream was ridiculous. It occurred to me for a horrible moment that I wasn't dreaming, but then I realised I must be, because no one would consider racing in these conditions. Then I realised they would be unlikely to abandon the race, because it would cost them a fortune.

I stopped laughing and came to the conclusion that I wasn't dreaming. So I sat in my car for about ten minutes, wondering if, in spite of everything we'd said, the consensus turned out to be to pull the horse we would be brave enough to do it. I decided we would be, and stepped out of the car into a large puddle, which hadn't been there when I pulled up. I swopped my shoes for wellies.

Walking on to the gallery above the parade ring, the place looked almost deserted, but on closer inspection you could see a few knots of frozen people huddled under the weighing room awning, or clustered by the Tote windows examining sodden newspapers. Rain was pouring off Arkle's nose as he stood overlooking the scene of his greatest triumphs. Now and then the occasional racegoer made a break for it, before being cut down by the icy crosswind. I headed for the Arkle Bar and had a stiff drink. The bar was in a state of shock: drenched, shivering racegoers wondered what had hit them, whether they, too, were dreaming – surely the day before had been warm, the weather forecast had been good. Had they somehow got lost en route? Had those RAC signs unwittingly directed them to the Arctic Circle? It was lucky no one from the meteorological office was there or there would have been a lynching.

Another drink. 11.30. There was nothing for it, I'd have to walk the course. My umbrella turned inside-out three strides out of the bar. I wrestled to put it right again, and the sight that greeted me hardly justified the effort. Half a dozen firemen were standing looking thoughtfully at an enormous puddle of water beside the last hurdle. My wellies spludged as I turned away and trudged round the sodden course. I rounded the home bend and past the first in the back straight.

Ahead of me a small crowd had gathered as another team of firemen was busy pumping water *out* of the water jump. I fell into step with someone, whom after a few moments I recognized as Tim Reed, who was riding High Edge Grey in the Gold Cup. We trudged on towards the next fence, and at least the rain was easing off. Put it this way: we could now actually *see* the next fence. Tim Reed had apparently recognised me.

'Don't suppose this was what you had in mind,' he said, the note of glee in his voice somewhat tempered by the obvious fact that this was not what he had in mind either. I noticed his hat had gone soggy and had settled over his head like a mushroom.

'How about you?' I grinned, returning the compliment. High Edge Grey liked fast ground and presumably this was why Tim was walking the course. God alone knew what I was doing there.

'It's not too bad,' he said, 'it's wet, but at least they'll go through it.' I nodded. We started up the hill, and immediately both of us almost fell over, feet sliding from under us on the sodden turf. I had to hold on to the running rail.

'Still think it's okay?' I asked, smiling. Tim had gone strangely silent.

'It is, uh, a bit wet,' he suggested.

We started down the hill, and had to walk several yards apart because we were splashing each other so much. Tim was now looking quite thoughtful as we slithered down the hill.

'Of course, there is quite a good race for my horse at Kelso next week,' Tim said thoughtfully.

Tim looked *very* thoughtful as the firemen seemed to be digging large holes in the course to try to get rid of the water. At any moment I expected several ducks to come in and land.

'I'll see you later,' said Tim, 'good luck.' He waved goodbye and headed for the weighing room.

I stayed behind and watched the firemen for a few moments. I didn't want to disappoint them or anything, but the puddle seemed to be getting bigger. Finally I headed back to the stand, and the PA announcement that greeted me was not encouraging: 'The trainer states that in the third race, Number Eight, High Edge Grey, will not run.'

Two drinks later I headed for the weighing room. I had a photograph I had promised I'd ask Simon to sign, but he wasn't there. Unfortunately I was promptly ambushed by a group of hacks sheltering from the rain.

'Are you going to pull him out?' they chorused.

I could see pencils hovering over notepads, so I chose my words carefully. 'It is very wet,' I answered, brilliantly.

'But he's going to hate this ground, you're going to have to pull him out. Aren't you?' said someone from the back. My own words came floating back to me, 'Come hell or high water.'

'Frankly,' I said, 'I'd be surprised if racing goes ahead. But if it does, I'm pretty sure David will want to run.'

I then spent a fruitless five minutes looking for Simon, and wandered back to the Turf Club to meet the family. As I walked in, I saw my father, looking like death warmed up and chain-smoking three cigarettes. I stopped as I heard a familiar voice over my shoulder. It was Richard Pitman, on television, doing a report for SIS. He was saying, 'It's stopped raining now and racing is definitely going ahead, but we hear that Richard Burridge wants to pull Desert Orchid out of the Gold Cup and David Elsworth wants to go ahead.' Oh I see, I thought. Here we go. I joined my father and he promptly lit another cigarette.

'This is unbelievable,' he said. 'We can't run him in this. Can we?' The tone in his voice was unmistakable. He was not going to pull Des out, but he hoped someone else would. Midge was also looking a little shell-shocked, and she noticed my wellies.

'Have you walked the course, Ricardo?' she asked.

'Afraid so,' I replied. I didn't elaborate. I don't believe in frightening people unnecessarily. I noticed my overcoat was starting to steam. I ordered another drink.

'What shall we do?' asked Midge. I knew Midge would be happy to go along with David's decision.

'Talk to David,' I said. 'It's up to him.' That day at Kempton four years ago floated back to me. I certainly wasn't in the mood to go through that again. I just wanted the decision to be made, and reached for the fast forward button in my mind, but couldn't find it.

'God I hope he pulls him out,' said Jimmy, lighting another cigarette.

I set off back to the weighing room with my photograph, and bumped into John Oaksey. 'Oh God,' he said sympathetically, 'what a nightmare, poor you.'

'You haven't seen David, have you?' I smiled.

'Afraid not,' he replied. 'Are you going to pull him out? I would.'

'It's up to David,' I shrugged.

A few yards further on I bumped into Mikey Seely. We exchanged a few uncomplimentary remarks about weather forecasters for a few moments, then he said, 'I've just been talking to

Dick Hern. He doesn't think your horse will be able to jump out of this ground. Are you going to withdraw him?'

I struggled on, with what was starting to sound like a litany. 'No,' I said, 'I'll talk to David.'

'I don't think anyone would blame you if you did pull out,' Mikey said.

This was odd. I had questioned whether we'd be brave enough to pull him out if we thought we had to, but everyone here seemed to be assuming he *would* be pulled out! I abandoned my search for Simon, and went looking for David.

'Anyone here seen David?' I rather foolishly asked the swelling press corps outside the weighing room.

'Why, are you going to pull the horse out?'

'Can we get this straight, you want to pull him out, but David doesn't?'

'Mightn't it be a mistake to pull him out before you've talked to David?'

WAITAMINUTE! I said I was looking for David to discuss the situation. Not, after all, that uncommon an event on the racecourse, an owner discussing his horse with a trainer.

'But you do *want* to pull him out?' someone chimed from the back.

I sighed and went back to the Turf Club, where Simon and Camilla, Johnnie and Pony, Simon and Juliet Bullimore were waiting. Simon Bullimore beamed at me. 'God this is bloody,' he said, smiling. 'What does David say about it?'

'Haven't seen him,' I replied.

'Christ, I hope he pulls him out, I've never wanted anything so much in my life,' muttered Jimmy. 'Can someone get me some cigarettes?'

We obviously formed a conspicuous group in the Turf Club and people kept pointing at us and whispering. It was now three-quarters of an hour before the Triumph Hurdle. As all anyone wanted to know was what David thought, and no one had set eyes on him, I thought I'd give it one last try.

I braved the press corps, this time just smiling at them, and gave an interview to Andrew Dagnall of *Pacemaker* and John Inverdale on Radio Two, in which I said that we appeared to have the high water I had mentioned, and hoped that hell was not about to follow.

Suddenly David appeared.

'Hi, David,' I said, 'I've been looking for you.'

'I know,' said David, 'I've been avoiding you. I hear you want to pull the horse out.' What?!

'No,' I protested, 'I just wanted to . . .'

'Come with me,' David said. 'I'm going to tell you why we have to run.'

'David, you don't need to tell me. If you want to run, that's fine.'

'Come on up to the Ritz Club box, we'll watch the Triumph Hurdle there.'

'David,' I said, 'it's not necessary.'

'Come on,' he insisted.

I hesitated for a moment and then I realised the press were watching us and it looked like we were having an argument. I went with David. In the Ritz Club box, we both had large whiskys and soda in our hands.

'Now,' said David, clearly not being about to brook any interruptions. 'I'm going to explain why he has to run. First, he has experience on his side, secondly he is the best jumper . . .' These arguments seemed rather familiar. They were what I had said myself a week ago. 'Thirdly, the ground won't bother him at all. And fourthly, he's the best horse in the race.'

'Fine,' I said, 'you've convinced me.' At that moment Alan Argeband walked up and shook my hand.

'Richard, I hear you're pulling him out, I'm sure it's the right thing.'

David turned and stared at him in complete disbelief for a moment, then exploded. 'Alan, I'm doing my best to persuade the owner to run the horse, and here you are talking crap, as usual!'

While David's back was turned giving the surprised Alan Argeband a bollocking, Max Kingsley approached and said, in his usual friendly fashion, 'I don't think anyone blames you for pulling him out, Richard, I hear the ground is desperate.'

David, overhearing this, paused mid-bollocking, did a double-take, and turned to Max Kingsley in renewed disbelief. 'Max, I know this is your box, but I'm trying to persuade the owner to run, and all I'm hearing is this crap about bad ground. This isn't bad ground, I've ridden on bad ground, and I can tell you this is not bad ground!'

I didn't point out that I was the only person here who had actually walked the course because it somehow would have seemed provocative. Anyway, I didn't need to. I just said, 'David, you don't *need* to persuade me to run, if you're happy, I'm happy.'

But David's bad mood deepened, especially when he was unplaced in the Triumph Hurdle, with Magnus Pym and Urizen, and he said, 'Look Richard, if you want to pull him out, pull him out, he's your horse.'

This supposed pep talk was going about as drastically wrong as any pep talk could do. David had started out by trying to persuade me to do something I'd already agreed to, but now seemed to be inviting me to do the opposite!

'David,' I countered for the umpteenth time, 'if you're happy, then I'm happy. Let's just stop *talking* about it!'

'You're obviously *not* happy, or we wouldn't be up here discussing it,' he said. Logic had disappeared. Ever since he'd arrived everyone had been asking him 'Is he going to run?' and David had countered with 'Of *course* he's going to run', but now it was getting to him a little. 'So if you want to pull him out,' he continued, 'pull him out. I just think you're making a big mistake. I understand your concern for the horse, but he's the best qualified to run in these conditions, and next year he might have a leg or something.'

This was one of the most ridiculous conversations I'd had in my life. For one moment something about David's manner suggested that even he was having second thoughts about running Des.

The point was not that he might get beaten – I never really thought he would win it, anyway – but that he might get killed, or injured, on a course and in a race I had never fancied much. Suddenly I started not to enjoy this at all. 'I think I'll go sit in my car,' I thought.

Instead, I walked with David back to the weighing room and found Simon. He was looking depressed after riding in the Triumph, and confirmed that the ground was atrocious. But he said that we might as well have a go, and if Des wasn't going or jumping, he'd just pull him up. That seemed fair enough, and we had a decision. But David rejoined us and suggested we go to talk to the other owners in the Turf Club. I was on my way out of the weighing room when Jonathan Powell grabbed me for an interview.

'I remember you saying at Sandown that the Gold Cup can be a terribly ugly race if the ground gets bottomless,' he said.

'I think it will be an ugly race today. I think we will have very tired horses, and obviously you worry much more about horses making mistakes, and you know this is such a popular horse, you're extra careful about not taking any unnecessary risks with him.'

'Bloody Jonathan,' said David, who had been watching this on television, 'he's just stirring it up. Now, let's talk about this.' He seemed happier again, and outlined what he'd said to me to the others, while I sat down and stared at a drink. Simon Bullimore was all for going ahead. So was Midge. Jimmy was more horrified by the prospect of having to make a decision than by the decision itself, but feeling himself in a comfortable minority, voted no. The needle swung round to me. This was ridiculous, half an hour earlier I'd been quite ready to run. But it was like having agreed to do something I never wanted to do in the first place. Having agreed to do it, I'd got locked into the comforting protection of rituals and schedules. I didn't have to think about it. But now I did have to think about it. After making the decision two weeks before, I now had to make it all over again. There was no point in bitching about it; here it was, my decision. Clarity arrives at moments like this, and I realised that deep down, heresy though this undoubtedly was, I didn't care if we ever won the Gold Cup or not. It wasn't the weather or the going. I just heard the same voice telling me to forget about Cheltenham that I had heard for years. But at the same time I recognised that I had ignored that voice ten days ago, so it wasn't the weather or the ground that worried me, it was just Cheltenham. Nothing had changed. I had been given one last chance to stop something, but I'd already made the decision. So I reached for the fast forward button in my mind, and this time found it.

'Let's do it,' I said.

'Well done,' said David, and grinned, patting me on the back.

Des looked the picture of health and power and ready to do the business as he was led round the pre-parade ring by Janice. Janice walked him into the saddling box and looked tense. Des stood trembling and peering out. Jimmy put the back of his hand out as usual and let Des take a chunk out of it. Everyone grimaced and turned away. Jane screwed up her face. She was still looking glamorous, despite the weather. 'Jimmy, I wish you wouldn't do that.'

'I'm sorry,' said Jimmy, nervously.

They went out to the parade ring, Janice on one side and Jinks on the other. I found a piece of chewing gum in my pocket and stuck it in my mouth, which was so dry I could barely breathe. My brother Simon and I joined Janice, Des and Jinks as they walked down the chute; then out to the course they went: Ballyhane, Bonanza Boy, Carvill's Hill, Cavvies Clown, Charter Party, Desert Orchid, Golden Freeze, Pegwell Bay, Slalom, Ten Plus, The Thinker, West Tip and Yahoo. 'And so the moment the whole National Hunt season has been gravitating towards . . .' murmured Julian Wilson. The sense of expectation was extraordinary.

I had lost my brother, so I stood alone on the grass. A couple of people recognised me and started to talk to me, but I just reached for that fast forward button. I was still preoccupied by what it was about Cheltenham that I dreaded. It was just a feeling, I couldn't really put a handle to it. It just felt like being taken somewhere I didn't want to go. But I wanted to be able to feel it, whatever it was, so I prayed that I could handle whatever was about to happen, and as always, the familiar glow of companionship flowed through me. The rain and the crowds disappeared. There was nothing now. The fast forward button clicked off. We were in real time.

The starter was shouting at the runners, 'Stay there, stay there!'

'They're under starter's orders,' boomed the PA.

'Wait a minute, sir, he's a spooky bugger this one,' Richard Rowe was suggesting about Ballyhane.

A few horses turned and came back in again.

The starter yelled, 'Come on.'

There was a great roar. I raised my binoculars. They were running.

Des looked pretty cheerful as he popped out of the mud and cleared the first. Simon had him on the outside and he took the lead at the second, doing a kind of false jump, a hitchkick, but still clearing it easily, enjoying the easy pace. Simon had him on the rail from Ten Plus and Charter Party, and at the third he was jumping well out of the ground. They streamed over the water, headed for the ditch and flowed over it. At the next on the far side, Golden Freeze fell. Then at the ditch Carvill's Hill fell. A great groan went up from the stands.

At the eighth, it was Des from Charter Party, Pegwell Bay and Ten Plus. Over the dreaded ninth he nodded, and so did the whole field. At the tenth The Thinker went sprawling. At the eleventh they seemed to be getting stuck in the ground, their breath clouding in the air. Des seemed to be toiling in the ground now, and Ten Plus went on and Cavvies Clown joined him on the outside. But Simon kept the rail.

On the first down the back straight, there were five in a line: Bonanza Boy on the outside, Slalom, Yahoo, Ten Plus and Des, behind them Charter Party and Cavvies Clown. John White pulled his goggles down. At the water Kevin Mooney on Ten Plus kicked on and went a length clear. With Charter Party going past Des now, Simon asked him to lengthen, and going into the ditch, Des put in a great leap which again put him upsides.

But Ten Plus forged ahead and, with Bonanza Boy being shaken up, Des, Charter Party and Slalom approached the sixteenth. Bonanza Boy made a mistake, leaving Ten Plus a length clear from Des, Charter Party and Yahoo. Kevin Mooney kicked again, and went three lengths up. At the final ditch, Slalom unseated John White, but Des put in a great leap; the course was taking him off the rail and he was now outside Ten Plus. Kevin Mooney kicked again, but Simon hadn't moved. This was the place Des always lost his races at Cheltenham; this was the crunch.

Cavvies Clown hit the next, and now the race looked to be between Ten Plus, Desert Orchid, Charter Party, Yahoo and Bally-hane on the outside. Kevin Mooney was really asking Ten Plus now, and went a couple of lengths clear, but Simon hadn't moved on Des. You could see three lengths between them. Kevin pulled his goggles down as they approached the dreaded downhill fence, and clearing that, took his stick out and gave Ten Plus a smack as they went down the hill and went a couple of lengths clear; behind him Simon still hadn't moved and was gaining. Des had weathered his worst moment and moved upsides Ten Plus. Both horses were in the air together at the third last, but Ten Plus didn't rise high enough and came crashing down, leaving Des in the lead. Then

Yahoo came up on his inside – Yahoo, ridden by Tom Morgan who had beaten us the year before on Pearlyman.

The ground was hurting now: great breaths hanging in the air, horses going up and down on the spot. Des's ears were flat back. If there was betting on the result now, there wouldn't have been a penny for Des. He looked beaten.

Des was desperately tired and, hating the ground, started to drift right. Simon took out his stick. Yahoo was saving yards going up the rail but Des was drifting and drifting to the right. Simon gave him a slap, Des straightened out and set himself for the second last. He jumped it half a length down, and started to drift right again, Simon hit him again and again he straightened, and now, coming to the last, a few strides off it, the grey changed his legs, pricked his ears, climbed over the fence, and set off up the run in half a length behind Yahoo. Both horses were desperately tired, but that prick of the ears at the last said so much about the grey horse. He was still in there, still battling. This was no day for exuberance, for showing off. Now the flashy bugger was running on raw courage. He was fighting; he was battling. Peter O' Sullevan was yelling into the microphone, 'But Desert Orchid is rallying, he's trying to come again.'

The horse who had drifted right all his life now, began to drift *left*, leaning on Yahoo, intimidating him, like he did to pretenders on the gallops. 'He's beginning to get up, he's beginning to get up,' yelled Peter O'Sullevan, and Simon momentarily had to stop riding him and pull him off, or he would have pushed Yahoo through the rails. The crowd was going berserk, and now Des was going on, inches, then feet, then a neck, and as the finishing post got closer, Des started to draw away. Peter O'Sullevan yelled, 'Desert Orchid wins the Gold Cup!' and Simon punched the air in triumph. A stride past the finishing post Des pulled up and pricked his ears.

Life goes into a sort of juddering slow motion. The first impression is of noise, barely human noise, like the crashing of waves against rocks. Then Richard Dunwoody on the third horse, Charter Party, grasps Simon's hand and just holds it and holds it. Tom Morgan on Yahoo shakes Simon's hand, then pats the grey horse on the neck. All the time the noise builds. Janice is in floods of tears. I pick her up and carry her down the chute towards the course. Simon gives a clenched fist salute to the crowd, and pulls the grey horse's ears, but Des resents it, as if to say, 'Bugger off, leave me alone.' The two Hunt horses supposed to lead the winner down the chute to the winner's enclosure baulk at the yelling mob ahead of them, and back off, but Des just swaggers in casually, Janice leading him, me on one flank, my brother Simon on the other. It's chaos, everyone is yelling and slapping the horse. I yell at Simon Sherwood, 'This will never happen again to any of us!' He smiles, nods. Now we can't move, the crowd is closing in, we have to shoulder our way through like rugger players. The crowds part as we shove our way into the winner's enclosure, the noise redoubles, everywhere you look people are applauding, yelling, screaming, cheering. Both my pregnant sisters-in-law are being squashed against the barrier. Finally we're all in the winner's enclosure except David Elsworth, because the gateman doesn't believe he's the trainer, though the winner's enclosure is full of people we've never seen before.

Jimmy is in tears, slapping the horse and talking to him. Johnnie Burridge raises both arms to the heavens in triumph. The grey horse just pricks his ears and considers the crowd. Some clown manages to put a tweed cap on his head but not even this indignity puts him off. Colin Brown embraces Janice. David Nicholson gives the horse a congratulatory slap. Everybody gives the horse a slap. David hovers behind the action, out of the limelight, but the line holding back the press is bulging. The noise from the crowd is getting louder, though the rain has blown up the TV sound. Three cheers for Desert Orchid. And again. And again. The grey's ears remained pricked, sweat steams from his flanks, now covered by a thin white and red sheet which reads 'Tote Cheltenham Gold Cup – Winner'. And there it is, for all to see, on the state of the art electronic number board:

Tote Gold Cup. 3.30. 1. Desert ORCHARD.

About this time I realised I was still chewing my piece of gum, as my mum shook my overcoat sleeve and told me to take it out, because I was about to receive the prize from the Queen Mother. 'No,' I said, 'Dad's going to do that.'

Jimmy was as happy as I've ever seen him. All the doubts and pain he felt over the years were swept away by the feeling that

he'd accomplished something – bred the winner of the Gold Cup
– that he never thought he could do, that he didn't think was
possible. The contradictions that ruled his life were settled for a
few brief moments in that cauldron of noise. The Queen Mother
chatted to Janice and patted Des, and now it was time for the
prize giving.

'Horses away,' said a voice, and the crowd booed. Eventually
Janice led Des out of the parade ring and away to the dope box.

The applause went on and on, for Jimmy, for David, for Simon.
No one could remember such emotion on a racecourse, even
hardened hacks were rumoured to have been crying. It was simply
one of the great days of sport, and no one who was there will ever
forget it. For a horse to have achieved what he had, to be so
widely touted, then win, didn't explain it. It was the way in which
he won it, the way in which everybody identified with him, and, it
is not overdoing it to say, loved him. It was a mass, joyous and
uncomplicated display of love that day, and everyone felt part of
it. Wherever we went, people were grinning and slapping us on
the back. Everyone there, on that appalling, cold, wet day, just
wanted it to last and last for ever.

Slowly reality filtered through. First came the rumour that two
horses had been killed in the Gold Cup. Then just one – Ten Plus.
That was enough. The day started to pall. We started to compare
what we were feeling with the emptiness that Ten Plus's connections must be feeling. I'm sure they wouldn't have denied us
our moment of glory, but it did put it in perspective. It had been
a tough race after all: thirteen starters; five finishers; one horse
killed.

Eventually the day was over, and the stands were emptying, and
I went to see Des. Janice was about to load him into the horsebox,
and a small crowd had gathered. Des was clean and dry now, but
tired, and a racegoer on the way out saw me and shouted, 'If Ten
Plus had stood up you'd have been slaughtered.' It was a macabre
choice of words, and it didn't matter that I disagreed.

Three-quarters of an hour later the Turf Club was emptying. I
had been on a fruitless search for the Gold Cup itself, but it had
already been packed off to the engravers. I was alone, sober now,
waiting for some people to turn up to whom I'd promised a lift.

I warily spotted an unsteady figure lurching rather aggressively towards me, but he was so comically drunk with his bashed trilby and crumpled coat that I couldn't help smiling.

'You know,' he said in a friendly-aggressive manner, as he clamped a hand on my shoulder. Then his face lit up in a broad grin. 'You know, I wanna tell you something. I had fawty parns on Yarhoo at thirty-three to one – and I was shouting for your bloody hawse on the run in!' And with that he grinned and lurched off.

David had invited me back for the night. Whitsbury had more or less exploded at the same time as Cheltenham, but you could still hear the boom long after Cheltenham had gone quiet. The drinks had been on the house at The Cartwheel and the place was awash with journalists and TV crews. Chris Harper had never seen anything like it. David, Rodney, Janice and everyone in David's yard was interviewed, all much the worse for wear. David was asked whether he was confident Dessie would get up. 'Well,' said David, 'I was certainly more confident when I was watching the video.'

I had a meal with the other owners at the Fossebridge Inn, and arrived at Whitsbury about three am, after everybody had gone to bed. Jane had left the lights on and the spare room door open. I spent half an hour reading that morning's papers and feeling what a long, long way we'd come in eighteen hours. I went to bed. The next morning there was an unbelievable deluge of publicity – front pages on all the papers, TV crews, radio interviews. I had to go back to London for a script meeting, but before I left, I did an interview with Malcolm Foley of the *Daily Express*. In it, I said I thought Des was a gift from God. The remark came out as a gift from 'the Gods'. This remark was later used to peddle a porcelain statuette of Des: 'A Gift from the Gods'. Perhaps this example of the way a declaration of faith in a higher authority could be turned into a commercial endorsement was a sign of things to come.

As we started to take stock of what happened, we concluded that from a cold-blooded point of view, it was just about Des's worst performance of the season. But that didn't matter much; he had won the King George and the Gold Cup in the same year. Des himself seemed very well, in fact, as bright as a button, and we had to decide what to do with him next.

Five days later we combined my brothers Simon and Johnnie's birthday party with a party to celebrate the Gold Cup, to which everybody we could think of was invited and during which everybody who did come had too much to drink. A minibus conveyed a dozen lads from Whitsbury. Janice was there with her boyfriend Paul Holley. Rodney and Shirley were there. Martin Chilton, in charge of the lower yard at Whitsbury, was there. And, of course, David and Jane, and Simon Sherwood were there. We were all interviewed – for some reason that escapes me a camera crew was there – and Janice was asked what she thought should happen now. She giggled and protested it wasn't up to her. We persisted.

'Take him home,' she said.

22

⚜

Over the Top

WE DIDN'T TAKE HIM HOME. Perhaps we were getting carried away, but Des seemed unbeatable – in the dry and in the wet, from two to three miles five, in handicaps and conditions races. We dreamed of further glory. Only Arkle had done the King George/Gold Cup/Whitbread treble in the same season, and we thought Des had a chance of emulating him. David wasn't happy with the Whitbread, though, as he thought the ground would be too firm by the end of April, but he saw no reason why Des shouldn't have another race, and a week later he nominated the Martell Chase at Liverpool. Des still seemed to be 'on a high', and David was always keen to strike while the iron was hot.

However the shock waves were still reverberating from Cheltenham, and it sometimes seemed that the whole country had stood still for those final few moments of the Gold Cup. Certainly anyone watching the beginning of BBC coverage of the Liverpool meeting expecting the usual introduction followed by shots of horses in the paddock was in for a shock.

It started with Rodney cantering Desert Orchid at Whitsbury, in slow motion, to a roll on a kettle drum. It then dissolved to another slow motion shot of Des eating some grass, then another slow motion shot of him galloping, then another, then another, all accompanied by the plaintive Ennio Morricone score from *The Mission*. Desert Orchid seemed to be stuck in permanent slow motion as the captions appeared: Racing from Aintree: Featuring the Martell Chase: *Starring* Desert Orchid.

Seeing this later, David groaned. No wonder things didn't go quite right that day. We weren't finished yet, either. Several more slow motion moments were followed by shots of David's horsebox arriving at Haydock, and Julian Wilson picks up the commentary.

Janice leads Des into a box and gives him an apple as Julian explains this is 'Desert Orchid's secret overnight location'. It didn't seem like much of a secret. Janice leads Des into another box and grins at the camera, but we're not finished yet. Morricone is replaced by Level 42, as we reprise Desert Orchid's early hurdling and steeplechasing career, and end with a flourish at Cheltenham. Finally we're back at Liverpool as Simon rides Des out on to the track.

It was all very nicely done, but it was certainly true that a kind of madness had descended, and if you can define madness as a lack of detachment, we were all guilty of it. Everywhere we went, people stared, newspaper headlines screamed, cameras rolled.

We started to feel self-conscious. Things we had been doing for the last six years now seemed faintly ridiculous – gathering at the pre-parade ring beforehand in our lucky clothes, crowding into the saddling box and giving the horse a pat, Simon Burridge and I walking down with Des to the course. All privacy had vanished.

The scrapbook, which I'd started all those years ago with my rather feeble page and a half, now threatened to run to over 110 pages on the Gold Cup alone. I stared at this mountain of newspapers in alarm. To hell with that. It might be bad luck not to do the scrapbook, but who had the time?

The problem was, it wasn't just the coverage that was over the top. It was also the horse.

The Martell Chase, called the Chivas Regal Cup the previous year, was a conditions race, and as a result of winning at Cheltenham, Des had to carry top weight of eleven stone thirteen. Seven horses took him on, most notably Yahoo and Charter Party. After seeing so much of the horse in the media, it was almost a shock to be confronted with the real thing again. He looked well, bouncing around the paddock, and he'd picked Janice up by the jacket and thrown her across the box while he was being tacked up, which was a good sign, though possibly not for Janice. He looked fresh going down to the start, too, and tried to tank off with Simon.

In the race he looked good, bowling along in front, skipping over his fences, though Simon was not entirely happy with him.

Starting out on the second circuit, he began to worry a little. He had to ride him into the plain fence in front of the stands, then ride him over the water jump. None of this, I should add, was apparent from the stands at the time: the horse appeared to be going well.

He set off round the bend, still going well, still in the lead, and straightened out for the first in the back straight. Charter Party was about a length down on him on his outside. Des seemed to meet the fence about right, perhaps he was a little close to it, and brushed through the top of it. He landed a little steeply. It was the sort of straightforward 'mistake' he had made dozens of times. Jumping fences at speed, especially at this level, requires rapid 'adjustments' on take off and landing. A good jumper, which Desert Orchid certainly was – he had never fallen over fences – makes these adjustments as a matter of course.

But on this day he didn't. He didn't adjust, he didn't stick out a leg, he just crumpled on landing, went down on his nose, and flipped over.

Desert Orchid had fallen. So had Charter Party beside him. Two Gold Cup winners falling at the same easy, unremarkable fence, in a race which had also claimed the Gold Cup winner of three years before, Dawn Run. The other jockeys looked as surprised as the crowd.

It was not a bad fall, and Des, in typically agile fashion, bounced to his feet and set off in pursuit. I was watching from the stands, and thought the fall had been so easy that there must be something seriously wrong with him. Anyway, one minute I was on the grandstand, the next I was running down the track like an idiot. The grey horse came cantering down the track, and a man in a trenchcoat caught him and handed him to me. He seemed to be fine. Ahead I could see Janice, David and Peter Maughan hurrying towards us looking worried, and I handed Des over to Janice, Peter took the tack off, and that was that. In the meantime, Yahoo, who had gamely collared Delius on the run in and won the race, was practically ignored, which was a little tough on him.

Simon wasn't hurt, and gained some compensation by winning the John Hughes Memorial Chase over the National fences on Villierstown in great style, and a couple of hours later said he was retiring. We thought we might change his mind later. It seemed almost unthinkable. But Simon, who had originally planned to ride professionally for just two seasons before taking up a new career as a trainer had now ridden for four seasons and won two King Georges, two Whitbreads, one Gold Cup, one Champion Chase, and had scaled such heights on Desert Orchid that there was nowhere to go but down. He'd lost his appetite for the day to day slog at the small jumping tracks; he had also had his fair share of injuries and was happy to get out in one piece. If he quit now, he would be quitting at the top.

His ten rides on Desert Orchid marked quite possibly one of the most exhilarating partnerships in the history of jump racing. There was such a complete understanding between horse and rider that they appeared to be able to do almost anything. In his ten rides on Desert Orchid, Simon had won nine; *Nine Out of Ten* later became the title of his autobiography. It was a good title, but we, and I'm sure the horse if he had been able to, would have given him ten.

So with Desert Orchid having involuntarily retired two jockeys in as many years, we had to find a replacement for next season. We chucked a few names at each other but soon realised there was only one man we wanted, Richard Dunwoody. He was retained by David Nicholson, but the Duke had always been an admirer of the horse, and we thought he might be prepared to release Richard. David said he'd approach David Nicholson and Richard Dunwoody in due course, but there was no hurry. There was a long hot summer ahead of us. That's what we thought, anyway.

23

The Price of Success

BUT CHELTENHAM WOULD NOT GO AWAY. Des stopped off at Cheltenham on his way home to receive another Bravest Horse of the Year Award from Piper Heidsieck, and also, incongruously but touchingly, the award for 'the greatest contributor to National Hunt Racing'. The Queen Mother had been a previous winner. Janice and Rodney had to cope with the mixed emotions of receiving the awards and then seeing their charge disappear for the summer. By common consent Liverpool had come too soon after Cheltenham, but Des looked magnificent, as hard and polished as marble.

He was unanimously voted National Hunt Horse of the Year for the third time, and won just about every award going. A certain proportion of our Gold Cup money went in dry cleaning bills as we attended one black-tie function after another. At one of these David said, 'Dessie is a wonderful horse and it gives me a great sense of pride to think that so many people get so much pleasure from watching him run. But if I wasn't his trainer, I think I'd be sick of hearing the sound of his name!'

Des was certainly still getting his fair share of press coverage even though he was now in a field. Whereas six years earlier we would have struggled to give him away, his performance at Cheltenham seemed to have enthused half the country. The correspondence pages of the racing press were filled with tributes to him or calls for his retirement. When someone wrote to the *Racing Post* suggesting that people only liked him because he was grey, such a volume of scorn and contempt descended on him that the *Post* was forced to close the correspondence on the subject. He was mentioned in *Spitting Image*, he was sought for commercials, and he had clearly become that rare thing, a 'crossover' sporting hero. People who knew nothing about racing knew about Desert Orchid, and really identified with him.

In fact so many people felt that they 'owned' him that they also assumed responsibility for his failures. Following Liverpool we received dozens of guilt-ridden letters in which the various correspondents blamed themselves for his fall. They hadn't been wearing their lucky clothes, or they had been to see him in the flesh, or they had had a bet on him – in one way or another they had broken their own rules and tempted fate, and they were responsible. Superstition, of course, is the curse of ownership. Since there is almost nothing you can do to affect the result of something that means so much to you, you invent a connection, however unlikely.

Hundreds of letters poured through our collective letter boxes, most of them touching testaments to how much Desert Orchid meant to the writers, but I couldn't begin to see how I'd be able to answer them. It was just as bad for David, or more accurately for Chris Hill. Chris was busy enough at the best of times, but now he was staying at his desk till nine o'clock every night wading through sacks of mail, only to find another sack waiting the next day. We were all rather accessible: our addresses were in the phone book, though I don't suppose it would have made much difference if they hadn't been. Chris got plenty of letters addressed simply to Desert Orchid, c/o David Elsworth, and one envelope I received was addressed to Richard Burridge, owner of Desert Orchid, High on the Moors, Somewhere in Yorkshire. A friend of mine decided to join in the fun, and sent me a postcard from Australia addressed to Richard Burridge, Desert Orchid, England. It arrived in six days.

So while the object of this adulation munched away in a field with an enviably free diary, we were being driven mad. It was now the middle of May, and the Cheltenham Gold Cup would not go away. We had sent off what spare photos we had, but barring moving or leaving the country, our only other option appeared to be to become organised, and Midge offered, to our immense relief and gratitude, to see what she could do. 'Dessie gets his fan club' ran the headlines the next day.

What we would have all done without Midge I do not know.

She was magnificent. She had taken a back seat before, but now she stepped into the glare of the limelight. In an uncomplicated, efficient way she set about organising the club. She had to start by working out what we could offer. Desert Orchid was just munching grass, and there was not much you could say about that. Not for the first time or the last, the demand for information about him outstripped the supply. She decided to stage an open day; she didn't know whether anyone would actually want to come to Leicestershire to see a horse in a box, but she was prepared to organise a day if they did.

Within a couple of weeks Midge had received several hundred applications. Suddenly there were forms to order, photographs to organise, and insatiable demands to be met. She branched out into sweatshirts and tea towels and set up an 0898 Desert Orchid Hotline. There are various publications around which advise prospective owners what may be involved when you put a horse into training, but I'm willing to bet that setting up a fan club for your horse does not appear in them.

Midge still found it hard to believe that she owned one of the great jumpers of all time, and thought it a small thing to share him. Though it would have been tempting to tell everyone to go away, it would also have been rather ungracious, and we supported her. It is one thing being behind someone, though, and another being in the front line. One thing became clear: if you don't have enough members, you lose money, and the fan club was losing money hand over fist. Then a great friend of Midge's, Johnny Hippisley, came to our aid. He could see that even without Midge taking a penny for all the work she was doing, the fan club was heavily in debt, but the idea of a horse having a fan club intrigued him enormously, and also presented a challenge. Johnny was a theatre producer, so he applied his entrepreneurial skills to see if he could get the fan club to make a profit, as it would then be in a position to support various charities such as the International League for the Protection of Horses, and the Brooke Hospital in Cairo.

They set about organising the open day: together they contacted the police, hired a band, organised videos, arranged parking for 500 cars, and hired marquees. My sister Frances and several family friends were drafted in to steward this event.

Jimmy's nerves had not been improved by all this – for a start things had not gone smoothly with Desert Orchid. His corns became infected and he was hobbling lame. It was now late May and Des was not ready to go to Flintham. And with the open day already set for July and an appearance at a black-tie do for the PDSA slotted in before it, Jimmy was locked into fixed dates, something he had never been before. Finally he scrambled Des over to Flintham in the first week of June, with his half-sister Indian Orchid as company for the first time, and Jim Stone again kept an eye on things.

The whole thing was becoming a little frantic, though. TV stations wanted this shot and that shot; the press kept wanting progress reports; the phone never stopped ringing with fan club members reporting that the printers for some extraordinary reason had printed at the bottom of a photo of Colin Brown riding Des 'Desert Orchid ridden by Oliver Sherwood'.

The sight of the muddy, plump figure in the field with his ears pricked inquisitively towards Jimmy as he leant over the gate on his regular visits to Flintham always did something to raise his spirits – but the pleasure was fleeting. He, like the rest of us, had begun to wonder what we'd done when we'd agreed to run him in the Gold Cup.

June shot past, and Des was brought back and cleaned up by the girl who now worked for Jimmy, Sally Buck. Midge and Johnny worked round the clock to get everything organised, and Jimmy spent hours with Des on the horsewalker, thankfully away from the telephone and the giving of directions to Ab Kettleby. By now the garden looked like a fairground: the horses' field had been turned into a carpark, and Desert Orchid's sisters, Peacework, Tudor Orchid, Irish Orchid and Indian Orchid, were drafted in as the supporting cast and were now all in boxes trying to eat the cardboard name tags pinned to their doors.

The fan club day was free to members, but Midge and Johnny still didn't know if anybody would actually turn up – they did, in their hundreds. They queued at Des's stable door for pictures and a pat; they lined a parade ring, and Jimmy and Midge struggled with a loud-hailer as Des was led round. There were schoolgirls and grannies, racing buffs and pensioners. They got there in cars and buses and trains, organised carpools and overnight stays, got out of sick beds and postponed holidays, and most amazing of all, seemed to have a wonderful time as they reviewed races and swopped memories of where they were at this race and that race. It was like an extended family, presided over by Desert Orchid, who rose to the occasion and acted as if it was no less than he deserved. It was really a very funny, friendly day. Crazy, but touching.

By now I was also filming the event for Channel Four. In the weeks after the Gold Cup my phone had never stopped ringing with news of one proposed enterprise after another, and when people were kind enough to offer us a royalty, we gave it to charity. I don't know whether anybody made much money out of all these enterprises, but I rather doubt it, as there were so many of them. But when I learnt that no less than four films were being proposed, I decided to get involved. There did seem to be a demand for a film about Des, and though it was a little complicated trying to fit it into the other work I was supposed to be doing that summer, it would mean we could control what access could be given to Des, and not mess up his preparation for the next season. The idea of the film was simply to take Des round the calendar from the Gold Cup to his first race of the next season to show how much work goes into producing a horse fit to run on a racecourse, and also in a small way to show how many people's lives Des had affected. It was to be shown on Christmas Eve, and we knew that we had to appeal to a broad audience who did not necessarily know anything about racing or about Desert Orchid.

We completed the first two blocks of shooting in Flintham and at the fan club open day, and prepared for three days in Yorkshire, then Des got the cough. It took a couple of weeks for him to recover, and we were about to send him back when David's yard also got the cough, and David had to close down for a few weeks.

David, Janice and Jinks eventually turned up to get him, and Des disappeared whinnying into the mist to embark on yet another season. It was a touching scene, but much as we all loved the horse, it was actually a relief to get rid of him. He had had a rather more relaxing summer than we had!

Three weeks later we went down to Whitsbury to shoot Des on the gallops, and David, who was also starting to be driven slightly mad by all the attention, was in rather a sombre mood, wondering out loud whether Des might have peaked. I also interviewed Chris Harper, the owner of the stables, who said he had seen nothing like it. Once upon a time Whitsbury had been a sleepy Hampshire village, but now it was alive with people cruising up and down the lanes trying to catch a glimpse of Desert Orchid. People had been turning up all summer when Des wasn't there, and some of them were quite happy just to see his box. David occasionally found people wandering into his yard and had to throw them out. It was becoming difficult for David to treat Desert Orchid as just another horse, but fortunately he was more than up to it.

David had originally targeted the Terry Biddlecombe Chase for Des's comeback race, but the autumn stayed warm and dry, and the ground was too fast to work him, let alone race. We eventually went down to film Des for his one and only schooling session, and recorded the first time Richard Dunwoody sat on the horse. Richard was excited at the prospect. An Ulsterman, he had hit the headlines as an amateur when riding four winners in an afternoon at Hereford. Then he had won the Grand National on West Tip, and had gone from strength to strength. He was originally retained by Tim Forster, and had once ridden Ragged Robin, but now worked for David Nicholson with a second retainer for Nicky Henderson, and both trainers had sportingly agreed to release him whenever necessary.

Richard was a wonderful jockey with a quiet style that had a touch of poetry to it, and I suppose as he climbed on the grey horse for the first time we looked for some sign that he was experiencing something special. But if he had shown it, it would probably have been faked. After all, Richard rides hundreds of horses every season. Probably behind the eyes the brain clicks instinctively, noting the head carriage, the length of neck, the responsiveness to shifts of weight, but these are physical sensations and difficult to describe.

Rodney explains about how to stop getting carted and Richard listens, really listens, nods. With a grin at the camera he's off. Paul Holley on Wink Gulliver, an iron grey, is beside him as they stick their noses over the fences. Des likes this, a fence. He eyes his jockey sideways a little, and decides he likes the quiet hands.

Back to the start of the run in to the first of the schooling fences, and they're off, Des fighting for his head, climbing up an invisible staircase as his hind legs tuck in behind him, into power drive as he's off. Richard is immediately more familiar in his riding pose, head level, looking at the fence as the power builds up behind him. Flick, flick, crash, flick, flick. It's over, Des is galloping away, with Wink Gulliver trailing behind him. David is relieved that's over. These schooling sessions make him nervous, and they're even worse when they're being filmed. Richard rides back, grinning. He enjoyed it, lucky man. He calls Des 'the grey horse'. What does he like about him? Power. Then he adds, intelligence . . .

We're not just switching jockeys this year, we're switching colours. The old woolies shrunk so much at Cheltenham they would hardly fit David's young daughter Jessica, and another set has been ordered by Chris Hill. Jockeys don't like new colours. They spit on them and stamp them on the floor.

The clock was counting down to Des's first race after Liverpool, the Silver Buck Handicap Chase at Wincanton, which turned into a two horse race between Des and Roll-A-Joint, the previous year's Scottish National winner, and we were all as nervous as sheep as we drove into Somerset.

Richard put up with the hoopla in a relaxed fashion, but the scenes before and after the race took some believing. The papers had been full of it for weeks before and half the photographers and sports news teams in the country seemed to have descended on Wincanton. Ian Renton, the Clerk of the Course, let us film wherever we wanted so I had nothing to complain about. But, and perhaps I noticed this more because I was trying to film the event, you couldn't get near the horse for cameramen. I'd given my crew instructions to stay back out of the way, but all they were filming was the back of other photographers' heads. The problem wasn't confined to professionals. At every fence people shot off instamatics, with an explosion of flashes. I suppose if there was one horse that was immune to photography it was Desert Orchid, but I wondered what would happen if a flash exploded in the eyes of a young horse as he was about to take off.

Anyway, Des won in a canter, Richard reported himself delighted, and a few weeks later he turned out in the Tingle Creek Chase which had by now been established as his annual warm-up for the King George.

Again the papers were full of it, and Des got applauded everywhere he went. When once upon a time we were almost alone with our nerves and the grey horse at the pre-parade ring, now we were surrounded by enthusiasts happy to miss the race before to get a peek at their hero. It seemed more like a public appearance than a horse race. And then Des was beaten by Long Engagement, who was receiving two stone.

There was a sort of stunned reaction in the winner's enclosure afterwards, and a stunned reaction in the press the next day. David said it felt like someone had died. Long Engagement got almost no attention in spite of the fact that he'd won. However often we'd told his new fans that Desert Orchid was just a racehorse with no divine right to win, we got the impression no one really believed us, that this was some sort of joke. They learnt it that day at Sandown. He was beaten. No big deal, he'd come on for the race, and with all the doubts about the ground – Sandown was almost cancelled – we were grateful to have got two races into the horse.

And yet, and yet ... It was one of the many ironies of that summer that I'd set out to record a typical summer in the life of a horse, but in every way it was not typical. He got the cough, then David's yard got the cough, and then he had been the victim of a strange accident on the gallops ...

Amongst the many other stars in David's stable was the magnificent chaser Barnbrook Again, a deep-chested eight-year-old gelding who had never failed to finish in the first three in any of his races over fences and hurdles, including the Champion Hurdle, and but for leg problems would probably have doubled his winning tally. Some people at Whitsbury, notably Chris Hill, regarded him as at least as good as Des, if not better. Simon Sherwood had ridden him the previous season and said that he was potentially the best chaser he had ever ridden; but there was a gap between potential and achievement. If there was one chink in his armour it was that he was perhaps not quite as tough as the grey horse, and because of this I always fancied in a showdown Des would prevail.

With two such stars in the same stable, there was a certain amount of friendly rivalry between us and Mel Davies, the owner of Barnbrook Again, who was as dotty about his horse as we were about ours. Mel had shown enormous belief in Barnbrook after he had broken down, remortgaging his house to buy out his partners, and now his faith was paying off. I put my foot in it one day when a remark intended as a joke had found its way into print, namely that I didn't mind Desert Orchid and Barnbrook Again being in the same race as long as they went to the course in the same box, as Des would psych him out on the way to the track. Mel wasn't amused.

In one sense it was true that Barnbrook Again was not as competitive as Des. To try to break him of the habit of settling in behind the grey horse on the gallops, David decided to send Barnbrook Again and a galloping companion out before first lot so that 'Barney' would have the benefit of an empty gallop without the grey horse throwing his weight around.

Des plainly resented this. He was used to being first out and he didn't like the idea of anyone preceding him. About a month before his first race, he had been walking back from the gallops when he spotted Barnbrook Again's galloping companion walking ahead of him on the road back to the stables. Barnbrook Again was well ahead, but his companion, either because he wasn't as talented in the walking department, or because he had been exhausted by trying to keep up with Barney, had fallen behind, and Des, walking at his usual brisk pace, was closing on him and began to eye him dangerously. Des slowly closed the gap, eventually drew alongside, and before Rodney could stop him, went for him. Des had not chosen his ground very carefully though, and slipped, did the splits, crashed down on the road and, as Rodney rolled clear, galloped off. He returned half an hour later, covered with mud, looking very pleased with himself, with all the skin scraped off one hock. Rodney was a little anxious. Des had really done the splits when he'd come down.

Then at Wincanton, for the first time, he returned with speedy cuts. These are cuts on the inside of the back legs caused by the back legs 'overrunning' the front legs, with the front shoes actually cutting the inside of the leg just below the stifle. Des had never had them before. At Sandown he got more speedy cuts. It seemed there might be a problem. And though Des was now hot favourite for a third King George, he would have to be at his best to win it.

I have to say that I immediately thought of George Armatage, and as I was going down to Whitsbury anyway with the tape of the Channel Four film I'd finished, I decided to talk to David about it. David listened good-humouredly to the suggestion that George come down to his yard. I asked him, if he was still worried, to give Michael Stoute a call. He said he would.

I went home and waited for David's call. Three days later he phoned. He'd talked to Michael Stoute, who had given George a glowing recommendation. David would allow him into the yard and take it from there.

I called George and he agreed to come down when he could. A week later, only seven days before the King George, I got a call from Nancy. George would be arriving on the 8.10 Newcastle to Heathrow flight.

In one sense I was dreading what might happen when we got there, because I simply had no idea what would happen. If David was in a bad mood that morning he was quite capable of throwing George out of the yard, and George, equally blunt, would probably have called him enough names to make it unlikely that he, or for that matter I, would ever be welcome again. In another sense and for the same reasons, I was looking forward to it. I sensed some drama in the air. But I decided that it would be better to be prepared, so I invited Simon Bullimore to come down with me, and he accepted. In the end this proved a nightmare for him, as instead of being in London that morning he was in Brussels and had to be back there for a meeting that afternoon. However he was determined that we should try to sort this out, if we possibly could, and said he might be able to fly over in the morning and fly back in the afternoon.

'It's up to you,' I said. 'But I think it would be a help if you could come.'

He hesitated for a moment. 'Yes,' he said, 'it is important. I'll come.' He laughed. 'I must be mad. We all must be mad.'

I somehow managed to meet both planes and drove Simon and George down to Whitsbury. We arrived at the yard; Jane made us a cup of coffee and telephoned David in the office to say we were there. David pulled up and came striding into the kitchen, grinning broadly.

'Hello, Richard,' he said. 'Hello, Simon.'

Simon and I shook hands with David.

'David,' I said, 'this is George Armatage.' David paused for a second, his eyes twinkling.

'Hello, George,' he said. 'I've heard a lot about you.'

'Aye,' said George, his eyes twinkling back, 'I've heard a lot about you too, Mister Elsworth.'

'Have you?' said David, smiling. 'I should think you'd like to take a look at this grey horse.'

David walked across the yard to Dessie's box with George limping beside him. Des was standing watching all the goings-on with his usual curiosity. David opened the door. Outside the lads were preparing for the second lot.

'Ooh, looks grand sir, grand.' George patted him on the head and Des snorted at him, searching for a peppermint. David purred back at Des and took his rugs off. George hobbled round him and looked at him from behind.

'Whoa old fellah,' he said.

David started elaborating on his plans for the horse in the remaining six days before the King George. George listened, without commenting, then said, 'Can you fetch me a headcollar Richard?' I obliged. George ran his fingers down the horse's spine, and hitting a spot, Des went down sharply at one side.

'Aye,' said George, 'he's out. If you'll just leave him to me, sir.' David looked at George, then looked at me. This was it. This was the moment. Simon and I watched without having any idea of what would happen next.

David paused, looked at George again, then shrugged and walked out. If I ever had any doubts that David was a great man, they disappeared in that moment. It was one of the single most gracious, sporting and magnanimous gestures I have ever witnessed. I knew how David felt, and I knew how much he hated to climb down. We stood outside the box, and I just said, 'Thank you, David', though I could have hugged him, not only for letting George deal with the horse, but also for the wonderful way he had dealt with it.

David started talking about the second lot parading round in front of him. After a few moments there was a bang on the door and I let George out. Des was standing as before.

'Is he all right now, George?' I asked.

'Well, he was in a bad way,' he said. 'His back was wrong. Now, let's have a look at these shoulders.'

For some reason, George never minded anyone watching him do the shoulders. David put the rugs back on and watched with mild interest as George ran his fingers down the horse's shoulder and Des trembled violently. 'Aye, that's out, too,' he said. He walked round to the other side and did the same thing. 'He's out there, too. Poor old fellah.' He walked round to the other side and performed a routine that, though I'd watched it done plenty of times, I could not describe fully. He sort of carved his thumb down the horse's shoulder, then slapped it, then repeated the original movement and there was no shuddering.

'Aye, sir, he's fine now. He'll be right now. Just give him three days walking and he'll be right as rain. He'll win the King George for you now.'

David gave no indication whether he believed a word of this or not, just nodded, smiled, and said, 'Right, George. Have you got to go?'

'We've got an hour,' I said.

'Good,' smiled David. 'Let's go and have a look at some *good* horses.'

We all went up to the gallops to watch second lot and David and George got on famously, discussing the various young horses as they cantered past. Then it was time to go; David shook George's hand, and thanked him for coming.

'Of course,' said David to me and Simon, his eyes twinkling, 'I don't believe a word of it.'

'That's okay,' I said. 'But thanks all the same.'

'Yes,' said Simon, 'thank you.' Simon had been equally touched.

'Tell me, George,' said Simon, as we drove back to the airport, 'if you don't mind me asking, why don't you let anyone see what you're doing?'

'Because it's so simple,' said George, 'anyone could do it. I'd lose my livelihood.'

'Why do you let people see you doing the shoulders?'

'Oh, because you couldn't get that from watching.'

To be honest, neither Janice nor Rodney noticed much difference in Des, but this strange world of bad backs that we had stumbled into dealt with only that two or three per cent at the top end of a horse's performance, that lengthening of a stride on the run in, that ability to jump a fence flat out after galloping three miles that perhaps made the difference between winning and losing.

We now approached the normal Boxing Day festivities in an appropriate mood, as did the sports writers for whom Desert Orchid's appearance at Christmas had become an annual jamboree, though perhaps something of a nightmare for sub-editors as they struggled to come up with headlines that avoided all the 'White Christmas', 'Christmas cracker' clichés of previous years.

There were a few musings about whether Des's exhausting run in the Gold Cup followed by his fall at Liverpool had taken the edge off him, and whether Richard could pick up where Simon had left off, but basically he was a warm order to win. There was, at the same time, quite understandably I think, evidence of a professional weariness of a very British variety that was later to come to the fore much more. Des was increasingly attracting a fanatical 'new element' into racing, and while nobody could deny that Des was the real thing, or that he was good for racing – in some ways he was the embodiment of National Hunt racing – there was none the less a feeling that he was threatening to dominate the sport to the exclusion of all the other horses. So it was, in a way, something of a relief to the sportswriters when he had been beaten at Sandown. It punctured the myth of invincibility, and turned him back into a racehorse. Now, in the face of despondent 'Dessie fans' journalists could re-engage their enthusiasms, pick up their form books, and argue that he was still by some way the best horse in training and the likely winner of the King George.

On the face of it, Des's biggest rival was Barnbrook Again. There was a certain amount of doubt whether Barnbrook Again would stay the three miles, and though the style of Barnbrook Again's victories suggested he would stay, David was not confident. Against that was the fact that the King George always rewarded class, and Barnbrook Again had class in abundance. He also had the jumping brilliance, the turn of foot and the flamboyance that frequently characterised winners of the King George. Even taking Desert Orchid out of the picture, the past winners of the race represented the cream of the cream – more so than the Gold Cup really – and Barnbrook Again's inclusion in that pantheon would be no less than he deserved. In some ways, too, it was unfortunate that coming from the same stable as the grey horse, he didn't always receive the credit from the outside world that he deserved.

One of Barnbrook Again's assets was that he not only handled Cheltenham but he also thrived on it, and I suspect that very few people at David's yard would have backed the grey horse to beat him at Cheltenham. But here opinion was divided: some people felt that the younger Barnbrook Again could depose Desert Orchid, who at ten was not likely to be getting any better. So even within Whitsbury this started to have the appeal of a grudge match, the winner to be the best horse in training – well, till the next time. Chris Hill was understandably going purple over all the inquiries about Desert Orchid and was forced to point out that they did train other horses there, most notably one Barnbrook Again who might well beat him.

Yahoo, his challenger in the Gold Cup, was lining up but his recent form didn't inspire much confidence (3P) and Kempton's flat track wouldn't draw on his stamina. Bob Tisdall, from the same stable, was entered only in case Wetherby was abandoned. Pegwell Bay certainly commanded respect, as he had speed but not necessarily stamina, and Kempton would have seemed ideal except for the fact that it was right-handed, which according to Tim Forster didn't suit him. The final contender was Norton's Coin, trained by permit holder Sirrell Griffiths. Richard Dunwoody had ridden Norton's Coin the previous season and thought him a nice horse, but this was his first race of the season and he still looked burly in the paddock beforehand.

I thought there was only one danger to Des, and that was Barnbrook Again – and they were travelling to the races in the same horsebox. Hamming it up in the parade ring, Des looked tough, a fighting machine, head bowed, glancing up to eye his crowd, sweat breaking out on his neck. Richard was smiling; he looked confident. This was his first really good chance at winning a King George.

As the race started, Des did not jump with his usual fluency to begin with, but perhaps realising his shoulders and back were not hurting, he started to stretch out and reach for his fences in his familiar way, and with Richard sitting quietly on his back, settled in the lead. His jumping was fluent now, and Barnbrook Again was on his tail, but the crowd were waiting for the race to start in earnest. Turning away from the stands for the first time, Des seemed more interested in the crowds than in the race, and as he came to the second last ditch, the twelfth, he stared at two photographers standing on stepladders; he was still looking at them when he was supposed to take off, and completely missed the fence, crashing through it. Richard did well to keep Dessie balanced, but at least that woke him up. He stopped playing to the gallery and started concentrating on the race. He stretched down the back straight, and coming to the fourth last they started closing on him.

Richard let him take a breather round the bend, then pressed the button and, ears back, he shot forward, and it was him and Barnbrook Again flat out down the straight for the last three. Very few horses could live with Desert Orchid's power over these three, and in a matter of strides it was all over. To an incredible roar from the crowd, he skipped over the last and sprinted away for an eight length win from Barnbrook Again. Simon Bullimore received the trophy and we all trooped up to the Rank box thinking they must be getting sick of the sight of us, but they seemed as pleased as ever. I remembered standing in that box for the first time and talking to Monica Dickinson, and saying we still had a long way to go to compare with Wayward Lad. I suppose Desert Orchid had come that long way now: he had equalled Wayward Lad's record of three wins.

David's record also looked extraordinarily impressive. In the last six years he had trained three winners and four seconds – a record almost as impressive as Michael Dickinson's training of the first five home in the Gold Cup of 1985, when you consider what a feat it was just getting Des to the track in good shape four years running.

Mel Davies was understandably disappointed as Brendan Powell, who rode Barnbrook Again, said he didn't think the horse quite stayed, and various Cheltenham plans were raised without any conclusions being reached. David mooted Des's next race as the Victor Chandler Chase, then Des coughed, and that was it for the time being. Desert Orchid coughing made the front page of *The Times*.

In the meantime, a new decade was dawning, and a poll in the *Racing Post* gave Des the honour of being the top jumper of the Eighties. We had come a long way since that novice hurdle at Kempton eight years before. In a letter to the *Racing Post*, Peter Hicks wrote:

> Desert Orchid has caught the public's imagination: he has put steeplechasing back on the map: he it is whom people flock to see perform heroic deeds at his beloved Sandown Park, Kempton Park and (at long last) Cheltenham.
>
> Desert Orchid is Jump Horse of the Decade. Like Coe, Maradona and Ballesteros, Dessie is the symbol for his sport in the 1980s.

Desert Orchid was indeed famous. But he was about to become even more famous for a race he didn't even run in.

24

A National Debate

Perhaps the strangest thing about the Grand National was that we never really discussed it. For a few weeks the racing pages became consumed with a passionate debate about it, but the owners and trainer hardly discussed it at all! The year before, Seagram, the Grand National sponsors, were hosting a press conference at Whitsbury, the fortifying substances had been flowing, and David had said he might run Desert Orchid in the Gold Cup and the National that season, but later he had rung to apologise and to tell me he didn't mean it.

I also later heard of one evening when Simon Bullimore had kept David up late into the night till he promised he'd never enter him in the National. I knew Jimmy was against it, and Midge wasn't keen either, because we all just assumed it was the wrong race for Des. It was left-handed. It was a handicap, and it seemed pretty obvious that Des would get over twelve stone, and carrying twelve stone plus over four and a half miles is obviously harder than carrying it over two or three miles, especially going the 'wrong' way round. Even more significantly, the National comes only three weeks after the Gold Cup, and on the evidence of the year before, that wasn't enough time for the old boy to recover.

The Grand National is, of course, a very special race, by far the most popular race in Britain, and perhaps in the world. This is partly because it is perceived as a lottery, with the big drop fences frightening the life out of everybody, and the additional hazard of loose horses leading to the popular feeling that it's not necessarily a race for top class horses. In other words, you don't just need to be good, you need to be lucky. Had anyone asked us, I think we all would have said that we thought Des would jump round all right, though I do remember Neville Crump coming up to me once at Edinburgh and saying that in his opinion Desert Orchid would overjump, and as he had trained three National winners, you had to respect his opinion. I suppose we would have conceded that with Des we had to be a little bit careful. If he had run in the race and hurt himself, which he could have done in any race, the stakes were high. It might have damaged the National.

But I hadn't actually discussed any of this with David till one grey day in January when I went down to Whitsbury to film an interview with him. David was his usual articulate self, and afterwards we had a drink before I had to go and interview Colin Brown and Simon Sherwood. We talked about this and that, I finished my drink, and as I was on my way out of his living room, David said casually: 'By the way, the National closes in a week. How would you feel about entering him?'

'I thought we were going for the Whitbread,' I said.

'Well, the Whitbread's a hard race,' he said, 'but the National, you know, well people make a lot of fuss about it, but it's not a particularly good race. I'd say it was easier to win than the Whitbread. And Des would jump round okay, you could bank on it.' We kicked it around for a couple of minutes, and I told him what I thought about it being too close to Cheltenham, and being left-handed, and Des being given too much weight, and so on, and he didn't seem to disagree, but he still wanted to enter him. I reminded him I thought the other owners were against it.

'Yes,' conceded David, 'but I'm not sure they're looking at it straight. We know he'd stay the distance, he'd jump round . . .' He continued persuasively.

'But you wouldn't run him in the National with top weight three weeks after the Gold Cup, would you?' I said.

'I don't know,' said David. 'Probably not.'

'And you know what I feel about running with over twelve stone?' I said. 'You've said it yourself, we've got to be careful about overfacing him in handicaps.'

'Well, he probably will get more than twelve stone,' said David. 'But we'll never know if we don't enter him.'

'Look, David,' I said, grinning. 'Are you sure this is a good idea? The chances of Des running in the National this year are almost nil. I think the other owners are against it under *any* circumstances. I'm against it if he gets more than twelve stone, which as you say he probably will. But even if he was *your* horse, would you run him three weeks after the Gold Cup?'

'But if we don't enter him,' he said, 'we won't have the option, will we?' I couldn't help laughing.

'I'll talk to the others,' I said.

'Fine,' said David, amiably.

That night David told the press he was going to enter Des for the National, and then went shooting for three days. All hell broke loose in the meantime. It made the headlines in the *Racing Post*. The first call I got was from Jimmy, and he was furious.

'What the hell is going on?' he demanded. 'I've never agreed Des can run in the National. We've never even discussed it!' I said I didn't know David was going to say anything till we'd had a chance to discuss it, but in any case Des wouldn't run if he also ran in the Gold Cup or if he had more than twelve stone.

'Well, as he is going to run in the Gold Cup, and he almost certainly will get more than twelve stone,' said Jimmy, 'it seems completely ridiculous to me.'

He had a point, and I couldn't really think of anything to say. Now the press got hold of me. I merely said that it was 'extremely unlikely' that Des would run, but David had sort of finessed me into defending his point of view. Obviously I couldn't say we had no intention of running him because then why were we entering him?

Desert Orchid in the National was the story of the hour, though, and I had this vision of David chuckling away, and there then followed a ludicrous public 'debate': newspaper polls, editorials and 0898 phone-in rip-offs of the should he/shouldn't he run variety. The overwhelming majority was against it. Dessie was 'too precious' to be risked in the National, though this in itself was a little curious. Red Rum was still the best known horse in the country, and he had gained his reputation entirely from running in the National. The press, and 'public opinion' interpreted by the press, became obsessed with the safety issue. Furthermore, the press now suggested that 'public opinion' was making us back down. It was true that earlier I had unwisely said, at Wincanton I think, that whenever the subject of Des running in the National came up we got buried in hate mail, but it was meant to be a sort of joke. We did get the odd barmy letter on the subject but just tossed it in the bin. The fact was we had never even considered running Des in the race, so it wasn't courage we lacked but conviction.

The issue was blown out of proportion as the debate raged around us. Jimmy found all his time consumed with dealing with phone calls and letters accusing him of all sorts of things, and they *were* a little tricky to deal with. He could hardly be expected to defend a decision he didn't believe in himself. The whole debate became hopelessly polarised, too, and in a very odd way. All the people who didn't want Desert Orchid to run in the Grand National assumed he was going to run in it, and all the people who did want him to run assumed he wasn't going to run. Naturally, we were in the middle of this crossfire, attacked on the one hand for being heartless beasts and on the other for being spineless wimps. David didn't escape unscathed either. He received so many threatening phone calls that a special police guard had to patrol outside his house, while the object of all this speculation, Desert Orchid, dozed away a few yards from his kitchen window, blissfully unaware of the furore his public status was causing.

The Grand National weights were due to be announced a few days after the Gainsborough, so I presumed we'd all have a chance to have our 'discussion' at Sandown, but then the Gainsborough was cancelled, and Des was rerouted to the Charterhouse Chase at Ascot the day after the publication of the weights. That meant we wouldn't be able to get together to have a chat about it till *after* the weights were published. The day before, David declared his hand.

'Twelve two is right for Dessie' ran a headline in *The Sporting Life*, quoting David. I called him up. 'That's not what I think,' I said, 'and you know it.'

'Well let's hope he gets twelve four,' David laughed, 'and then we can just pull him out.'

I went to bed the night before the publication of the weights, determined not to react to any press enquiries next day. At half-past six the ansaphone went, and the Press Association boomed out 'Twelve stone two, what do you think?' At half-past twelve there were over twenty messages on my answering machine. I turned on Oracle for the next day's runners at Ascot, and the sound stayed on as the picture was replaced by text. As I waited

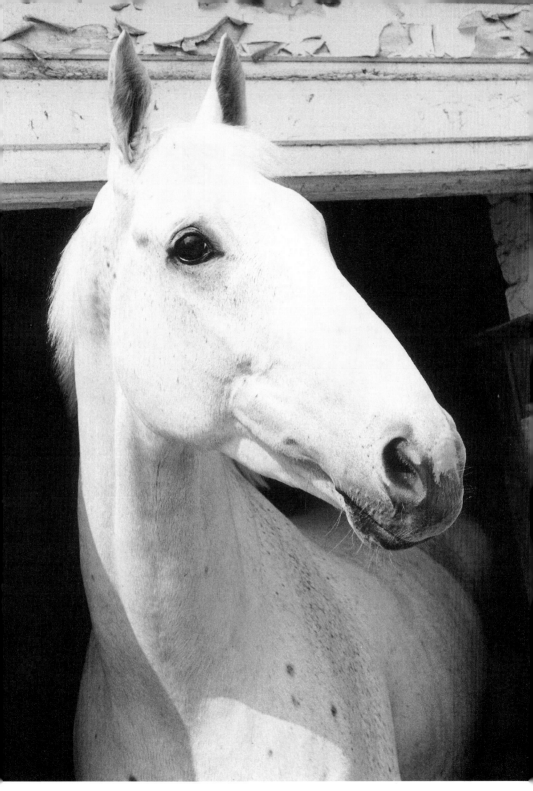

33   A wise old head. Now starting his eighth season in training, Desert Orchid looks out from a strange box as he waits to go back to Whitsbury which has temporarily closed down with the cough.

34 Desert Orchid galloping with fellow stable star and main rival for the King George, Barnbrook Again (Ross Arnott up).

35 His exercise completed for the day, Des knows his own way home.

36   New jockey Richard Dunwoody aboard Des before his annual hair-raising school over fences.
37   A spectacular leap at the second last at the Racing Post Chase at Kempton in February takes him clear for an eight length win with twelve stone three. His finest handicap performance.

38   Des manages to survive a terrible blunder at the last in the Irish Grand National in April 1990 to win by twelve lengths.

39   Des, led by his summer 'minder' Jim Stone, shows off in front of his fans at the open day at Ab Kettleby.

40   Midge Burridge
receiving the Agfa
Diamond trophy,
Des's last win.

41   George Armatage.

42   Simon Bullimore receiving
the King George trophy.

43   Simon and Camilla Burridge after Des wins the 1988
Whitbread.

44   Desert Orchid was beaten in his own race at Wincanton, but he's still the centre of attention. From left: Simon Burridge holding his daughter Felicity, Johnnie holding his daughter Amy, Midge's hat, Jimmy's hat, and Simon Bullimore.

45   Des showing his usual fire on the gallops, though his days at Whitsbury are numbered.

46   Three King Georges: 1986 (top) and 1988 (middle) with Simon Sherwood, and 1989 (bottom) with Richard Dunwoody.

47   The crowd goes wild as Richard Dunwoody rides Desert Orchid out to win a record-breaking fourth King George in 1990.

48   His final King George and his final race. Desert Orchid finishes alone, the glory all his.

for the runners to come up, I heard 'Desert Orchid is to run in the Grand National.' David was saying it was a very fair weight and the way was now clear for him to run. I turned over to the BBC News. Over pictures of me after the Gold Cup, a voice was now saying we were going to run the horse.

'The way is now clear?!' That was news to me. I turned on Ceefax. 'Desert Orchid to run in National. Owners all for it.' I thought I'd better answer the next three phone calls. They were from *The Sporting Life*, the *Racing Post* and the Press Association. I told them as far as I was concerned it was even more unlikely he'd run. Sitting in my office on a bleak day on the Yorkshire Moors, I saw Ceefax change in front of me. 'Desert Orchid *un*likely to run.' I can't deny it made me laugh. The whole thing was absurd. I called David, who wasn't in, and asked him to call me back. Jimmy called, and I told him we'd try to sort it out at Ascot the next day. The situation was further complicated by the fact that several trainers were outraged at how little weight Des had got. In comparative terms they were right, Des was better off than in a normal handicap. But as he wasn't going to run if he ran in the Gold Cup – and as far as I knew he was going to – then the comparative weights were irrelevant.

David didn't call that night and the next morning I was on my way to Ascot. I was in the seafood bar chatting to Mark Bradstock and Sarah Lawrence, when about twenty minutes before the first race David walked in, looking worried.

'Look, it's very wet out there, I think we ought to withdraw him.'

'Okay,' I said, 'whatever you think best.' But David had inadvertently flushed me out. Reporters jumped me, and I was led in front of the TV cameras. David shot off before I had a chance to talk to him.

The interview was shown that night. Julian Wilson started by asking me whether public opinion had swayed me. I said it didn't, again outlining my objections. Julian Wilson then concluded to camera that I *had* been swayed by public opinion!

The final twist in this saga happened the next day at Wincanton. During all this speculation Des had spent most of his time in a horsebox. He had set off for Sandown, then that had been cancelled, so he turned round and went back to Whitsbury. He had been to Ascot but had been withdrawn, so once again he had turned round. The following day he went to Wincanton. His actual racecourse performances seemed to be taking a back seat to his life in the media, which was, frankly, how it felt at the time, but racegoers gathered enthusiastically by the pre-parade ring with the cameras, waiting for him to appear before the two mile five furlong Racing In Wessex Chase. Everybody was very keen to see this horse who had been plastered over their newspapers for the last three days. A grey horse duly appeared and several rolls of film were shot off. The only problem was, it wasn't Desert Orchid but Imperial Champagne. Film was hastily reloaded. Now another grey appeared, and another roll of film was shot off. Only that wasn't Desert Orchid either. It was Mzima Spring. By the time Desert Orchid did appear, no one had any film left. Des won the race very easily by twenty lengths, but the press were much more interested in the National. As we *still* hadn't discussed it face to face, we adjourned to the bar.

David said he thought Des could win the race, but if we didn't want to win a National, that was up to us. Jimmy said he didn't want to be disrespectful, but he didn't think the National was the right race for his horse, and never had done.

David nodded and considered Jimmy for a few seconds. He began to see the toll the episode had taken on him, and for the first time questioned his decision to enter Des – not because he hadn't thought it the right thing to do, but because racing is supposed to be fun, and this clearly hadn't been much fun for Jimmy. He turned to me, and there was a different tone in his voice. 'You don't want to win a National either?' I said of course I would like to, but I thought running Des in the National three weeks after the Gold Cup wasn't a serious proposition, and if we weren't going to run him, then we might as well take him out now.

David understood, nodded and smiled. 'Okay,' he said. He went out and told the press. 'It has been decided by Desert Orchid's joint-owners and myself that the horse will not run in the Grand National this season. His target is the Gold Cup and then depending on how he comes out of Cheltenham, the Whitbread Gold Cup. The Irish Grand National is also a possibility.'

After racing David, Jane and I had dinner. 'Well,' he said, 'you cracked under the pressure.'

'Cracked?!' I laughed. 'What do you mean? I've said the same thing all along. If anyone was putting us under pressure it was *you*!'

'How was I putting you under pressure?' he asked.

'You said you were going to run him and we'd never even discussed it,' I said.

'I never said he'd run.'

'But you implied it, come off it.'

'I just thought we were going to leave the decision till after Cheltenham,' he said, smiling.

'But you wouldn't have run him in the National after the Gold Cup, would you?' I said.

'I don't know. I might have. It was an option.' He laughed. David loves taking people on. In spite of the chaos of the last few weeks, David had clearly enjoyed the episode.

'Well,' I said, 'I don't think you ever would have done.'

'Who knows?' said David. 'Who knows?'

And that was that. *The Guardian* continued to be interested in the story. Chris Hawkins had written earlier in the year that we had been mad to run Desert Orchid at Liverpool after Cheltenham last year, and now fellow correspondent Richard Baerlein took up the baton, and accused us of being crazy *not* to run at Liverpool after Cheltenham this year. Baerlein produced the same theory in Saturday's *Guardian*, in Sunday's *Observer* and in *The Weekender*, yearning for the type of old-fashioned owners who actually ran their horses. My brother Simon wrote a letter pointing out that we had, in fact, run Desert Orchid, usually at the highest level, in nearly sixty races. For some reason I was given credit for this letter, but that was okay, because Simon writes much better letters than I do.

In the end I don't believe there was any real disagreement. Following the Gold Cup six weeks later David said there was no question of him going to Liverpool for the Martell Chase because he hadn't recovered from the Gold Cup, so I don't think David would have considered running him in the National. All it boiled down to really was just one of those discussions about running plans between owners and trainers that takes place every day up and down the country. But with Desert Orchid, well, things were always a little different . . .

25

The Show Goes On

Considering the hysteria of the last few weeks, it was appropriate, I suppose, that Desert Orchid should now run in a race sponsored by a newspaper. The Racing Post Chase at Kempton had been started a couple of years before as a Gold Cup prep race, and in this confusing, interrupted season it was an opportunity we were very glad to have.

But on twelve stone three, including a three pound penalty, Des had to give two stone to the brilliant Delius, and two stone three to the rest of the field. Whenever Desert Orchid ran in a handicap these days, the riders of his opponents considered the prospect gloomily, knowing they would have to spend hours in the sauna to get down to the minimum weight of ten stone. Break out the Ryvita, boys, it's another hungry night in Lambourn.

Twelve stone three, of course, was near enough to his twelve stone two in the National to cause an intake of breath in certain quarters, followed by meaningful looks in our direction, but we would quite cheerfully have run him with twelve stone seven over three miles round Kempton.

The crowd was up forty-two per cent on the previous year (Channel Four commented that the *person* we had to thank for this was Desert Orchid). It turned out to be a pretty good show – that forty-two per cent may be back. David was very confident beforehand; he thought Des was as well as he'd ever been. As usual, Des set off in the lead. At the eleventh, he was taken on by Solidasarock, but Richard sat quite still. Coming to the fourth last, he accelerated, jumped it magnificently, and the race was on. Coming to the third last, Solidasarock looked cooked, and Des went on. Delius came out of the pack. Des was spectacular, but very low, at the second last, a little tired at the last, and galloped on to win by eight lengths from Delius, with future Grand National winner Seagram another eight lengths back in third, and Ballyhane leading the others another fifteen lengths away.

Richard Dunwoody was grinning from ear to ear. The grey had never felt better. Dominic Gardiner-Hill in the *Racing Post* argued that it was the best performance of Des's entire career, and went on to suggest that he had performed to a mark of 183, two pounds better than when beating Pegwell Bay at Sandown the previous year. And though it seemed unlikely at eleven, this suggested he was still improving. Gardiner-Hill concluded that 'the message was clear – there is not a staying chaser within ten pounds of Desert Orchid, who will take a world of beating in defending his Tote Gold Cup crown.'

Afterwards David said that he wished the Gold Cup was tomorrow and that he believed Des was even better than last year, and though it might be tempting Providence he couldn't see him being beaten.

After last year, though, we were not quite so sure we were looking forward to the avalanche of media attention that would surround Des's attempt on another Gold Cup. We felt we'd said more or less everything there was to say. Not that you didn't sympathise with the journalists. It must have seemed to them that they had been writing about Desert Orchid since the invention of the printing press. David signed himself up exclusively to *The Sun* which allowed him to give a convenient 'no comment' to anyone else, and I went skiing. *The Guardian*, presumably infuriated by not being able to get hold of either owner or trainer, printed a rambling, mean-spirited and pretty pointless put-down of the whole Desert Orchid phenomenon, trashing everyone involved, David, me, Jimmy, and proceeded to categorise all the 'fans' as dotty lunatics.

Other journalists were more imaginative, and Ian Wooldridge even interviewed the horse. Desert Orchid, in his piece, emerged as a rather jovial, military type. Talking about last year's Gold Cup, he 'said':

'Do you know why I won? Because the horse that headed me over the last fence was called Yahoo. I'd thoroughly snubbed him in the paddock, I can tell you, but there he was under the sublime misapprehension that he had a chance. I mean no one ever loses to a horse called Yahoo, does one? This year, of course, my opponents include Cavvies Clown, my stablemate here at Whitsbury. We're not close. He has the occasional touch of halitosis and takes *The Independent*. Occasionally, when I'm doing a television interview or chatting with Lord Oaksey or Peter O'Sullevan, he gives me this sort of pathetic look. I'm sure if you go up there now he'll talk to you for hours. A bit like some football clubs I could mention. Doing all right, but hardly a friend in the world. I see that Bonanza Boy is also mentioned as a conceivable rival. I simply choke on my lunch. I mean I have nothing against Bonanza Boy personally. Probably has quite a future with the Field Artillery. Extrovert, friendly, amusing. Reminds me a bit of Ron Atkinson. He'd run with four pounds overweight of gold bracelets on his hocks if they'd let him, but essentially, if I may say so, secondary modern. You see one has to be aware of one's status if you are to get anywhere in this life. I openly admit I have never been overburdened by modesty but then I'm Desert Orchid.'

As the days were counted down to the Gold Cup, Des was such a hot favourite that bookies started taking prices on how far he would win the race by, with the 9–2 favourite with Corals being seven to ten lengths.

But David's conviction following the Racing Post Chase was starting to evaporate, and as he is often right about these things, this was depressing. On the face of it, Des seemed to have an even better chance this year, the ground was faster and his run at Kempton suggested he was still improving. Although David didn't necessarily disagree, he was unwilling to commit himself to the conclusion that Des would win. This was mainly because he had a horse in his own yard whom he thought might beat him, and that was Cavvies Clown. Doubts had continued to be raised about Barnbrook Again's ability to stay three and a quarter miles round Cheltenham, and after a certain amount of agonising, David eventually persuaded the horse's devoted owner, Mel Davies, to run him in the Champion Chase again. Mel was always much better behaved than we were, and went along with his trainer's advice. But perhaps David had been telling him the same thing, i.e. that Cavvies

Clown would win. Cavvies stayed; he jumped; he acted on the course; he was in good shape after an easy win in the Jim Ford. While respecting David's views, I didn't rush out and back the horse. David has such a natural affinity for the underdog that he reacts against a presumed certainty, even if he's training it. And though he'd been to hell and back with Cavvies Clown over the steroids thing, he continued to believe in this game little horse with the enormous ears, and loved the sight of him trouncing horses who appeared to be twice his size.

As it happens, it was lucky that I hadn't put the mortgage on Cavvies, as on arriving at Cheltenham I bumped into Jo Ollivant, the owner of Cavvies Clown.

'Good luck, Jo,' I said, 'though I'm not sure you'll need it. David's been telling me we can't beat your horse.'

'That's funny,' she said, laughing, 'he's been saying the same thing to us about your horse.' David believes in preparing his owners for failure.

The countdown to Cheltenham was an exciting time for everyone at Whitsbury. Having the hot favourite for the Gold Cup made the nerves tingle, though it sometimes seemed hard to reconcile the sheer normality of the horses dozing in their boxes with the furore that awaited them at Cheltenham. The nerves had to remain steady though, there were so many things that could go wrong at the last moment. As the headlines rattled off the presses, it was people like Martin Chilton, in charge of the lower yard where Dessie was stabled, who checked the feed and the rugs and basically always kept an eye on things, who made all the difference. It was the dedication of everybody at Whitsbury that was the real bedrock on which those Cheltenham performances were built.

Principal opposition to Des this year came from Bonanza Boy, the impressive winner of the Welsh National; Toby Tobias, a brilliant young horse from Jenny Pitman's stable who had five straight wins till he'd unseated his jockey; Yahoo; Maid of Money, a very good mare from Ireland; Pegwell Bay, who had the ground he liked; Nick The Brief who had just won Ireland's 'Gold Cup', the Vincent O'Brien Chase at Leopardstown, in great style; our old friend Kildimo; Ten of Spades, representing the connections of last year's tragic faller, Ten Plus; and the outsider The Bakewell Boy. I've left one out, though, because he obviously had no chance. Norton's Coin was trained by Welsh permit holder and farmer Sirrell Griffiths, and he was only running in the Gold Cup by mistake. Sirrell had intended to run him in the Cathcart, but found he was not qualified for it, and by that time he had missed the deadline to put him in the Mildmay of Flete, so he thought he might as well have a go in the Gold Cup. We had beaten him by forty lengths in the King George.

The media pressure built to a crescendo. At least I didn't need to ring up David to find out about Des. I could read about him in the newspapers.

Des looked hot stuff in the saddling box beforehand, but everyone was tense. By now Carol Dunwoody had become a fully paid-up member of the distressed wives of Desert Orchid's jockeys. She was as nervous as a sparrow, and received a good deal of sympathetic support from Annie Brown and Lucy Sherwood.

The horses set off to the usual cheer. For the first circuit everything seemed to be going well. Ten of Spades was harrying Des, but Des seemed to be enjoying himself on the firm ground. Then turning into the back straight for the second time, something suddenly seemed to go wrong. I couldn't say what exactly, but Des's action wasn't as good, he wasn't bouncing in quite the same way. Coming down the hill, two horses were clearly going better: Toby Tobias and ... black and white hoops, green and white quartered cap, hang on a moment, what? Norton's Coin?

Coming to the second last, I still thought Des might do it. He was no further back than he was the year before. But he was flat, with nothing more to give, and though he plugged on up the hill, he was always going to be third to Norton's Coin and Toby Tobias. He pricked his ears at the post but he looked knackered.

It was a fairy tale result, though admittedly not quite the one we had hoped for. Sirrell Griffiths had got up that morning, milked his cows, then driven his 100–1 home-bred ex-point-to-pointer to Cheltenham – and carried off the greatest prize in the jumping calendar.

The public could not believe Desert Orchid had been beaten. In terms of sporting shocks it was compared with Mike Tyson's defeat by Mike Douglas and the English cricket team's defeat of the West Indies in the first test in Barbados. The American magazine *Sports Illustrated* cancelled their Desert Orchid cover, explaining that jump racing was obscure enough to Americans without trying to explain why a horse everyone thought was the best for twenty years had just come third.

'I'm Gobsmacked' ran the headline in *The Sun*, though David had certainly been preparing the readers for defeat. The bookies were ecstatic, they had been bracing themselves for a £10,000,000 pay-out if Desert Orchid had won.

David commented that it wasn't surprising Des had been beaten as he hadn't had 'the ideal conditions' of the year before! He did think, though, that the firm ground might not have helped Des, because it had neutralised his jumping and stamina advantages, and allowed the younger but less experienced horses' speed to come into play. We weren't too disappointed, because by now we were used to Cheltenham. We had gone through all this so often before – going there with such high hopes, running well but just not quite well enough. There was one consolation. The people who had been clamouring for Desert Orchid to run in the National now went silent. Des had been gutted by Cheltenham.

We wanted to give him one more race, to end the season on a positive note. It was a toss up between the Irish Grand National at Fairyhouse and the Whitbread Gold Cup. But David wasn't keen on the Whitbread, so we turned our eyes, with some enthusiasm, towards Ireland.

Roy Craigie, the Clerk of the Course at Fairyhouse, promised the grey horse a great reception, and though Des would obviously be carrying top weight of twelve stone, the race looked ideal. It was over three and a half miles on a right-handed track, and took place on Easter Monday, two weeks after Liverpool. We thought this would give Des plenty of time to recover from Cheltenham, but eight days before it, and a week after Liverpool, he still looked flat and David was concerned. We were going to fly Des over, and as this was very expensive, we didn't want to commit ourselves until we were sure he was right. On the other hand, we didn't want to voice doubts about his well-being, because that might encourage his opponents. We decided to use the ground as a focus for our anxiety – not that this wasn't an issue, it just wasn't the main concern.

So with the ground being the key factor, the phones started humming from Ireland, with all sorts of different opinions as to how fast the ground actually was. Roy Craigie had said it was 'good', though he added that he was watering it. Opinions raged violently between good and rock hard. The methods of evaluating going are never very scientific at the best of times, and in Ireland appear to be as idiosyncratic as water-divining. They certainly wouldn't have thought twice about the going at Cheltenham the year before, it was good jumping ground! David got a phone call from a complete stranger who lived in County Meath who informed him that he lived within five miles of the course and wanted to report that it was now raining. There were so many people wandering round Fairyhouse prior to delivering going reports that it must have looked like Piccadilly Circus. I began to wonder whether there'd be any grass left.

Then on the Thursday before, Des finally showed some sparkle, and Rodney gave him the green light. David was still not completely happy, but confirmed Des was going. He had originally planned to send Des over on the day of the race, but now decided to go the night before. Roy Craigie rescrambled his arrangements.

The fun started again as soon as we touched down at Dublin airport. Though Des had never been on a plane before, he whinnied once as they took off from Eastleigh airport, then calmly munched his hay all the way over, and now with a police escort, set off for the stables opposite Fairyhouse. Leaving him with two Gardi as night watchmen, we went to the boarding house where Janice and Peter were to stay. On the way there, I stopped off at a pub to book a meal. Though I had never been into this pub before in my life, it was like walking into a party I had left five minutes earlier. 'Hello, Richard,' various people hailed me. 'So you're here are you?' The next morning it just got better and better – I don't think the Pope could have got a better reception than Desert Orchid. Everybody wished us luck.

There were a few unflattering things in the press, mostly at the suggestion that Desert Orchid might be as good as Arkle. This debate had raged for years. As far as we were concerned, there will never be another Arkle. He was supreme, peerless, sublime. I only ever saw him on television, but the impression he made on me, and many others like me, will never fade, and his record speaks for itself. He towered above his contemporaries, and before he came along, they were considered pretty hot stuff, too.

The problem was some people had dared to mention Desert Orchid in the same breath as Arkle, and this got very short shrift, because apparently it is blasphemy to compare *any* horse with Arkle. In a couple of respects, though, the horses were comparable, because they were both, at their time, undisputed champions, and some way clear of the rivals, and they both attracted obsessive followings. The whole debate got pretty silly at times, especially when it was just used to put down Desert Orchid. Des had taken on all the brilliant horses of his day and beaten most of them, and you couldn't really ask for more than that. It was unreasonable to keep running him in races with ghosts. Janice summed up the whole thing best by saying that both Arkle and Desert Orchid were individuals, and we should be grateful for them both.

David spluttered into his coffee when he read a putative handicap in one of the Irish papers which suggested that Des was not only a stone and a half behind Arkle, but also inferior to no less than five Irish Grand National winners, and five pounds behind Brown Lad. That aside, the morning went well, and a friend of mine picked me up and whisked me through the traffic jams to Fairyhouse. Irish Distillers invited us to their box, and the feeling grew that this was a special day. Everywhere we went, people said thank you for bringing him over. Thank you. For what? For raiding your biggest prize of the year? Yes. Thank you.

David was getting increasingly jittery though as the afternoon wore on. He knew Des was right on the edge, and today he was running on hope rather than confidence.

As the horses came into the paddock, crowds gathered fifteen deep in anticipation. It got so bad that the great white one could not get through at all. The Gardi waded in and tried to make a path through the crowds. I was introduced to the great Pat Taafe, Arkle's rider, and he seemed to be almost as excited as everyone else to see Des. It was a wonderful moment. Being associated with Des was always like a rollercoaster, we sometimes didn't have time to realise just what he'd achieved. That day brought it home to us. We did own a great horse.

Des eventually appeared and the crowd applauded him into the parade ring, out of the parade ring and down to the start. Temporarily forgoing the joys of the Irish Distillers' box, I stood near the finishing post with my brother Johnnie and his wife Pony, but it was so crowded we couldn't actually see much.

Richard had had a couple of rides already that day, and said the ground wasn't too bad. He managed to line up on the inside, but Sara Cullen on Bold Flyer was determined not to surrender the lead to Des. She led over the first, but Des outjumped her at the second, and they were together for the next circuit. Bold Flyer gradually began to weaken and Des went on, and five out the pack was trying to close behind him. At the third last, Richard felt him 'go' and felt his feet were hurting. He was suddenly worried that Des would not last home. He glanced behind him and realised that the others were flat to the boards. Over the second last and one fence to go. Richard was nursing him now, trying to hold him together, but at the last fence, which is opposite the stand, Desert Orchid hardly rising at all ploughed through it. There was a great gasp from the crowd, but Richard stayed on, and Des recovered in a few strides, and galloped on to win by twelve lengths.

If the reaction of the crowd had been good before, now it was unbelievable. They mobbed him coming into the paddock, and Janice didn't have room to turn him round. Richard was thrilled: this win in Ireland gave him as much pleasure as any race he'd won on the grey, and David was very relieved. With something approaching a shock, he found he'd got away with it. Des had not only won another race, but had also won the Irish Grand National!

We got our prizes, made our little speeches, and while Des flew home, we went back to Dublin to celebrate. When I got back to the hotel, there was even better news. My mum phoned me and told me that my old mare Made For Life had won her first point-to-point. The Irish National and the Staintondale Maiden Point-to-Point, all within half an hour. Has there ever been such a double? I was getting carried away, and believe me, Dublin is the right place to get carried away in. Somehow, at about lunchtime the next day, I surfaced and went home. It had been another wonderful season.

PART FIVE

❧

Turning for Home

26

❧

A Long Hot Summer

Mʀ Fʀɪsᴋ ʜᴀᴅ ᴘᴜʟʟᴇᴅ ᴏꜰꜰ a brilliant double, winning the Grand National and the Whitbread, and the result of the Racegoers Club National Hunt Horse of the Year poll was in doubt. Janice had been groaning about this for weeks. She knew Des wasn't going to win it this year.

'Why not?'

'Because Mr Frisk is going to. Isn't he?'

'I'll bet you a fiver Des still wins it.'

'I haven't got a fiver.'

'I'll bet you a quid, Janice.'

Des won the National Hunt Horse of the Year Award for the fourth time running – a record. Janice never paid up.

The Racing World video on the jumping scene again featured Desert Orchid strongly, and in the closing section, Jonathan Powell took off his interviewer and presenter hats, and made a plea that next year Des be allowed to run in the Grand National.

Nobody had ruled it out. We'd agreed that he would not run in the Gold Cup and the National in the same season, but that was all. We could give Cheltenham a miss and go straight for the National. At twelve, the Grand National would certainly not be beyond the grey horse. It might even have suited him more at that age. But then shortly before the Irish National something happened, which was slowly, as we digested its implications, to take the Grand National off the agenda.

Des had returned from the Gold Cup with speedy cuts, and George came down three weeks after Cheltenham, and found a problem in Des's left shoulder. It was the same problem that he had put right a few times before. I asked George how he thought

Des had done it, but George could not give a definite answer. 'Could happen anywhere,' he said, 'in the box, in the field, on the gallops, jumping a fence. Anywhere.' However, this time we were able to pinpoint the injury more accurately. It was unlikely that Des had had a problem during the Racing Post Chase, and he had no speedy cuts after it. But by the time he'd finished the Gold Cup, he did have a problem. So that meant that he had done it sometime between the end of the Racing Post Chase and the end of the Gold Cup. As he hadn't done anything unusual in his build up to Cheltenham, it seemed probable that he put the shoulder out during the Gold Cup.

As I drove George back to the airport we discussed it, and realised that Des had seemed to have a problem after Cheltenham every year. Perhaps at long last this explained why he was not so effective going left-handed. Perhaps every time he went left-handed he put his shoulder out, and it did seem to me, looking back, that generally he had always been better on the first circuit than the second, and in particular he had seemed to lose so many of his races at Cheltenham as they turned into that far bend. George said this was possible, and only added that these things were more likely to happen on fast ground.

If this were the case, it put an altogether different complexion on the National. If he had a tendency to put his shoulder out turning left-handed, then he would surely do it at the Canal Turn, which is one of the sharpest left-hand turns in racing – and if he did, he would then be struggling for another circuit and a half under top weight, and would probably finish exhausted down the field. Des was so game he would never give up, and it might have been the end of him. We were all aware that approaching his eighth season in training we were starting to live on borrowed time, and had to be extra careful not to ask too much of him. We felt that it was not a risk it would be fair to ask Des to take.

We didn't talk to David about this at the time, and as events turned out there was no need to. But I think he would have given the idea a fair hearing, as he now got on very well with George. When George had been down to see Des, David asked him to look at two other horses, and they both subsequently put in very impressive performances. David asked George down later in the summer to check out all his horses.

Apart from a few minor problems with Des's feet, everything went smoothly at Ab Kettleby that summer. For the first time there were no corns. This was just as well, because Des was now 'locked in' to various dates. David Pipe at the Jockey Club had asked us whether we'd allow Des to form part of the Jockey Club's contribution to the parade that was being organised to commemorate the Queen Mother's ninetieth birthday. This was a mammoth event with 6,000 people from various walks of life in costume, on floats, leading animals and parading through Horseguards Parade while a choir of 500 sang in the background. It involved marching bands, armoured regiments, cheering spectators and a flypast of Battle of Britain planes. Rodney offered to lead Des up, so we got the grey horse out of his field, cleaned him up and sent him down to London in a horsebox. There was a certain amount of silly buggers as he was boxed back and forth from the Royal Mews to Wellington Barracks for the rehearsal, but when it came to the real thing, he loved it. He was positioned between the Poultry Club and the RSPCA and followed two of the Queen Mother's own horses, Whitbread hero Special Cargo and The Argonaut, and appeared to presume that the whole thing was being staged in his honour. He peered round and acknowledged the cheers of the crowd. It was extremely nice of all these people to turn out for him. The Poultry Club, the Aberdeen Anguses, Dr Barnado's and wait a minute, who was that – the Queen Mother had turned out to see him?

He now had another date ahead of him, the annual open day. Two thousand people turned up over two days, though the weather was appalling. They stood in lines for half an hour to wait their turn to see him and have their pictures taken with him in his stable. They waited in ranks eight deep round the parade ring. We auctioned racing plates for charity and they went for over £300 each. We auctioned two mangy lead ropes, guaranteed chewed by Desert Orchid, thinking they'd probably fetch about fifteen quid each. One went for £90, the other for £120.

Despite the weather, everybody seemed to have a good time. Desert Orchid did mean an awful lot to people, and always seemed to have a positive effect. There was something about him that always seemed to cheer people up. Richard and Carol Dunwoody turned up, as did Colin and Annie Brown, and Richard and Colin almost got cramp they signed so many autographs. One man told me he had been to every single open day going over the last few years, in Newmarket, Lambourn, wherever, and said that he had enjoyed this one more than any of them. That was a great tribute to Midge and Johnny Hippisley, but most of all to Desert Orchid.

A few days later Des came up to Yorkshire, but this year without Trevor. Clare was backed up by Celia Hammond, Jane Milburn and Henrietta Sedgwick. Henrietta had been a three day event rider till she had broken her back at Burghley, and was a wonderful rider.

It was a red hot summer, and I've always thought it got hotter on the moors than anywhere else: on two days running the thermometer in the stables climbed over 100°F. Bright, endlessly hot days were always relieved by a gentle breeze and cooler nights, and the horses seemed to relish it, especially since there are no flies up on the moors. While racing yards all over the country had to adjust their schedules to go out at five and six in the morning to miss the heat, we could continue to ride out in the middle of the day.

Then one day Irish Orchid kicked her brother, hard, on the forearm. There was a sickening crunch, and for a few moments Des was hobbling lame. I had visions that Desert Orchid's career had just ended. By the time we got back, he was walking sound, and after Clare had patched up the wound, Edmund Collins came and X-rayed him. He was okay, but plenty of horses' careers have ended with less.

A couple of days later he was fine, and everything else went smoothly. David was a regular visitor, especially at the Ebor meeting. This year he'd won the Juddmonte with In The Groove, and we celebrated, but next morning he cast a critical eye over Desert Orchid.

'He's bloody fat, Richard.' David was right. He was fat. And when he went back about two weeks later, I sensed we were in a certain amount of trouble.

'He's well,' David told me, 'looks magnificent – but he's as big as a house.' I realised what the trouble had been. For the first time he'd had nothing wrong with him, so he'd continued to put on weight all summer.

A couple of weeks later he was paraded at the Brent Walker

Festival of Racing at Ascot. He still looked fat. Things were made worse by the firm ground. The shift in the weather pattern was effectively buggering up the whole first half of the jumping season.

Des missed his intended first race at Wincanton, the Terry Biddlecombe Chase. Two weeks later David was still not happy with him. He was still fat and David hadn't been able to work him. But time was passing and he had to do something. He decided to send Des to Devon & Exeter for the Plymouth Gin Haldon Gold Challenge Cup Chase over two miles. 'My drinks' cupboard's getting empty,' he explained.

'He's back' screamed the *News of the World*, '(and we don't mean Lester Piggott).'

That year the new jumping 'pattern' had been initiated. A number of races now had Grade 1, Grade 2, and Grade 3 status and the prize money in these races had risen dramatically, with the (intentional) consequence that these races were more fiercely contended. This would be no pushover. But what the hell, we thought, he may not be fit, but what can beat him at level weights over two miles on a right-handed track?

Devon & Exeter is a lovely track, and one of the biggest courses in England, but the spectating facilities are not exactly extensive, so after traffic jams for miles before the race, you couldn't move in the stand. Half the West Country had turned up to see Des.

Richard had to decide beforehand whether to ride Des or Waterloo Boy, the two mile star of David Nicholson's yard. Richard chose Des, and when Waterloo Boy fell, we thought this was going to be easy. But the pattern had attracted other good horses. Sabin du Loir, formerly a star of Michael Dickinson's stable and now with Martin Pipe, had been highly thought of till he'd developed leg problems, and at the age of eleven was better than ever.

Coming into the final straight, the crowd roared, as Des was four lengths behind Sabin du Loir and appeared to be gaining, but then he couldn't match Sabin du Loir's turn of foot, and finished six lengths second to him. It wasn't too bad, but of course the unspoken question was: was Des still the force he used to be?

'Is he over the top? Should he be retired?' grinned David,

tackling the problem head on. 'I thought I would get that in first before anyone else does. No, everything went right, except the result. They went a good gallop and he jumped well. He was beaten by a better horse on the day.'

Des was fine the next day, and David said we probably ought to think about Sandown again. But with the pattern upping the added prize money from £10,000 to £25,000 in the Tingle Creek, all the hot shot two-milers were heading there too, and we'd be giving them weight. Sabin du Loir, for instance, who'd just beaten us at levels, would be getting twenty pounds, Waterloo Boy sixteen pounds, and Young Snugfit twenty-one pounds.

'We're not going to win this, boy,' said David gloomily during our weekly phone conference two Sundays before. We mulled over the alternatives: there was the Peterborough Chase at Huntingdon the preceding Tuesday, which was a two and a half mile conditions race.

'I dunno, perhaps we should go to Huntingdon. But he'd have to stay overnight, that's the problem.' We agreed to talk later.

I talked to Richard, half hoping he'd say we'd be crazy to run in the Tingle Creek, but he didn't. Richard is canny enough to keep out of these things. He did say that he didn't think we could beat Waterloo Boy at the weights, and that he might switch horses. I suppose reading between the lines he *was* saying we'd be crazy to run in the Tingle Creek, but I didn't want it between the lines, I wanted it on the line. I called David a couple of days later and said I thought we'd lose Richard if we ran in the Tingle Creek.

'Well that's no problem,' said David, 'we'll get Brad.' Graham Bradley had been on our original shortlist to replace Simon.

'Does that mean we're going for the Tingle Creek?' I said.

'Oh, I dunno,' he said, 'I must be getting old, I'm not enjoying this as much as I used to. The nerves are going. I don't think either race is right for him, I'm not sure he'd win either of them.' The prospect of getting beaten at Huntingdon was even less appealing than getting beaten at Sandown, so we hummed and hawed.

'Well,' I said eventually, 'which race will set him up better for the King George?'

'Sandown,' said David, without hesitation.

'Fine,' I said.

Rodney gave me hell. His voice always rises a couple of tones when he's aggrieved about something. 'I don't know, I don't know what's wrong with you, what's wrong with Huntingdon!?'

'Too far,' I said. 'Horse doesn't like to travel.'

'Richard,' he said, 'this horse would travel to the moon and back and come out and win. He loves travelling. He can't win that race, you know, he just can't win it.'

'Dunwoody dilemma' screamed the headlines of *The Sporting Life*, with the news that Richard might do the ultimate unpardonable in jump racing in actually getting off Desert Orchid. 'Bradley gets Dessie job' announced the *Racing Post*, when Richard did.

Almost all our discussions about the grey horse were now set against a backdrop of furious interest by the racing press. As Des stood munching away in his stable, it always seemed incongruous that he was capable of generating so much newsprint. But there was something about him that just generated – what? – I don't know, but . . . nothing he did was ever routine, or boring. It was impossible, you thought, as you looked into that big black eye, that he could somehow be a conspirator in all this, that in some strange way we were all being manipulated to serve his appetite for publicity. Yes, of course, it was impossible.

Graham Bradley was delighted to get the job. Following his association with the Dickinsons, his career had been in the doldrums. David, with his natural feeling for the underdog, had to some extent rescued his career, but it wasn't just sentiment that inspired this. Graham Bradley was a magnificent jockey, with quiet hands and perfect balance. Along with Richard and Peter Scudamore, he was one of the best around. So Desert Orchid got his fifth jockey.

Brad was due to go down to Whitsbury to school Des the Sunday before to get used to the horse, but at the last minute David decided he couldn't be bothered. Nevertheless, David went ahead and said Brad had schooled him because it seemed less trouble just to say so, and Brad played along saying his schooling had gone perfectly. David was laughing when he told me. 'Another one for the book, Richard.'

But on the Thursday before the race, ironically two days after the Huntingdon race, Des trod on a stone. Rodney was pulling him up at the end of a bit of work, looking round to see how far ahead he was, and bang, Des put a foot on a stone, lame. The next day he was all right, more or less, and Saturday he was fine so nothing was said.

Des, however, was friendless in the market, but this was more due to a warning given by David a few days before when he said that the grey horse needed the race and might even come last. This proved pretty much right. But it wasn't his defeat that provoked comment, but the manner of it.

Everyone agreed that Des now needed 'waking up' over two miles, and Brad talked to both Richard and Simon Sherwood. Their advice was to make a lot of use of him, and that's exactly what he did. Brad, looking very good on the grey horse, set off like a scalded cat in front and, with his ears pricked, Des soared over the first fence, but just as he touched down, his ears flashed back, and stayed there. He sprinted for the second, and jumped it well, but his ears flashed back again.

Going down the back straight, the field gradually swallowed him up and he started going into the bottom of his fences. Then he got close to the pond and that was that. He finished last of the four finishers, four lengths behind Waterloo Boy, who was ten lengths behind Sabin du Loir, who was two lengths behind Young Snugfit.

Last, that was a new word in his vocabulary. Of course, at the weights he did come about top so it wasn't disastrous. But still . . . And then we noticed the speedy cuts.

Half an hour later I noticed Janice hurrying past the bar. 'What's up?' I asked. She looked worried, and looked around as if someone might be watching her.

'I'm going to get Elsie,' she said, 'Dessie's lame.'

We all trooped into the stable yard and Janice led him round. Des was going short on his near fore. It didn't look very serious, but he was definitely lame.

'Well,' said David, 'let's keep quiet about this.'

27

Business as Usual

'Desert Orchid Heads Off Into The Sunset', 'Sun Is Setting on Desert Campaign', 'Time for Dessie to Bow Out' ran the headlines the next day. You couldn't really blame the papers for taking that view, but perhaps they were over-reacting a little. David had been quite pleased with the performance, and considering his advance warnings that the horse would need the race and the fact that he was racing over two miles, it wasn't that bad. How many Irish Grand National winners could come back and do what he'd done? Watching the video in the knowledge that he was lame made the whole thing clear. His feet had been hurting. It had been the same in his first Whitbread, fence for fence.

I felt sorry for Graham Bradley, but he was as positive as ever, and the defeat didn't stick to him. As a matter of fact he rode a very good race. The bonus from our point of view, and possibly his, was that we now had a stand-in if for any reason Richard was not available in the future.

'He's much better,' said David, a few days later. 'In fact, he's bloody well. We'll win the King George. Are you going to bring down your man Armatage?'

A day's poulticing and a few days on the easy list had dealt with the bruised foot, and now there were just the speedy cuts to fix. George came down, and by now he and David were great friends. He dealt with a problem with Des's right shoulder, which gave us further cause for confidence, and a couple of days later Rodney galloped him against Landyap over seven furlongs. Landyap had recently run in the Hong Kong Cup, and Des beat him. We were quietly confident.

David didn't tell the press Des had been lame; there was no

point. He would simply have suffered death-by-a-thousand-phone calls, and the pressure leading up to the King George was bad enough without that.

But the fact that people were now starting to question Des's invincibility was almost a relief, and it felt like the old days again. He no longer just 'had to turn up' to win, and we could start banging the drum for our horse again amidst the general gloom of his presumed decline.

We were looking forward to the King George. A fourth King George, though . . . It was almost impossible to believe the old boy was really attempting a fourth King George.

Celtic Shot was the horse people were backing. He'd run up a string of three wins, he'd won a Champion Hurdle and he could be even better over fences. Toby Tobias, who had beaten Des in the Gold Cup, attracted some support when he was declared a definite runner, but Jenny Pitman hadn't been able to get a run into him. The Fellow, trained by our old friend François Doumen, was over from France, though he was young at five. Sabin du Loir had beaten us at levels first time out, but wasn't quite as good over three miles, though Panto Prince was a danger, as he had almost never been beaten at Kempton. It looked like it would be a tough race.

Around this time, Tim Neligan of United Racecourses rang up, and said he'd like to put a full size statue of Desert Orchid at Kempton and did we object? Of course we didn't, though we did suggest it might be odd for the horse to encounter a full scale statue of himself on the way out to the track. Tim said it would take them over a year to do, so there would be no question of it happening in a hurry, but that they'd like to get it finished before the King George next year.

Maybe as a result of this, or maybe not, gradually confidence in Des's opposition began to wane. 4–1 disappeared and showed no signs of re-appearing. It was one thing to say Desert Orchid was in decline, but quite another to find something to beat him. We were all being disgustingly positive, and his reputation started to intimidate people again. Could anything really beat Desert Orchid – round Kempton – at level weights – over three miles?

Not all the press had deserted him, either, and the growing confidence we had in him was reflected in his starting price of 9–4.

It was a horribly wet day, and the ground had become soggy. Perfect jumping weather!

Des looked like he appreciated it, strutting around the paddock with his neck arched. The TV pictures were foggy with mist as they lined up at the start, with Richard hoicking at Dessie's neck to get him on the inside. The tapes went up, and Prize Asset went on over the first two, and turning into the bend, Des was fourth behind Prize Asset, Sabin du Loir and Panto Prince. The ground was pretty filthy, and he was soon spattered with mud, but he seemed to be going – and jumping – better than at Sandown. Turning into the straight for the first time, Sabin du Loir, with his ears pricked, went three lengths up. Richard looked relaxed, and though they didn't appear to be going very fast, the field was getting strung out behind them. Mark Perrett on Sabin du Loir kept his three length lead over the next three fences and into the bend, and lined up for the first down the far side. Sabin du Loir hit it hard, and sprawling on landing, hit the deck. For a moment it looked like his flailing legs would bring down the grey horse, but in a remarkable feat of agility, Des side-stepped him and galloped on. His ears were pricked now and he was jumping superbly. Behind him Toby Tobias was overtaking The Fellow and Des was three lengths up, as Richard gave him a slap down the neck. Des put in a brilliant leap over the fourth last and went into the bend five lengths up. The crowd started to roar. Behind him Mark Pitman on Toby Tobias wasn't making much progress.

Into that famous Kempton straight, and Des cleared the third last beautifully. Toby Tobias was beaten as Des went eight lengths clear going to the second last. Again he jumped it well and went ten lengths up. Graham Goode bellowed into the microphone, 'The crowd's going absolutely wild!' One fence to go between Desert Orchid and racing history, and a record that would probably never be beaten. He soared over it and set off, ears back, for the line, as the ten lengths turned to twelve, and the crowd went berserk. Graham Goode, who had called home so many of his famous victories, was yelling 'This was *his* race, Desert Orchid, watch history being made, roars of applause, the King's in his counting house, Desert Orchid's blooming, he's been here before, Desert Orchid the winner, marvellous!'

Des pulled up with his ears pricking to what must have been

the biggest roar ever heard at Kempton. Richard stroked his neck and trotted back, and Janice, tears in her eyes, caught hold of him. Only four horses out of nine starters had finished, and Des had beaten Toby Tobias by twelve lengths, with The Fellow five lengths back in third, and Celtic Shot seven lengths back in fourth. He had won a fourth King George.

David was grinning as he walked Des into the winner's spot. It was a great piece of training, and everybody paid tribute to him and to Rodney, watching at home. David said simply he was proud to be the grey's trainer. Des stood in the middle of the continuing applause, his face spattered with mud, his ears pricked, as the family engulfed him. Paul Hayward wrote in *The Independent* the next day: 'There is an end to the film that is Desert Orchid's racing life, but someone seems to have lost it. Watching him win a record fourth King George VI Chase yesterday made you think the thing is stuck in replay mode.'

Afterwards David said he was not entering him for the National, and though we still hadn't discussed it, that was fine by me. Jenny Pitman came up in the Rank box afterwards and said that she hadn't wanted to say anything before the decision was made because it wasn't her business, but she was sure it was the right thing to do. The last time she had run Corbiere with all that weight, it nearly broke her heart. She had looked into his eye after the race and had seen right to the bottom of him. She said he was never the same horse again.

No one could have been a bigger fan of the horse than Jenny, and no one was a bigger fan of the National. Of course everyone would have liked to have seen the grey horse jump those National fences, but that was too glib to take at face value. The chapter had closed on Des in the National.

After the King George it was assumed that with Des's advancing age, he would be given a break. But David regarded the obvious with suspicion. If you own a horse trained by David Elsworth, you learn to listen to the way he insinuates, almost casually, an unusual idea into the argument, as if he's just thought of it, and thinking this is a discussion, you start to discuss it. Only you find it isn't a discussion at all, you're being told what's going to happen. I don't remember a single occasion in all those years when I managed to change his mind about a single thing. In other words, with David, you have to learn to expect the unexpected, and then you have to learn to see the unexpected as perfectly normal, as inevitable. So I wasn't surprised by his next suggestion, and I also knew there was no point in arguing about it.

'I think we'll run him at Ascot, Richard, in the Victor Chandler.' This meant two miles, top weight.

'Fine,' I said.

I didn't think Des had much chance of winning, but it wasn't such a crazy idea. The alternative was doing nothing, and with his various problems now sorted out, he was bound to do a lot better than at Sandown. But David also had runners in the Ladbroke Hurdle race at Leopardstown the same day.

'I think I'll go to Ireland, though. I'll send Rodney.' Er, was that really such a good idea? 'Yeah, gives us an excuse if we're beaten,' he laughed. This turned out to be a fiendish bit of Elsworth logic. Rodney was the one who'd objected most strongly to his charge's participation in this event and now he was going to Ascot to front the enterprise. David was highly amused at the idea.

Rodney never looks particularly cheerful even when he is cheerful, but that day at Ascot he seemed very gloomy as he stood buried in his sheepskin coat.

'Hello, Richard,' he said, 'what do you think about this then?'

'What do you think?' I countered.

'Hasn't got a hope,' he said. 'I don't know why you think he has.'

'Me?' I said.

'Yes, Elsie said it was your idea.'

I laughed. If David ever gets fed up with racing, he definitely has a career in politics.

It was a cold, sunny January day, somehow reminiscent of Des's early hurdling days, and I think it occurred to all of us this might be his last visit to Ascot. The whole of the second half of the season was like that, tinged with a kind of poignancy that recalled the wide-eyed early days with the horse.

His opponents were Young Snugfit, the grey Blitzkreig from Ireland, Katabatic and Hogmanay. Des had to give seventeen pounds to Young Snugfit and twenty-four pounds to the rest of the field, a tall order considering the doubts about his efficiency over two miles these days, but he looked well, so it was still possible. Anything was possible with Desert Orchid.

Richard had the rail and let him run into an early lead, but the others were close up and then Hogmanay took the lead and squeezed him up a little on the bend. At the first down the back straight, Hogmanay fell, impeded Des a little, and Young Snugfit and Blitzkreig went on. Hogmanay continued riderless, and started to get in Des's way all the way down the back straight, with Richard, now relegated to third, having to duck and dive to avoid Hogmanay. It was the same story after Swinley Bottom, with Hogmanay continuing to get in his way, and Des probably lost three or four lengths trying to get past him. Coming into the straight, though, Des was not going to win. He was last by several lengths, and ahead of him Young Snugfit and Blitzkreig had flown. He fought all the way up to the line, and as Blitzkreig just beat Young Snugfit, with Katabatic third, Des was three lengths behind in fourth. Two miles was too short for him now, and he was not disgraced. Katabatic went on to win the Champion Chase at Cheltenham, and since we had to give him twenty-four pounds and only failed to beat him by a length, at the end of the season Timeform again made Des their top two mile chaser. It was sad not to win, though poor old Rodney took much of the blame. We left Ascot thinking it would be unlikely we would ever be back with Desert Orchid.

It was the same story at Sandown three weeks later. Most of my favourite days with the grey horse were at Sandown: the sight of him jumping the first ditch in the straight, the sight of him storming up the hill, the way the noise of the crowd built all the way from the pond fence to the finishing line.

Today Des was attempting to match the great Burrough Hill Lad's record of three victories in the Gainsborough, now sponsored by Agfa Diamond. Given the number of photographs of him in circulation, it was appropriate that the race should be sponsored by a film manufacturer.

Des was trying to give fifteen pounds to Nick The Brief, and twenty-one pounds to Ten of Spades and Kildimo. His handicap mark had fallen to 177, but it would still be tough to win his ninth race here. It was a freezing day, but enough people had left their armchairs to come to Sandown to make it an occasion. Des got his familiar round of applause in the paddock and on the way down to the start, but John Upson, Nick The Brief's trainer, wasn't too happy about this. When Nick The Brief had performed disappointingly in the previous year's Gold Cup, he had thought the reception given to Desert Orchid before the race had put his horse off. He might have been right, but considering all Desert Orchid had achieved over the years, it wasn't surprising people wanted to show their appreciation.

Three miles round Sandown probably now suited Des even more than Kempton, and he went off favourite at 4–6. With no other front runners in the field, Des was allowed, for a change, to bowl along in front, and seemed happier at this pace. He was a stirring sight as he flew down the back straight, measuring his fences, and looked wonderful coming past the stands for the first time. Ten of Spades was not jumping well and was losing touch, but Kildimo and Nick The Brief were on his tail as he went down the back straight for the second time. You do not need many horses – two will usually do – for a great race at Sandown. The last three fences bring the runners together and the uphill finish often transforms races. Coming to the pond, Nick The Brief made his challenge on the outside, and Kildimo ranged up outside him. Richard bustled up the old grey, and neck and neck they went for the second last, with Nick The Brief apparently going best. Nick The Brief got his head in front going to the last, but Des fought back and the three horses were in the air together. Again Nick The Brief went on after the last, but the crowd's roar seemed to lift Des, and with Richard riding away for all he was worth, the years dropped away, and the grey horse was fighting his way up that Sandown hill again, in front of his crowd, and in as good a finish as he ever produced at Sandown, won going away by three-quarters of a length. It was a replay of so many days at Sandown – the crowd rushing to the winner's enclosure, Des nodding furiously as Peter Maughan took the tack off and Janice led him around and around. We thought he was as good as ever, but David wasn't so sure. 'Dessie had to take his coat off' he pointed out, and he also said he wasn't enjoying it as much, and he wasn't sure Des was either.

Back at Whitsbury, Chris Hill suggested the performance was at least on a par with his beating of Pegwell Bay two years earlier, and in many respects, the two races were identical. David relented a little, saying that it was very difficult to be objective, and perhaps it was just him that was getting old. It was hard to be detached and with Rodney and Janice continuing to feel good about the horse, he conceded he might be wrong. On the other hand, he felt he should not subject the horse to too many hard races from now on, and said he would attempt to regain the Gold Cup and that would probably be that for the season. We all now recognised Des's racing days were numbered.

We'd discussed his retirement before, but only in a general sense. We wanted to retire him at the top, and not let him slide into a slow decline. Though Des loved jumping and galloping, it would not be doing him any favours to keep him going past his prime, and it would only hurt his reputation. About eighteen months before I had suggested the 1991 King George could be his last race. It would be a few days before his thirteenth birthday and, paradoxically, though the King George was regarded in some circles as the top staying chase in the calendar, it was just about the easiest race for him. Three miles round Kempton at level weights was perfect, so if he couldn't win that, given his position at the top of the handicap, he couldn't win anything. We had to get him to Kempton next year fit to run and didn't want to tempt fate by announcing the plan in advance, although we all agreed what that plan should be. I hoped that we would have one last attempt at the Whitbread, but we would see.

Soon after the Gainsborough, Nick The Brief won the Vincent O'Brien Cup at Leopardstown in a canter, and though his rivals all fell, it had been an impressive performance and made Des's defeat of him giving him fifteen pounds look all the better.

We braced ourselves for a final onslaught on the Gold Cup. It would be pure Desert Orchid to lose the Cup one year, then regain it the next. Celtic Shot jostled for favouritism with him; he was a brilliant horse who loved Cheltenham, but there were doubts as to whether he would stay the three and a quarter miles of the Gold Cup if it turned out to be wet. Arctic Call had won the Hennessey, but this race represented a step up at the weights. Cool Ground had won the Welsh National and was improving, but at that stage he had not proved he was more than a very good handicapper. Nick The Brief we had beaten at Sandown; Yahoo we had beaten two years before at Cheltenham; The Fellow we had beaten at Kempton; but the Gordon Richards pair of Twin Oaks and Carrick Hill Lad looked dangerous. Norton's Coin, like so many Gold Cup winners, had not blossomed since, and had refused at Leopardstown after receiving a kick during the race. Party Politics, like Arctic Call, was stepping up in class; Kildimo we had beaten and another French challenger, Martin D'Or, looked to have little chance. Finally there was Garrison Savannah, a horse whom Jenny Pitman had bought because he reminded her of her great favourite, Corbiere. He had had problems though, and had had only one race that season. Jenny had given him a course in acupuncture and sent him swimming to try to get him fit for the big race.

The unknown ingredient at Cheltenham is the ground, but this year it looked like it would be perfect jumping ground. It was not as fast as the year before, but not so wet as to suit the mudlarks like Cool Ground and Carrick Hill Lad. We felt the old boy had a good chance as we descended on Cheltenham. He had at least got to know the place pretty well.

There was a fresh, grassy smell to the air that day; the sense of spring was not far away. We could have walked through the rituals blindfolded: gathering at the pre-parade ring, waiting outside the saddling box as David tacked Des up, joking nervously in the parade ring, then that lurch in the stomach as Richard rode him down the chute and out to the track. Taking up our familiar positions on the lawn, the memories of that day two years earlier were never far away: time slowing as the horses become specks in the distance as they walk around at the start, the buzz of the crowd settling, the bark of the commentator announcing 'They're under orders', the sense of 50,000 pairs of eyes focused on one thing, the start of the Gold Cup.

Once again, they were off. Once again, we abandoned all our hopes, all our bravado. This was Cheltenham. We would be happy if he came through it in one piece. Richard had lined the grey horse up on the inside, and set off at a sensible pace, sharing the lead. Going round the bend, Arctic Call went on, with Des a couple of lengths behind, dwarfed by the enormous Party Politics.

Down the back straight they went, and though Des was jumping well, his ears were back. Perhaps he resented not being in the lead, but he didn't seem entirely happy, and when Arctic Call made successive mistakes at the two in the home straight, and Des briefly hit the front, his ears still didn't go forward. He jumped into the lead at the first in the back straight, but his ears stayed back, and though he was going well off a loose rein, he lost ground at the sixteenth, and was suddenly swamped by four or five horses.

He tucked in behind Nick The Brief, Celtic Shot and Carrick Hill Lad, and started to battle on, but five from home he was also behind Garrison Savannah and The Fellow. Richard brought him round on the outside at the fourth last, and he jumped it well, taking advantage of a mistake from The Fellow to go briefly into second behind Celtic Shot as Richard steered him hard into the left-hand bend. Again he fell back; at the third last he was fourth, but jumped into third as Carrick Hill Lad broke down. Garrison Savannah took a three length lead and Des was squeezed between The Fellow on his outside and Celtic Shot on his inside, and dropped back to fourth as he battled on round yet another of those left-handed bends.

Straightening up, the race was lost. Like the year before, two horses had gone clear, and as Garrison Savannah fought out the finish with The Fellow, Des plugged on. His speed had faded with the years, his experience neutralised by the fast ground, his stamina sapped by those terrible bends, but still he plugged on, reaching for his greatest quality, the quality which remained undimmed and triumphant after all those miles and all those fences – his great, indomitable, and magnificent courage. Perhaps it was a little thing, perhaps it was a very great thing indeed, but he plugged on, never surrendering, attacking that hill, and stayed on into third place, beating Celtic Shot and all those other younger horses. At the line, for the first time, his ears were pricked. Cheltenham had beaten him again, but he was too proud and too brave to surrender. He just looked pleased it was over.

He'd given his all. Once again he'd beaten the fancied horses, but two others had beaten him. It was so familiar. Cheltenham had struck again, but it had struck for the last time. As Janice led him into the horsebox Des pricked his ears and looked round. 'Say goodbye, Dessie,' she said.

The Whitbread looked a forlorn hope, and again the weather

turned against him when it stayed dry at Sandown. David kept him going, but after a couple of weeks he called it a day. No Whitbread for Des. It hurt. Perhaps we had seen him run for the last time at Sandown. I rang David from Ireland.

'Are you sure we're doing the right thing, David?'

'I'm sure.'

I paused. So many things went through my mind; for the first time I felt the pangs that I knew would come, that I might never again see him coming up that Sandown hill, or hear the roar of the crowd as he jumped the pond. There was so much I wanted to say, so much I wanted to do with Desert Orchid before it was too late. But I just said, 'Okay, David. And thanks for another great season.'

'It's been great, hasn't it?' he said. 'We'll miss him when he's gone.'

28

❧

A Sense of Loss

WHEN DES CAME HOME that summer, we all knew this was the last time we would be going through the rituals we had evolved over the years. Richard Watson looked at his corns; he was a little worried that he'd spotted some hyperflexion in his left front joint, and George Armatage found his shoulder was out. It was a cold, miserable spring with the wind blowing from the east, and with the deadline of the open day approaching, it was impossible to get him to Flintham, so he stayed at Ab Kettleby. David was keen to get him back a couple of weeks early for the following season, so we shuffled his schedule forward. For the first time in five years, though he was still the top steeplechaser, he lost his Horse of the Year National Hunt Award to the hurdler Morley Street.

His popularity was increasing, though, and along with the usual requests to turn out at various charity events, we agreed to take him to Downing Street to deliver a petition protesting against the removal of the 'minimum values' legislation which currently protected horses against being exported live for slaughter. It was appropriate that Des, blessed with talent and soundness all his life, should try to do something for less fortunate horses.

He had been in from the field a week and doing an hour and a half a day on the horsewalker when we drove him down to London. A box was provided by the Blues and Royals off Horseguards Parade, and Des watched quizzically as the cavalry horses shuffled past in full regalia. He took the whole thing so calmly he was offered a job as bugle horse. His retirement options were increasing. Last time he had been in London, he had been offered a job as a police horse.

John Oaksey led him into Downing Street, and the traffic

roared past as he strolled up Whitehall. With his ears pricked, he marched up Downing Street and stood patiently while his picture was taken, pausing only on the way back to leave a deposit outside the Chancellor's house. A few months earlier a Gallup poll had established that in fact Desert Orchid was better known than the Chancellor. Eighty-four per cent of the people polled had heard of Desert Orchid and only seventy-seven per cent had heard of Norman Lamont.

Lamont countered in his budget speech in the House of Commons, 'I was surprised to read that I am almost as well known as Desert Orchid and I haven't yet run in the Gold Cup. Actually, Desert Orchid and I have a lot in common. We are both greys, vast sums of money are riding on our performance, the opposition hopes we will fall at the first fence, and we are both carrying too much weight. The crucial difference is that Chancellors are never favourites.' He then put VAT up by two and a half per cent to seventeen and a half per cent, which put a further burden on the breeding and training industry.

This was not the first time Des had been mentioned in Parliament. A couple of years earlier Sir Anthony Myers was put up against Mrs Thatcher and it was generally considered he was a 'stalking horse' candidate. 'Who is this "stalking horse"?' asked Norman Tebbit. 'He's no Desert Orchid, is he?'

Meanwhile, Philip Blacker was already well on with his life-size sculpture commissioned by United Racecourses. He wanted to capture the sense of a coiled spring as Des walked around the paddock, and the problem of the colour also preoccupied him. Various solutions were proposed, then the foundry Philip was using came up with some acids which would turn the bronze to grey. He was excited by the results.

One superstition that permeates racing is: don't ask anyone to paint your horse while he's still racing, something always happens to him. Of course there were dozens, perhaps as many as fifty, paintings or prints of Des in existence, but we hadn't contributed to them. However, we were contributing to this one in the sense that we were giving Philip as much access to the horse as he wanted, and Midge and Jimmy were worried.

Des floated through his fan club appearance – this year someone came from Argentina – and went up to Yorkshire. Clare always called him 'old man', but at twelve he was getting old. His back was dipping, and perhaps he was a little quiet. He was always so switched off in Yorkshire, though, we couldn't really tell. To wake him up, we abandoned the easy tracks across the moors, and rode him up steep bank sides. His balance was remarkable. I used to jump off the mare I was riding and lead her, but Clare shook her head and said she'd be fine on Des's back, thank you. He was like a cat, pivoting from one section of rocky track to another and enjoying it. He still wouldn't cross anything that looked like a puddle; with any other horse we would have insisted, but with Desert Orchid you make exceptions.

Bearing in mind his weight problems of the year before, I put him on a diet. Not a strict diet – he had twenty-four pounds of food a day, and most of that was hay – but a diet none the less, and he was furious.

Then Mary Reveley came to lunch one day and told me that George Armatage was dying. He had become very thin, and when he finally agreed to go for a check-up, he was told he had inoperable cancer. We were devastated. George had been such a tower of strength over the years that it was difficult to imagine things without him. I went to see him, and his eyes still burnt with that old strength and intelligence. He was too ill to make his rounds any more, but he wished us luck, and hoped we could find someone to help Des on what would be his last season. It was a very sad day, and driving away from George's house, it felt like something was ending.

Then Clare told me about John Patterson, who had treated a horse of Charlie Booth's. He was also a vet, and did Arthur Stephenson's horses, as well as the Ramsdens's and a few other trainers', and was the course vet at Newcastle. Everyone spoke highly of him, and when I met him I could see why. He was one of those rare people who radiate a kind of wonderful, enthusiastic intelligence. As a vet he had pioneered a lot of the work on trace minerals, and to begin with he had not believed that what George did was possible. However, as he lived close to him, he began to see so many miraculous 'cures' that he became a believer and taught himself to do what George did.

George kept his secrets to himself, but John explained exactly what he did. We suspected Des was not quite right, as he was not straight at the trot; John found his pelvis was out, and used the horse's own strength to click it back. He found a different problem with Irish Orchid and put her right. John was a great admirer of George's, and recognising his absence left an enormous vacuum, did his best to fill it.

The horses had also been found by Edmund Collins to be anaemic and short of copper, and Edmund gave them a tonic. Apparently it was a widespread problem; no one really knew why, but there was a general suspicion it had something to do with modern farming. It was getting much harder to get horses absolutely right. David came to stay a few weeks later and though he had won some big races, he'd had a difficult time earlier in the summer when none of his horses had been quite right. The recession was also biting hard, and it added to the feeling that something was changing. I don't think many people in racing surveyed the future with quite as much optimism as they had a few years earlier.

David was pleased Des wasn't too fat, but shook his head as he considered him. He said he might be imagining it, but he thought Des's back legs were looking old. He drew a picture. They used to look like this, he said. Now they looked like this.

John Oaksey came up to ride out one day and, having seen the grey horse fighting his way down to the start before most of his races over the years, thought he might have his hands full, but Des just lobbed round the roads like an old hack. It was a perfect August morning, and that summer all the summers seemed to blend together: bright blue skies, the familiar snickering and pricked ears as we walked out of the house towards the stable, the click of hooves on asphalt, the cars pulling over, the ride past familiar houses and familiar faces. But life was moving on, turning a notch, the summer was slipping by.

Now it is late August. The light has gone by half-past eight. The heat and wind of the summer is replaced by a dull serenity as the seasons change. The heather has turned brown.

It is the last time we shall be sending Dessie south. The poignancy of the end of the summer is pointed up by a feeling that something is coming to an end. The anchor is shifting. Life will be a little different from now on. The end has begun.

29

The Dying of the Light

THE RETURN OF THE GREY HORSE to Whitsbury marked the end of the summer for us and the beginning of the jump season for David's yard. Over the years David had switched more and more to the flat, but the lads who had been with him for years still enjoyed the jumps, and were pleased to see the old grey back again. To begin with he was a little quiet – perhaps we had overdone the 'diet' – and David's daughter Jessie rode him back from the gallops one day, with David walking by his side. After a week, when Rodney gave him his first serious piece of work, he exploded, and Rodney felt the familiar aching arm muscles.

Rodney always had the measure of him, though it was an entertaining contest. Out of the trees and up the hill came the grey horse, ears pricked, the power down, he fought his companion. Rodney, his eyes twinkling, rode him on a long rein, Des sticking his head out to one side, and as they went past Des seemed to be thinking that he had him, but a few strides further on he'd suddenly stop and walk on, looking puzzled – he was sure he had had Rodney that time . . . maybe tomorrow.

United Racecourses had contacted us in the summer with a view to naming a race after him, if possible a race he could run in. David and I thought perhaps a two and a half mile chase at the early December Sandown meeting would be ideal. There were no really perfect prep races for the King George, i.e. conditions races at a right-handed track at the beginning of December, but Tim Neligan called at the beginning of September to say the search for a suitable race for him at Sandown had failed. The race planners considered there were already two prep races for the King George, the Rehearsal Chase at Chepstow and the Haydock race, and though nobody seemed to regard them as prep races in anything but name, that was that. Apart from the King George and the Gainsborough and a couple of races at Wincanton, there were actually very few three-mile races that suited Des. In handicaps he was always giving lumps of weight away and almost all the conditions races, especially in the second part of the season, were at left-handed courses. It was ironic that despite him being the biggest draw in jump racing, there were actually very few places we could take him. Then Ian Renton from Wincanton called and suggested renaming the Terry Biddlecombe Chase after Desert Orchid.

Wincanton was David's local track, and we had many happy times there over the years. But now the pressure was on to get him fit for his own race in late October. Again the weather was against him.

It had probably been against him for the last eighteen months. He was definitely not as happy on fast ground now, and the only two times it had been soft, the King George and the Gainsborough, were the only two races he had won. We had another dry autumn, and David was struggling to get the work into him on the firm ground. He was aware, we were all aware, that we were living on borrowed time, as we tried to get him back to his best for one last crack at the King George. But the combination of Des's trimmer figure and a little rain in the middle of October made the trip to Wincanton feasible. Desert Orchid was to join a select few to run in a race named after him.

At Wincanton it was the usual madness, clogged roads, hastily commissioned overflow carparks, people jammed eight deep round the pre-parade ring. David, perhaps anticipating the scrum, went to Newbury to saddle three runners, and watched the race on SIS. In his place he sent Rodney Boult. Rodney, mindful of his reputation, was as nervous as a squirrel. To be one of the main contributors to the horse's success over the years and yet to be so unwelcome on the racecourse was an odd state of affairs, and I'm afraid we showed him no mercy.

The race had lured some serious rivals, notably Sabin du Loir from Martin Pipe's stable, who had beaten him in the Plymouth Gin Haldon Gold Challenge Cup at Devon & Exeter the previous season. We could count on him being fit, too, and were hopeful rather than confident of beating him. That was pretty much the way it turned out. Des ran well, but Sabin du Loir was fitter, and leading throughout, accelerated off the bend, and Des had no answer on the fast ground. Everything but the result was right. The old horse still had his enthusiasm, and he was on target for Kempton.

We juggled alternatives for his next race. There was the Silver Buck at Wincanton, but that came a little too soon. Then there was the Rank Trial Chase at Kempton. That came a little too late to fit in another race after it. In the meantime Philip Blacker had finished his statue, and that was due to be unveiled at the Kempton meeting on 21 November. Four days before it, George Armatage died at home in Northumberland.

His funeral was on the 21st; as I travelled up to it, I could not help noting the irony that the man who had done so much to help Desert Orchid over the years was being buried at the moment that a statue was being unveiled to the grey horse. Perhaps in some way it would stand as a memorial to his achievements, as well as to all the other horses he had helped over the years. Desert Orchid was the best loved and most successful jumper of his time. But the basis for that durability was so slender. He was very lucky to have George travel all those miles to put him right over the years.

Other alternatives to Dessie's last race before the King George included the Long Walk Hurdle at Ascot. We discussed it for a few days, and then decided that in spite of the distance he'd have to travel, the Peterborough Chase at Huntingdon, a Grade 2 conditions race over two and a half miles was the easiest race.

Then we were at Huntingdon. To jump from the relative seclusion of a phone conversation a week earlier in London to the middle of that meeting was very strange. Thousands of people had turned up, and you couldn't move, but the easy race we had anticipated had evaporated. Sabin du Loir was taking part again, as was Norton's Coin. Des looked interested as he walked round this new parade ring beforehand, but he was starting to look old. His legs were turning hairy in his old age.

Spectators lined the pre-parade ring ten deep while the previous race was running. Des was applauded down to the start and Richard was wearing some new silks that day.

We knew Peter Scudamore was going to take us on, and as the tapes went up, Sabin du Loir and Des went flat out for the first fence. But instead of standing off, Des put down, hit the fence, and he was a length down going to the second. He stayed that way down the back, but was still going well coming into the straight for the first time, though Sabin du Loir looked very relaxed in the lead on the fast ground. There is an open ditch right in front of the stand at Huntingdon, and everyone was expecting a spectacular jump from the two leaders, but at the last moment Sabin du Loir jumped across Des, and Des put down and hit the fence and went into the bend a couple of lengths down. It was a bad omen, and he seemed to be guessing a little at his fences down the back. Sabin du Loir went clear coming into the home straight. Richard shook Des up and got after the old boy; he didn't look like he'd make it, but he fought on to the line. Sabin du Loir won easily by four lengths, and Norton's Coin just held on to beat Des by a short head. Afterwards he was blowing as hard as I'd seen him for years. It was getting hard, and again there were the speedy cuts. I went and saw him an hour later. He looked very tired, and flinched when I touched his stifle. He must have really clobbered that first fence. David went to see him half an hour later. He was fast asleep.

It took two hours to get out of the carpark. It was worse than Cheltenham with cars bumper to bumper in the gloom, exhausts steaming, heaters blaring. Des had put 5,000 on the gate. Clerk of the Course Hugo Bevan said he had been waiting all his life for a day like this at Huntingdon.

The countdown to the King George began in earnest. We didn't know whether we would retire him after it or not, but on balance, after Huntingdon, we thought we would. David wanted to leave the decision to us, though he added again that he wasn't enjoying it as much and didn't think Des was. The enthusiasm was still there, but the ability and strength was slipping away. He was starting to look over the hill, but as David pointed out, it had been a very big hill he'd been up, and he might still be good enough to win a fifth King George. I felt it might be worth considering a break after Kempton, then a short spring campaign culminating in either the Irish National or the Whitbread – Des seemed to need further than three miles these days. David felt he would not be able to give the weight away and thought his advancing years would adversely affect his stamina. So with that option out of the way, there was nowhere to go after Kempton.

We all wanted to separate the retirement issue from the King George: the pressure leading up to Boxing Day would be bad enough, without it being accompanied by the hype if it were known beforehand that it would be his last race. Besides, racing was an uncertain business. There was no need to make a final decision till we had to.

Our confidence started to grow. Huntingdon had straightened Des out, and he was fizzing and popping on the gallops. Perhaps he was kidding us, but Rodney thought again he was a powerhouse, a biting, kicking machine.

Richard Dunwoody had a difficult decision to make. In a situation uncannily reminiscent of Colin Brown's decision all those years before, he had to choose between the brilliant young pretender in the shape of the unbeaten Remittance Man and the old stager and four times champion. Remittance Man could be anything, but lacked experience, and trainer Nicky Henderson could only get one race into him before the King George.

Remittance Man was favourite, and Richard's dilemma deepened. Des galloped with Oh So Risky, David's Champion Hurdle hope and a useful flat horse. Des took three lengths out of him, and Oh So Risky could not claw the distance back. He was clearly getting back into the groove at the right time, but Richard wanted to leave his decision till the last moment so we put Graham Bradley on stand-by. A week before the race Richard called and said he would be riding the grey horse. Desert Orchid's price for the King George shortened half a point. Now there were just the speedy cuts to sort out. John Patterson came down on the Saturday before the big race, with five days to go, and found one shoulder was out, which explained the speedy cuts.

I went down to Whitsbury on Christmas Eve with Simon Bullimore because I thought it might be the last time I would ever see Des on the gallops. It was a glorious winter's day, the New Forest was sprinkled with frost, and Des was at the head of affairs as Rodney cantered him round the loop to warm him up, standing up in his stirrups to stop him off a long rein. We set off to the end of the gallops in David's Range Rover full of dogs, and stood shivering in the early morning sun.

David said it was tough for him to put so much pressure on Des. 'I have to get after the bugger. I don't like it, but it's not fair to him if we don't. We won't be doing any favours being kind to him here.'

Des appeared out of the mist galloping with Floyd and Big Beat. He took a couple of lengths out of them at the start, then they closed up at the four furlong marker. Then Des took off, and as he stormed past, he looked as powerful as I had ever seen him, and he was fifteen lengths clear of Floyd. Rodney was grinning. He was really pleased with him.

The scene was set for the King George, as Desert Orchid walked back after what was probably the last piece of work he would ever do at Whitsbury. All those miles over all those years were going to be tested one last time at Kempton on Boxing Day.

'The job's done,' said David. 'Now it's up to him.'

30

The Last Lap

As we set off to Kempton Park, from our separate homes, we all knew this was probably the last time we would be going to cheer on the grey horse. As much from habit as superstition we had got used to the rituals. At half-past six Janice mucked out, and at seven she changed his rugs and loaded him on to the box. The horsebox left Whitsbury at half-past seven and got to Kempton at quarter-past nine. Des, who no longer needed to roll every time he got to a racecourse, stood waiting patiently for his race to come up.

Simon Elsworth, who had stood guard outside his box for the last four years, no longer had a stable pass and so was not allowed to this time. He still kept an eye on him from a distance. David left Whitsbury at half-past nine and battled through the traffic clogging the roads.

I did the scrapbook the night before, got up at eight, read the papers, put on a grey suit, blue shirt, grey tie, picked up my old brown overcoat and set off through the quiet London streets. As you get closer to Kempton, you find yourself glancing into the other cars on the road, wondering if they're going to the same place as you. Then you see the signs to Kempton Park. The pulse quickens – once more into the cauldron of emotion.

A traffic jam was already forming at half-past ten, and the gateman, after nine years and nearly fifty visits to Sandown, Kempton and Ascot, refused to believe I was the owner of Desert Orchid and claimed eight owners had already gone in. I had no idea who they were, but it looked like they would have to find another way of getting themselves parking from now on.

The life-sized statue of Desert Orchid stood on the tarmac as we walked through the members' gate. We would see if it was bad luck. Philip Blacker was worried that it was too light, too ribby, but he had measured the horse up after Cheltenham; I thought it was pretty wonderful. Throughout the day people stopped and had their photos taken beside it. We had come a long way from the first fall in January 1983, nine years before.

Rank's sponsorship of the race was ending. They had begun sponsoring the meeting the first year Desert Orchid had won. This last year of their sponsorship coincided with his last run in the race. Six years. Desert Orchid had been running in the King George for six years.

I stood on the Rank balcony after the second race. Balloons drifted into the cold blue sky. Cars were still forming a queue to get in after the second race. The place was bursting at the seams, 29,000 people went to Kempton that day, a record. I talked to David briefly before the third race. Someone had offered to set up a match between Des and Carvill's Hill at either Kempton or Cheltenham, and this might have provided Des with exactly the kind of second half of the season opportunity we had been looking for. David suggested whatever happened during the race we take some time to think about it before making any decisions about his retirement.

We went and stood at the pre-parade ring as the runners cantered down for the third race. The best King George for ten years people were saying, but with the exception of Remittance Man, Docklands Express and Foyle Fisherman, the others had run in the race before. I personally did not think it was as good a race as the King George between Des, Forgive 'N Forget, Wayward Lad, Combs Ditch and Bolands Cross – Bolands Cross at the time had pretty much the same reputation that Remittance Man had now – but racing is all about differences of opinion, and it was still a bloody good race. Remittance Man could be anything, but he would be subjected to more pressure throughout the race than he had ever been before, and any inexperience in his make-up would be found out. Sabin du Loir, despite looking very impressive and more or less unbeatable over two and two and a half miles in the first part of the season had yet to win over three, and I felt the biggest dangers would come from The Fellow and Toby Tobias, the second and third the previous year. The Fellow had, after all, failed by only a nose to win the Gold Cup, and though this looked on the short side for him, he would be assured of a fast pace and fast ground, and could be assumed, at six, to be better than he was the year before. Toby Tobias was also a tough, brilliant horse and could be expected to have improved by the same amount that the grey horse had declined in the intervening year. Docklands Express was something of an unknown quantity: he had won the Whitbread after the controversial disqualification of Cahervillahow, but it was generally assumed that he would need more than three miles and was running for fun.

Peter Maughan, Jinks and Simon Elsworth were standing in the entrance to the stable box, waiting for David to come back from the weighing room with Richard's tack. As Janice walked him round, Des, like in so many pictures of him these days, looked a little furrier than before. The profile was getting a little blurred.

Des was applauded into the parade ring, and though the bounce was not as pronounced as in his youth, he looked very powerful and broke into a sweat. Richard looked calm, but Des continued to sweat freely as Janice and Peter Maughan walked him past the packed stands for the last time. He was drifting in the market, too. The professional punters felt it was beyond him, though you got the feeling that they would not have begrudged him this final victory. We took up our normal positions on the lawn below the stand. It was a bright, sunny day, and there were no visibility problems barring the crowds and the carousel in the middle of the course.

The whole process was so familiar that we had to remind ourselves this was probably the last time we would ever see him on a racecourse. The crowd buzzed as the starter called the runners in. For the last time we stared out at that grey figure across the flat landscape of Kempton Park.

Richard had not managed to get the rail at the start, but as Sabin du Loir shot off, and Des went with him, Des was soon far enough clear to move in. He jumped the first two fences well, and went into the bend about a length and a half down on Sabin du Loir. At the third Des put in a magnificent leap, and the crowd roared as he took three lengths out of Sabin du Loir and went a length and a half up. He was ahead at the next, but Peter Scudamore gradually eased his horse back up on the outside to take the lead at the fifth, and that was the way they stayed all the way down the back and into the straight. The rest of the field was going comfortably behind them, all the horses going well within themselves, and the mixture of applause and cheering that greeted the horses as they galloped past the stands was tinged with the expectation of the drama that lay ahead.

Over the water they went, with Des hanging off the rail to look at the crowd, then at the next, he made a mistake, a bad mistake. He seemed to take off too early, and instead of reaching for the fence as he would have done in his youth, he landed in the middle of it, and hit it very hard. It was a similar mistake to the one he had made at the last at Fairyhouse when he had been tired.

Richard kept him balanced, but Des had dropped right back and looked as if he might have hurt himself as he was now struggling a little. At exactly that moment the others speeded up, and Des went into the bend fourth or fifth, and ran into further trouble when Mark Perrett on Docklands Express took the rail, and Des ran into the back of him.

Again the pace quickened, and again Des struggled to keep up, his ears were back now and Richard gave him a slap on the neck. Ahead, Sabin du Loir seemed to be tiring, but behind him Remittance Man, The Fellow, and Docklands Express were full of running. Going into the fourth last Graham McCourt on Norton's Coin drifted into the rail, and now Des was last, as the field stormed round the bend into the finishing straight.

Watching from the stands, we knew it was over. Perhaps it had been that mistake, perhaps it was the fast ground, but we knew he could not win. He was still running on, and could have got third or fourth, but somehow the spark was not quite there. The crowd, so desperately wanting to shout him home one last time, went a little quiet for a few moments, but then soon began to roar again – this was the King George after all – as the leaders approached the third last. Sabin du Loir looked cooked, but Remittance Man seemed full of running, and cleared the fence well; beside him Sabin du Loir crashed to the ground. Des was about three strides behind them and on the outside and seemed to be setting himself for a big jump – then halfway into his take-off stride he did something he had never done before. He seemed to lose confidence, put down again, and hitting the fence with his chest, crashed through it, landed on his nose, and sent Richard Dunwoody hurtling into the ground. He had fallen.

There was a kind of strangled roar and yell from the crowd – it had been a terrible fall – and they were torn between watching the leaders and looking back at Des to see if he was all right. Thankfully Des didn't keep anyone guessing for too long. He hauled himself to his feet, inadvertently kicking Richard, and set off after the leaders, who were now approaching the last.

Still suffering from shock – people could imagine him being beaten, but not falling – the crowd started to roar again as, in a closer finish than there had been for six years, The Fellow collared Remittance Man and Docklands Express after the last, and won going away, in record time – he had taken four seconds off the course record.

Someone had tried to catch Des, but he was not to be denied his final moment of glory. He side-stepped him, and cantered, ears pricked, past the stand to an incredible roar of relief and affection, almost as big a cheer as the winner received. The old showman had upstaged the others, even in defeat, and he looked strong and fresh again as he passed his public for the last time. Peter Maughan caught him and handed him to Janice, and she wiped away the tears after she could see he was all right. Des had made it easy for us. There was no question now but that we would retire him, and we would merely delay the decision to the next day so as not to overshadow The Fellow's achievement. Twenty-five years to the day on which Arkle had run his last race, Desert Orchid was retiring in the same race – and it seemed fitting that he had cantered alone past the stands, the glory all his and his alone. He had fought for the last time with the brightest and the best and not been disgraced. His spirit was undiminished. His years and all the miles he had galloped had finally caught up with him, but even in defeat he had risen to the occasion. He had surprised us, right up to the end, and again stolen the show. Here I am, that triumphant gesture seemed to say. Here I am. Desert Orchid.

It was chaos afterwards and many of the people who had only arrived half an hour before his race now turned round and went home again. Des seemed fine afterwards, except for a scrape on his hock, but Richard had had such a bad fall that he gave up his rides for the rest of the day. He could reflect that right up to the end

Des had made it a memorable day for him, if for the wrong reasons. As the red tail-lights of the cars snaked endlessly towards the exit, and the light went, we gathered in the Rank box for the last time and toasted the grey horse.

It was dark now, and there was a dull red glow in the sky as he was loaded into the horsebox for the last time. Janice patted him on the nose, and grinned at me and shrugged. Her life would be different from now on. All our lives would be. There was nothing else to say really. The silly old bugger had said it all. He was tired. He was ready for another kind of life.

Next morning I talked to David. The only question was how best to make the announcement. I decided it would be best to call the Press Association. I asked to be put through to the racing desk. What was it about, they wanted to know. Desert Orchid, I said. The phone was passed to someone else.

'John Lees,' said the voice. There was a short pause as I think we were both probably aware that this was somehow a significant moment.

'It's about Desert Orchid,' I said.

'Yes?' said John Lees.

'He's retired.'

31

A New Life

On 8 January 1992, Des returned to Jimmy at Ab Kettleby where he had grown up. The cycle was complete. He had fallen in his first race at Kempton in January 1983 and in his last race at Kempton in December 1991, nearly nine years later. The first fall had gone almost unnoticed; the last made the TV news and the front pages of the national newspapers.

In between he had raced 170 miles over 850 fences and 160 hurdles, and walked, trotted and galloped thousands of miles preparing for those races. Miraculously he retired as sound as the day he first went to Whitsbury, and though the old routine of training punctuated with glory days at the racetrack had slipped away, his brilliant career had run its course to the end. He had lost just the race that none of us can win, the race against time.

David rode Des on the gallops a few days before he left, and to his relief the grey horse didn't try to cart him, but behaved himself when he realised that he wasn't required to do any work that day. David, perhaps more than any of us, could measure his life with this horse. He had had him for nine years, nearly a fifth of his own life, and most of his training career. When we sent Des to him all those years ago, it was because we thought he was a good trainer, but we have since come to realise what a lucky decision it was. I doubt anyone else could have risen to the challenges Des presented with quite the same wit, style and honesty as David. Above all, David is a sporting man, gracious in defeat and victory, and always big enough for both. Like all of us, he identified with the grey horse, loved his toughness and combative spirit, his courage and style, and he served the grey horse well. He will go on to other triumphs, but it is unlikely he will ever have another horse quite like Desert Orchid.

For everyone at Whitsbury life would be a little different. The sight of those familiar pricked grey ears and big black eyes staring out of his box had gone for ever but life moves on, and within minutes of his departure the ante-post favourite, Seattle Rhyme, was moved into his box, the focus for a new set of dreams.

Rodney and Janice would miss Des, but could look back on his time with a mixture of relief and pride. He had made them both famous, but in a deeper way had allowed them to realise the dreams shared by so many dedicated people working in racing up and down the country. They were relieved to see him retire safe and sound. And though none of us would ever see Des race again, he had left us all with so many memories . . .

Colin cantering him down to the start with his arm muscles screaming. Simon riding him up between his ears, holding him together, poised, balanced, crouching into the drive position after the last fence as the crowd erupted. Richard grinning his gap-toothed smile as he rode in the mud-splattered grey after another win, shaking his head in admiration as the applause seemed to go on for ever . . .

Des himself powering up the Sandown hill with his ear pricked, those last three fences at Kempton where he neither asked nor gave any quarter, the open ditches down the back at Wincanton and Ascot, which made you tremble to watch even though you were half a mile away. The final hill at Cheltenham, and that gut-churning day when he won the Gold Cup. The goofy smiles of the crowds as he walked past, sawing at his bit, prancing on his toes, breaking out into a sweat and trembling in the saddling box. The family gathering in the parade ring, the explosion of joy as he stormed past the finishing post. The way he pricked his ears, looked at the crowd, and rose to his triumphs. His willingness and his pride, his arrogance and his humility. His power, his enthusiasm, his energy and his purpose.

The spotlight that had shone on him so brightly over the years had briefly illuminated us all, and had changed our lives. Jimmy, now freed from the relentless anxiety of Des's racecourse appearances would be able to take stock, and come to terms with that most complicated of things, the realising of a dream.

It would be the same for all of us – to be so intimately concerned with such an extraordinary phenomenon meant that in some ways we were the last to realise what Des had done. We could be left in no doubt now, as even in retirement the offers flooded in for appearances at horse shows and racecourses.

His great popularity undoubtedly had something to do with the video age in which we live, and thousands of miles of videotape would remain to testify to his concrete, tangible achievements – his shattering of the prize money record, his four King George victories, his four successive National Hunt Horse of the Year Awards. The videos would also testify to an almost unprecedented versatility. He had been as brilliant a jumper of hurdles as he was of fences; he had been the champion from two miles to three miles five furlongs; he had won on firm ground and heavy ground; he had quite simply succeeded at everything he attempted.

But in another sense his achievements have been more elusive and less tangible, and he started to pass into legend long before his brilliant career was over. He generated so much emotion, touched so many lives, encouraged so many people, moved them, and exhilarated them, that this, perhaps, is why Desert Orchid would endure: we identified with him, because he seemed to represent the best part of us all: his courage, his style, his charisma, his talent, his refusal to quit. I said it all those years before, but this time I can be quoted correctly: he seemed to be a gift from God.

He gave us everything he had to give, and that was more than we had any right to ask. He scaled the heights and stayed there, year after year, and we shall all remember the generations of brilliant horses he battled over the years, and the way he proved himself again and again, season after season.

He will never again do what he probably loved doing most, galloping and jumping fences in public, but he is an intelligent horse, and perhaps he realises that it is time for a new life, a world of softer colours and gentler emotions. We will spoil him and continue to glow in the happy recollection of all the wonderful days he has given us, and we will try to make his retirement a long and happy one.

He still has half his life ahead of him, and the genius inside him will, we hope, only fade slowly. We will not make too many assumptions about Desert Orchid. Even after all these years there is something unknowable and mysterious about him. He has always surprised us.

All we can say after all this time is that he is, he has been, a great horse. A great grey horse.

APPENDIX I: RACE-BY-RACE GUIDE TO AN ILLUSTRIOUS CAREER

Reproduced courtesy of the *Racing Post*

Desert Orchid
gr g Grey Mirage – Flower Child (Brother)
Placings: 111F1211131/241413-23F
D. R. C. Elsworth   **12 11-10**

			Starts	1st	2nd	3rd	Win & Pl
			70	34	11	8	£654, 066
®177	2/91	Sand	3m½f Gd2 Lim Hcp Ch good £20,700				
	12/90	Kemp	3m Gd1 Ch gd-sft £45,190				
	4/90	Fair	3m4f Ext List Hcp Ch good £55,200				
®182	2/90	Kemp	3m List Hcp Ch good £24,100				
	2/90	Winc	2m5f Ch gd-sft .. £3,850				
	12/89	Kemp	3m Champ Ch good £40,986				
®181	11/89	Winc	3m1f Lim Hcp Ch good £5,076				
	3/89	Chel	3m2f Champ Ch heavy £68,371				
®180	2/89	Sand	3m½f Featr Lim Hcp Ch good £19,340				
®180	1/89	Asct	2m Hcp Ch good £21,950				
	12/88	Kemp	3m Champ Ch gd-fm £37,280				
®176	12/88	Sand	2m List Lim Hcp Ch good £8,813				
	10/88	Winc	2m5f Ch good ... £3,694				
®170	4/88	Sand	3m5f List Hcp Ch gd-fm £45,000				
	4/88	Lvpl	3m1f Featr Ch good £16,040				
	11/87	Kemp	2m4f Ch gd-sft .. £7,503				
	10/87	Winc	2m5f Ch good ... £3,842				
®176	4/87	Asct	2m4f Hcp Ch gd-sft £7,142				
	2/87	Winc	3m1f List Ch soft £6,323				
®171	2/87	Sand	3m½f Hcp Ch good £15,666				
	12/86	Kemp	3m Ch soft £31,696				
®144	12/86	Asct	2m Hcp Ch good £6,801				
®137	11/86	Sand	2m4½f List Hcp Ch good £4,950				

12/85 Asct	2m4f Nov Ch good £5,639
11/85 Sand	2m Nov Ch good £3,759
11/85 Asct	2m Nov Ch fm ... £7,987
11/85 Devn	2m1f Nov Ch gd-fm £1,608
2/85 Sand	2m Hdl gd-sft £4,417
2/84 Winc	2m Hdl yield £6,059
2/84 Asct	2m Nov Hdl good £2,977
1/84 Sand	2m Hdl good £4,482
12/83 Kemp	2m Nov Hdl good £3,548
11/83 Asct	2m Nov Hdl firm £2,317
10/83 Asct	2m Nov Hdl firm £1,932
	Total win prizemoney £544,238

21 Jan83 Kempton 2m Nov Hdl £1,638
18 ran GOOD 8 hdls Time 4m01.2s
1 Boardmans Crown 4 11-0 M Bastard 6/1
2 Butlers Pet 4 10-10 B Wright[4] 50/1
3 Busaco 4 10-10 M Perrett[4] 9/4
F **DESERT ORCHID** 4 11-0 C Brown 50/1
behind when fell last
Dist: shd-1-1½-hd-8

24 Feb83 Wincanton 2m Mdn Hdl £645
22 ran GOOD 8 hdls Time 3m55.4s
1 Raise the Offer 4 10-10 J Francome 12/1
2 Hollymount 4 10-10 B de Haan 10/1
3 Ikoyi Sunset 3 10-10 W Smith 5/2
0 **DESERT ORCHID** 4 10-10 C Brown 9/1
Dist: 1½-5-2-2½-6

11 Mar83 Sandown 2m Nov Hdl £1,265
16 ran GOOD 8 hdls Time 4m09.0s
1 Diamond Hunter 5 11-5 S Smith Eccles 4/1
2 **DESERT ORCHID** 4 10-6 C Brown 7/1
headway 2 out, strong run flat, finished well
3 Emperor Charles 6 11-5 B de Haan 15/2
Dist: nk-3

25 Mar83 Newbury 2m½f Nov Hdl £1,501
14 ran HEAVY 8 hdls Time 4m26.6s
1 Applejo 7 11-0 J Lovejoy[7] 20/1

2 Destiny Bay 5 11-7 H Davies 7/4F
3 El Mansour 4 11-0 S Smith Eccles 20/1
7 **DESERT ORCHID** 4 11-0 C Brown 5/2
every chance 6th, ridden and weakened 2 out
Dist: shd 5-3-½-10

---

29 Oct83 Ascot 2m Nov Hdl £1,932
5 ran FIRM 8 hdls Time 3m49.6s
1 **DESERT ORCHID** 4 10-10 C Brown 11/8
made all, unchallenged
2 Lucky Rascal 4 10-6 P Double⁽⁴⁾ 5/4F
3 Sammy Lux 5 10-10 Mr P Schofield⁽⁴⁾ 13/2
Dist: 20-15

---

18 Nov83 Ascot 2m Nov Hdl £2,317
3 ran FIRM 8 hdls Time 3m52.2s
1 **DESERT ORCHID** 4 11-6 C Brown 1/2F
made all, mistake 6th, blundered 2 out,
unchallenged
2 Don Giovanni 4 11-6 J Francome 7/4
3 Gillie's Prince 4 10-11 W Morris⁽⁴⁾ 25/1
Dist: 15-30

---

2 Dec83 Sandown 2m5½f Nov Ch £4,885
9 ran FIRM Time 5m14.8s
1 Catch Phrase 5 11-4 R Rowe 9/4
2 **DESERT ORCHID** 4 11-3 C Brown 5/6F
mistake 2nd, led to flat, hard ridden
3 Flash Fred 6 11-4 J Lovejoy 16/1
Dist: ¾-10-15-10-2½

---

26 Dec83 Kempton 2m Nov Hdl £3,548
10 ran GOOD 8 hdls Time 3m47.8s
1 **DESERT ORCHID** 4 11-10 R Linley 7/4F
mistake 3rd, made all, unchallenged
2 I Haventalight 4 10-10 J Francome 5/2
3 Derby Dilly 4 10-10 J J O'Neill 9/1
Dist: 15-1-½-1-25

---

7 Jan84 Sandown 2m Hdl £4,482
6 ran GOOD 8 hdls Time 3m58.9s
1 **DESERT ORCHID** 5 11-11 C Brown 5/6F
made all, unchallenged
2 I Haventalight 5 11-11 J Francome 4/1
3 Horn of Plenty 5 11-7 H Davies 50/1
Dist: 8-15-2½-½-8

---

8 Feb84 Ascot 2m Nov Hdl £2,977
10 ran GOOD 8 hdls Time N/A
1 **DESERT ORCHID** 5 11-11 C Brown 11/10F
2 Hill's Pageant 5 11-1 K Mooney 12/1
3 Brown Trix 6 11-5 J Francome 7/1
Dist: 8-12-8-10-8

---

23 Feb84 Wincanton 2m Hdl £6,059
9 ran YIELD 8 hdls Time 3m40.1s
1 **DESERT ORCHID** 5 11-2 C Brown 2/1F
mistake 4th, made all, ran on well
2 Stans Pride 7 10-11 R Crank 3/1
3 Very Promising 6 11-2 B de Haan 8/1
Dist: 4-12-2-8

---

13 Mar84 Cheltenham 2m Hdl £36,680
14 ran GOOD Time 3m52.6s
1 Dawn Run 6 11-9 J J O'Neill 4/5F
2 Cima 6 12-0 P Scudamore 66/1

3 Very Promising 6 12-0 S Morshead 16/1
0 **DESERT ORCHID** 5 12-0 C Brown 7/1
led 3rd and 4th, weakened 5th
Dist: ¾-4-1½-¾-2

---

20 Oct84 Kempton 2m Hdl £3,915
10 ran GOOD 8 hdls Time 3m49.20s
1 Ra Nova 5 11-10 M Perrett 5/1
2 Janus 6 11-4 R Rowe 14/1
3 **DESERT ORCHID** 5 11-10 C Brown 2/1F
led tl appr last
Dist: 1½-4-½-15-6

---

15 Dec84 Ascot 2m Hdl £4,819
5 ran GD-SFT 8 hdls Time 3m56.00s
1 See You Then 4 11-8 J Francome 11/10F
2 Joy Ride 4 10-8 S Smith Eccles 8/1
3 **DESERT ORCHID** 5 11-8 C Brown 5/1
chsd ldr: led 2 out: one pce
Dist: 2-5-15-25

---

26 Dec84 Kempton 2m Hdl £15,572
7 ran GD-SFT 8 hdls Time 3m59.30s
1 Browne's Gazette 6 11-3 D Browne 11/8F
2 **DESERT ORCHID** 5 11-3 C Brown 10/1
lw: mstke 3rd: led to 2 out: rdn nt qckn
3 See You Then 4 11-3 J Francome 2/1
Dist: 15-10-8-8-10

---

12 Jan85 Leopardstown 2m
Ext Gd 1 List Hcp Hdl £24,393
20 ran GOOD Time 3m52.4s
1 Hansel Rag 5 10-0 A Powell 14/1
2 Bonalma 5 10-0 B Sheridan 11/1
3 Another Shot 7 10-12 Mr T M Walsh 14/1
13 **DESERT ORCHID** 6 12-0 C Brown 11/1
Dist: 2½-2-shd-3-1¼

---

2 Feb85 Sandown 2m Hdl £4,417
8 ran GD-SFT 8 hdls Time 4m08.20s
1 **DESERT ORCHID** 6 11-5 C Brown 2/1F
mde all: qcknd 3rd: r.o wl
2 Mr Moonraker 8 10-10 B Powell 5/1
3 Infielder 6 10-11⁰1 J Francome 10/1
Dist: 10-1½-¾-hd-15

---

12 Mar85 Cheltenham 2m Hdl £38,030
14 ran GOOD 8 hdls Time 3m51.70s
1 See You Then 5 12-0 S Smith Eccles 16/1
2 Robin Wonder 7 12-0 J J O'Neill 66/1
3 Stans Pride 8 11-9 S Morshead 100/1
P **DESERT ORCHID** 6 12-0 C Brown 20/1
lw: chsd ldr tl wknd appr 6th: t.o whn p.u bef 2 out
Dist. 7-3-1½-2½-shd

---

8 Apr85 Chepstow 2m Hdl £8,480
7 ran HEAVY 8 hdls Time 4m07.00s
1 Browne's Gazette 7 11-13 D Browne 8/13F
2 Ra Nova 6 11-9 M Perrett 9/1
3 Stans Pride 8 11-4 S Morshead 5/1
P **DESERT ORCHID** 6 11-9 b¹ C Brown 20/1
prom: mstke 9th: ev. ch 3 out: btn whn mstke next
Dist: 1½-3-¾-20-dist

---

13 Apr85 Ascot 2m Hcp Hdl £3,834
8 ran GOOD 8 hdls Time 3m59.70s

1 Comedy Fair 5 10-5 J J O'Neill 7/4F
2 Rhythmic Pastimes 5 10-2 S Smith Eccles 5/1
3 Mister Golden 5 10-1 J Duggan 10/3
F **DESERT ORCHID** 6 12-0 C Brown 9/2
mde all: clr whn fell last
Dist: 1½-1½-10-20-2

---

19 Oct85 Kempton 2m Hdl £3,830
6 ran FIRM 8 hdls Time 3m41.40s (fst7.9s)
1 Wing and a Prayer 4 11-3 S Sherwood 7/2
2 Life Guard 4 11-3 J Frost 25/1
3 Monza 7 10-9 R Rowe 13/2
F **DESERT ORCHID** 6 11-4 C Brown 4/9F
led: qcknd 5th: wl clr whn fell 2 out
Dist: 1½-10-20-5

---

1 Nov85 Devon 2m1f Nov Ch £1,608
5 ran GD-FM 12 fncs Time 4m17.80s (slw0.9s)
1 **DESERT ORCHID** 6 11-0 C Brown 4/5F
lw: j.w: mde all: unchal
2 Charcoal Wally 6 11-7 R Linley 6/5
3 Pridden Jimmy 6 11-0 b B J Wright 33/1
Dist: 25-dist-25-30

---

15 Nov85 Ascot 2m Nov Ch £7,987
4 ran FIRM 12 fncs Time 3m52.80s (fst2.3s)
1 **DESERT ORCHID** 6 11-4 C Brown 4/9
mde all: qcknd appr last: easily
2 Cocaine 7 11-4 C Mann 9/2
3 Yacare 6 11-4 R Rowe 7/1
Dist: 12-dist-2

---

30 Nov85 Sandown 2m Nov Ch £3,759
5 ran GOOD 13 fncs Time 3m59.60s (slw1.4s)
1 **DESERT ORCHID** 6 11-4 C Brown 4/11F
lw: mde all: comf
2 Taffy Jones 6 10-12 P Barton 5/1
3 Evening Song 6 10-7 R Goldstein 33/1
Dist: 7-5-8-30-?

---

14 Dec85 Ascot 2m4f Nov Ch £5,639
6 ran GOOD 16 fncs Time 4m55.20s (slw2.9s)
1 **DESERT ORCHID** 6 11-11 C Brown 5/4F
mde virtually all: blnd 14th: unchal
2 Evening Song 6 10-7 R Goldstein 50/1
3 Play Boy 6 10-12 J Duggan 3/1
Dist: 20-4-10-2

---

10 Jan86 Ascot 2m Nov Ch £7,037
3 ran GD-SFT 12 fncs Time 4m04.00s (slw8.9s)
1 Pearlyman 7 11-4 P Barton 5/1
2 Charcoal Wally 7 11-4 G McCourt 5/1
U **DESERT ORCHID** 7 12-0 C Brown 4/11F
led tl blnd & uns rdr 5th
Dist: dist

---

1 Feb86 Sandown 2m Nov Ch £7,680
6 ran HEAVY 13 fncs Time 4m07.00s (slw8.8s)
1 Berlin 7 11-10 D Browne 5/2
2 **DESERT ORCHID** 7 11-10 C Brown 10/11F
led 3rd to 10th: rdn 11th: rallied flat: r.o wl
3 Allten Glazed 9 11-5 G Bradley 7/1
Dist: ½-15-hd-30

---

11 Mar86 Cheltenham 2m Ch £21,215
14 ran GD-SFT 12 fncs Time 3m53.30s (fst8.0s)

---

1 Oregon Trail 6 11-8 R J Beggan 14/1
2 Charcoal Wally 7 11-8 B Powell 11/1
3 **DESERT ORCHID** 7 11-8 C Brown 11/2
led 2nd to 10th: rdn 2 out: unable qckn
Dist:¾-8-8-5-shd

---

25 Mar86 Sandown 2m4½f Nov Ch £3,993
6 ran GD-SFT 17 fncs Time 5m12.40s (slw7.7s)
1 Clara Mountain 7 11-8 H Davies 2/1
2 **DESERT ORCHID** 7 11-8 C Brown 10/11F
blnd 1st: led 3rd to last: rdn: r.o
3 Whiskey Eyes 5 10-9 M Harrington 5/1
Dist: 1½-15-20-½-8

---

12 Apr86 Ascot 2m4f Nov Hcp Ch £11,108
13 ran GOOD 16 fncs Time 4m54.40s
(slw2.1s)
1 Repington 8 10-3⅛4 K Mooney 9/1
2 Just Alick 7 10-0 B Powell 10/1
3 Garfunkel 7 10-3 R Dunwoody 14/1
5 **DESERT ORCHID** 7 11-7 C Brown 5/1F
*led fr 4th: blnd 13th: hdd appr last: 2nd & wkng
whn mstke last*
Dist: 2-2½-¾-2-12

---

1 Nov86 Sandown 2m4½f List Hcp Ch £4,950
4 ran GOOD 17 fncs Time 5m15.00s (slw10.3s)
1 **DESERT ORCHID** 10-3 C Brown 7/4JF
made all: ran on well [op 13/8 tchd 15/8]
2 The Argonaut 8 10-0 S Shilstone 9/4
3 Very Promising 8 12-0 R Dunwoody 7/4JF
Dist: 4-3-bad

---

15 Nov86 Ascot 2m4f Gd2 Hcp Ch £18,584
6 ran GOOD 16 fncs Time 4m55.80s (slw6.4s)
1 Church Warden 7 10-7 R Dunwoody 12/1
2 Berlin 7 11-0 D Browne 9/2
3 Amber Rambler 7 11-5⅛7 R Rowe 9/2
4 **DESERT ORCHID** 7 11-6⅛7 C Brown 7/4F
*chsd ldr tl mistake 11th: ev ch 2 out: rdn & unable
qckn flat [tchd 2/1]*
Dist: 1½-4-hd-30

---

13 Dec86 Ascot 2m Hcp Ch £6,801
8 ran GOOD 12 fncs Time 3m58.50s (slw3.4s)
1 **DESERT ORCHID** 7 11-5 C Brown 7/2J
*led 3rd until 5th: led 8th until 10th: quickened &
led appr last [op 3/1 tchd 9/2]*
2 Charcoal Wally 7 11-3 B Powell 4/1
3 Little Bay 11 11-10 P Tuck 7/2J
Dist: 12-2½-hd-6-25

---

26 Dec86 Kempton 3m Ch £31,696
9 ran SOFT 19 fncs Time 6m18.90s (slw20.4s)
1 **DESERT ORCHID** 7 11-10 S Sherwood 16/1
*made virtually all: quickened 2 out: comfortably
[op 12/1 tchd 20/1]*
2 Door Latch 8 11-10 R Rowe 10/1
3 Bolands Cross 7 11-10 P Scudamore 9/2
Dist: 15-6-1-3

---

7 Feb87 Sandown 3m½f Hcp Ch £15,666
6 ran GOOD 22 fncs Time 6m12.70s (slw6.5s)
1 **DESERT ORCHID** 8 11-10 C Brown 11/4
*made virtually all: quickened 2 out: comfortably
[op 9/4 tchd 3/1]*

2 Stearsby 8 11-4 G McCourt 3/1
3 Bolands Cross 8 11-0 P Scudamore 9/4F
Dist: 10-3-12-bad

26 Feb87 Wincanton 3m1f List Ch £6,323
4 ran SOFT 21 fncs Time 7m00.70s (slw47.3s)
1 **DESERT ORCHID** 8 11-11 C Brown 1/2F
*made all: mstke 11th: blnd 14th: quickened 19th:
very easily* [op 2/5 tchd 4/7]
2 Mr Moonraker 10 11-7 B Powell 4/1
3 Fire Drill 12 11-7 P Richards 50/1
Dist: 12-dist-15

18 Mar87 Cheltenham 2m Gd 1 Ch £25,775
8 ran GOOD 12 fncs Time 3m59.10s (fst2.2s)
1 Pearlyman 8 12-0 P Scudamore 13/8F
2 Very Promising 9 12-0 R Dunwoody 3/1
3 **DESERT ORCHID** 8 12-0 C Brown 9/4
led to 2 out: every chance flat: not quicken [op 15/
8 tchd 5/2]
Dist: nk-3-25-3-20

8 Apr87 Ascot 2m4f Hcp Ch £7,142
7 ran GD-SFT 16 fncs Time 5m05.20s (slw12.9s)
1 **DESERT ORCHID** 8 12-4 C Brown 7/4F
*led to 12th: mstk 13th: hard rdn & rallied 2 out: led
last: r.o. wl* [op 6/4 tchd 2/1]
2 Gold Bearer 7 9-10 G Landau (4) 33/1
3 Sign Again 9 10-3[2/3] R Dunwoody 10/1
Dist: 2-3-2½-25-2

25 Apr87 Sandown 3m5f List Hcp Ch £32,250
9 ran GD-FM 24 fncs Time 7m12.00s (fst1.5s)
1 Lean Ar Aghaidh 10 9-10 G Landau[(4)] 6/1
2 Contradeal 10 10-0 K Mooney 5/1
3 Broadheath 10 10-6 P Nicholls 14/1
P **DESERT ORCHID** 8 12-0 C Brown 7/2
*mstks: chsd ldt tl 13th: blnd 14th: in rear 16th: blnd
& p.u. 19th* [op 3/1]
Dist: 5-7-6-2-15

29 Oct87 Wincanton 2m5f Ch £3,842
3 ran GOOD 17 fncs Time 5m19.60s (slw10.3s)
1 **DESERT ORCHID** 8 11-8 C Brown 1/7F
made all: very easily [op 1/8 tchd 1/6]
2 Sugar Bee 9 11-8 H Davies 6/1
3 Britannicus 11 11-1 D Morris 25/1
Dist: dist-dist

18 Nov87 Kempton 2m4f Ch £7,503
3 ran GD-SFT 17 fncs Time 5m18.00s (slw18.9s)
1 **DESERT ORCHID** 8 11-10 C Brown 1/5F
made all: unchallenged [op 1/6 tchd 2/9 in place]
2 Bishops Yarn 8 10-10 Richard Guest 7/1
3 Galway Blaze 11 10-10 S Sherwood 8/1
Dist: 12-1

5 Dec87 Sandown 2m List Lim Hcp Ch £8,796
5 ran GOOD 13 fncs Time 3m58.2s (slw2.1s)
1 Long Engagement 6 10-2[2/6][2/2] R Dunwoody 3/1
2 **DESERT ORCHID** 8 12-0 C Brown 10/11F
*chased ldr, led 10th & 11th jumped right last,
unable to quicken* [op 4/5 tchd Evens in plcs]
3 Amber Rambler 8 9-10 K B Walsh[(4)]5/1
Dist: 3-15-8-20

26 Dec87 Kempton 3m Gd1 Ch £31,400
9 ran GOOD 19 fncs Time 5m59.9s (slw2.0s)
1 Nupsala 8 11-10 b[1] A-M Pommier 25/1
2 **DESERT ORCHID** 8 11-10 C Brown Evens F
*led and mistake 3rd, led 15th until 17th, weakened
approaching last* [op 4/5 tchd 11/10]
3 Golden Friend 9 11-10 D Browne 20/1
Dist: 15-3-1-20

6 Feb88 Sandown 3m½f Lim Hcp Ch £20,450
11 ran HEAVY 22 fncs Time 6m40.1s (slw34.9s)
1 Charter Party 10 10-11 R Dunwoody 10/3F
2 Rhyme 'N' Reason 9 10-7 B Powell 7/2
3 **DESERT ORCHID** 9 12-0 C Brown 7/2
*led until 1st, led 7th until 11th, mistake 12th, led 13
until 2 out, unable to quicken flat* [op 7/2 tchd 4/1]
Dist: 8-nk-12-2-20

25 Feb88 Wincanton 3m1f List Ch £7,572
3 ran GD-SFT 21 fncs Time 6m43.5s (slw33.9s)
1 Kildimo 8 11-11 G Bradley 2/1
2 **DESERT ORCHID** 9 11-11 C Brown 1/2F
*jumped well, led until approaching last, not
quicken* [op 4/6]
3 Burrough Hill Lad 12 11-11 R Rowe 9/1
Dist: 1½-dist

16 Mar88 Cheltenham 2m Champ Ch £39,836
8 ran HEAVY 12 fncs Time 4m7.4s (slw8.0s)
1 Pearlyman 9 12-0 T Morgan 15/8F
2 **DESERT ORCHID** 9 12-0 C Brown 9/1
led to 2 out, hard ridden, ran on flat [op 7/1 tchd
10/1]
3 Very Promising 10 12-0 R Dunwoody 4/1
Dist: 5-1-2½-6-2

7 Apr88 Liverpool 3m1f Featr Ch £16,040
4 ran GOOD 18 fncs Time 6m2.5s (slw0.4s)
1 **DESERT ORCHID** 9 11-5 S Sherwood 3/1
jumped well, made all, stayed on well [op 9/4 tchd
7/2]
2 Kildimo 8 11-5 G Bradley 2/1F
3 Weather The Storm 8 11-13 T J Taaffe 8/1
Dist: 8-12 dist

23 Apr88 Sandown 3m5f List Hcp Ch £45,000
12 ran GD-FM 24 fncs Time 7m19.5s (slw6.5s)
1 **DESERT ORCHID** 9 11-11 S Sherwood 6/1
*led until 21st, led 22nd, hard ridden last, ran on
well* [op 9/2]
2 Kildimo 8 11-12 J Frost 6/1
3 Strands of Gold 9 10-0 P Scudamore 6/1
Dist: 2½-4-6-2-¾

27 Oct88 Wincanton 2m5f Ch £3,694
5 ran GOOD 17 fncs Time 5m14.2s (slw4.9s)
1 **DESERT ORCHID** 9 11-8 S Sherwood 2/7F
made all, well clear from 10th, easily [op 1/3 tchd
1/4]
2 Bishops Yarn 9 11-8 Richard Guest 9/1
3 Golden Friend 10 11-8 D Browne 5/1
Dist: 15-½-4-dist

3 Dec88 Sandown 2m List Lim Hcp Ch £8,813
5 ran GOOD 13 fncs Time 3m59.3s (slw3.2s)
1 **DESERT ORCHID** 9 12-0 S Sherwood 5/2

blundered 9th, made all, quickened 11th, very
easily [op 2/1 tchd 3/1 in a place]
2 Jim Thorpe 7 10-8 M Dwyer 3/1
3 Panto Prince 7 10-10 B Powell 4/1
Dist: 12-½-bad Postmark: 179/147/148

---

26 Dec88 Kempton 3m Champ Ch £37,280
5 ran GD-FM 19 fncs Time 5m50.00s (fst7.9s)
1 **DESERT ORCHID** 9 11-10 S Sherwood 1/2F
mistake 14th, led until 9th, led 13th until 16th, led
2 out, comfortably [op 4/11 tchd 8/15]
2 Kildimo 8 11-10 J Frost 8/1
3 Vodkatini 9 11-10 Peter Hobbs 7/1
Dist: 4-5-4-1½ Postmark: 168/164/159

---

14 Jan89 Ascot 2m Hcp Ch £21,950
5 ran GOOD 12 fncs Time 3m59.9s (slw6.1s)
1 **DESERT ORCHID** 10 12-0 S Sherwood 6/4F
led 3rd to 5th, led and mistake last, hard ridden
and rallied flat, led close to home [op 5/4 tchd 13/*
8 in plcs]
2 Panto Prince 8 10-6¾4 B Powell 3/1
3 Ida's Delight 10 10-0¾4 P Dennis 66/1
Dist: hd-8-10 Postmark: 179/157/143

---

4 Feb89 Sandown 3m½f Featr Lim Hcp Ch £19,340
4 ran GOOD 22 fncs Time 6m18.8s (slw13.6s)
1 **DESERT ORCHID** 10 12-0 S Sherwood 6/5F
led until 11th, led 2 out and last, quickened and
led near finish [op 1/1 tchd 5/4]
2 Pegwell Bay 8 10-10 C Llewellyn 4/1
3 Kildimo 9 10-13 J Frost 2/1
Dist: ¾-2½-25 Postmark: 180/161/161

---

16 Mar89 Cheltenham 3m2f Champ Ch £68,371
13 ran HEAVY 22 fncs Time 7m17.60s (slw40.4s)
1 **DESERT ORCHID** 10 12-0 S Sherwood 5/2F
jumped well, led to 14th, left in lead 3 out, soon
headed, quickened and led flat [op 11/4 tchd 7/2 in*
a place]
2 Yahoo 8 12-0 T Morgan 25/1
3 Charter Party 11 12-0 R Dunwoody 14/1
Dist: 1½-8-dist-dist Postmark 169/167/159

---

6 Apr 89 Liverpool 3m1f Featr Ch £20,094
8 ran SOFT 18 fncs Time 6m18.6s (slw16.5s)
1 Yahoo 8 11-5 T Morgan 5/1
2 Delius 11 11-5 B Dowling 12/1
3 Bishops Yarn 10 11-5 Richard Guest 13/1
U **DESERT ORCHID** 10 11-13 S Sherwood 5/4F
led until fell 12th [op 11/10 tchd 11/8]
Dist: 10-10-2½-dist
Postmark: 167/157/147/144/-/-

---

9 Nov89 Wincanton 3m1f Lim Hcp Ch £5,076
2 ran GOOD 21 fncs Time 6m29.0s (slw19.4s)
1 **DESERT ORCHID** 10 12-0 R Dunwoody 2/9F
jumped well, made all, canter [op 1/7]
2 Roll-A-Joint 11 10-4 I Lawrence[3] 4/1
Dist: 12 Postmark: 158/125/-

---

2 Dec89 Sandown 2m List Lim Hcp Ch £10,040
4 ran GD-FM 13 fncs Time 3m57.1s (slw1.0s)
1 Long Engagement 8 10-0 B Powell 9/2
2 **DESERT ORCHID** 10 12-0 R Dunwoody 1/2F
led to last, unable to quicken

[op 1/3 tchd 4/7 in a place]
3 Prideaux Boy 11 10-0 J Shortt 4/1
Dist: 2½-2-8 Postmark: 146/171/141

---

26 Dec89 Kempton 3m Champ Ch £40,986
6 ran GOOD 19 fncs Time 6m04.30s (slw6.4s)
1 **DESERT ORCHID** 10 11-10 R Dunwoody 4/6F
made all, mistakes 12th and 13th, quickened 2
out, comfortably [op 4/6 tchd 8/11]
2 Barnbrook Again 8 11-10 B Powell 13/2
3 Yahoo 8 11-10 T Morgan 11/2
Dist: 8-7-3-6-15 Postmark: 168/160/153

---

8 Feb90 Wincanton 2m5f Ch £3,850
7 ran GD-SFT 17 fncs Time 5m25.2s (slw15.9s)
1 **DESERT ORCHID** 11 12-0 R Dunwoody 3/10F
led to 5th, led 7th to 9th, led approaching 3 out
easily [op 1/4 tchd 1/3]
2 Bartres 11 12-0 M Bowlby 33/1
3 Mzima Spring 11 11-1 B Powell 16/1
Dist: 20-1½-5-1-25 Postmark: 145/125/110

---

24 Feb90 Kempton 3m List Hcp Ch £24,100
8 ran GOOD 19 fncs Time 6m00.10s (slw2.2s)
1 **DESERT ORCHID** 11 12-3⅗3 R Dunwoody 8/11F
jumped well, led to 11th, led 3 out, soon clear [op
4/6 tchd 4/5]
2 Delius 12 10-3 Peter Hobbs 6/1
3 Seagram 10 9-11 N Hawke[3]33/1
Dist: 8-8-15-4-1 Postmark: 183/147/136

---

15 Mar90 Cheltenham 3m2f Champ Ch £67,003
12 ran GD-FM 22 fncs Time 6m30.9s (fst6.3s)
1 Norton's Coin 9 12-0 G McCourt 100/1
2 Toby Tobias 8 12-0 M Pitman 8/1
3 **DESERT ORCHID** 11 12-0 R Dunwoody 10/11F
led until 16th, every chance 2 out, not quicken [op
4/6 tchd Evens in a place]
Dist: ¾-4-7-12-1 Postmark: 164/163/159

---

16 Apr90 Fairyhouse 3m4f Ext List Hcp Ch £55,200
14 ran GOOD Time 7m30.9s
1 **DESERT ORCHID** 11 12-0 R Dunwoody EvensF
2 Barney Burnett 10 10-0 b B Sheridan 16/1
3 Have A Barney 9 10-2 T J Taaffe 7/1
Dist: 12-1½-nk-nk-½ Postmark: 178/138/138

---

6 Nov90 Devon 2m1f Gd2 Ch £16,233
5 ran GOOD 12 fncs Time 4m17.40s (slw3.1s)
1 Sabin du Loir 11 11-0 P Scudamore 7/2
2 **DESERT ORCHID** 11 11-0 R Dunwoody
EvensF
went 2nd 6th, every chance, 10th until ridden and
beaten approaching last [op Evens tchd 11/10]
3 Setter Country 6 10-9 W Irvine 100/1
Dist: 6-20-15 Postmark: 127 + /121 + /96

---

1 Dec90 Sandown 2m Gd2 Lim Hcp Ch £15,703
5 ran GD-FM 13 fncs Time 3m51.6s (fst4.5s)
1 Young Snugfit 6 10-7 J Osborne 7/2
2 Sabin du Loir 11 10-8 M Perrett 5/2
3 Waterloo Boy 7 10-12 R Dunwoody 11/8F
4 **DESERT ORCHID** 11 12-0 G Bradley 5/1
led to 6th, in rear from 9th [op 5/1 tchd 6/1]
Dist: 2 10-8 Postmark: 160 – 159/153/161

26 Dec90 Kempton 3m Gd 1 Ch £45,190
9 ran GD-SFT 19 fncs Time 6m12.1s
(slw14.2s)
1 **DESERT ORCHID** 11 11-10 R Dunwoody 9/4F
always prominent, left in lead 13th, ran on well
[op 6/4 tchd 5/2]
2 Toby Tobias 8 11-10 M Pitman 4/1
3 The Fellow 5 11-10 A Kondrat 10/1
Dist: 12-5-7 Postmark: 168/156/151

12 Jan91 Ascot 2m Gd2 Hcp Ch £30,282
5 ran GD-SFT 12 fncs Time 3m55.1s
(slwl.3s)
1 Blitzkreig 8 10-4 T Carmody 11/4
2 Young Snugfit 7 10-11 J Osborne 11/4
3 Katabatic 8 10-4 L Harvey 7/2
4 **DESERT ORCHID** 12 12-0 R Dunwoody 9/4F *led*
until after 2nd, outpaced 4th, ran on one pace from
2 out op 7/4 tchd 5/2 in a place]
Dist: 1-2-3 Postmark: 154/160/151/172

2 Feb91 Sandown 3m½f Gd2 Lim Hcp Ch £20,700
4 ran GOOD 22 fncs Time 6m20.5s (slw15.3s)
1 **DESERT ORCHID** 12 12-10 R Dunwoody 4/6F
led to 3 out, led flat, driven out [op 2/5]
2 Nick The Brief 9 10-3 R Supple 11/2
3 Kildimo 11 10-7 R Stronge 8/1
Dist: ¾-1½-dist Postmark: 173/157/149

14 Mar91 Cheltenham 3m2f Gd1 Ch £98,578
14 ran GOOD 22 fncs Time 6m49.8s (slw12.6s)
1 Garrison Savannah 8 12-0 b M Pitman 16/1
2 The Fellow 6 12-0 A Kondrat 28/1
3 **DESERT ORCHID** 12 12-0 R Dunwoody 4/1
always prominent, led 11th to 16th, ridden and
lost place 17th, stayed on from 2 out [op 5/2
Dist: shd-15-2½-hd-2½ Postmark: 165/165/150

24 Oct91 Wincanton 2m5f Gd2 Ch £15,775
7 ran GD-FM 17 fncs Time 5m05.70s (fst3.6s)
1 Sabin du Loir 12 11-8 P Scudamore 8/11F
2 **DESERT ORCHID** 12 11-8 R Dunwoody 7/4
chased winner, every chance 13th, no impression
[op 6/4 tchd 2/1]
3 Shannagary 10 11-0 A Tory 14/1
Dist: 6-3½-shd-dist-25 Postmark: 144/138/126

26 Nov91 Huntingdon 2m4f Gd2 Ch £15,475
4 ran GOOD 16 fncs Time 5m00.2s (slw2.9s)
1 Sabin du Loir 12 11-19 P Scudamore 4/7F
2 Norton's Coin 9 11-9 G McCourt 11/2
3 **DESERT ORCHID** 12 11-9 R Dunwoody 5/2
chased winner, jumped slowly 8th, ridden
approaching 2 out, unable to quicken [op 6/4] Dist:
4-shd-dist Postmark: 164/160/160

26 Dec91 Kempton 3m Ch £44,170
8 ran GOOD 19 fncs Time 5m46.4s (fst22.1s)
1 The Fellow 6 11-10 A Kondrat 40/1
2 Docklands Express 9 11-10 M Perrett 25/1
3 Remittance Man 7 11-10 J Osborne 3/1F
F **DESERT ORCHID** 12 11-10 R Dunwoody 4/1 *led*
3rd to 6th, mistake 11th, ridden 14th, weakened
16th, in rear when fell 3 out [op 3/1] Dist: 1½-2-8-25
Postmark: 156/154/152/144/119-.

Flat Form

1 May85 Ascot 2m Gp3 £15,171
11 ran GOOD Time 3m28.78s (slw2.0s)
1 Longboat 4 8-8 W Carson[3] 10/1
2 Gildoran 5 9-3 B Thomson[1] 7/1
3 Spicy Story 4 8-8 Pat Eddery[1] 6/4F
0 **DESERT ORCHID** 6 8-8 B Rouse[7] 33/1
led 12f: 4th st: wknd over 2f out
Dist: nk-nk-7-3-nk

APPENDIX 2: FAMILY TREE

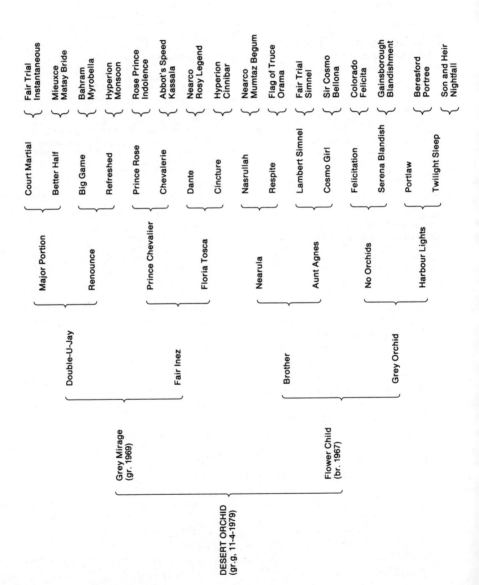

INDEX

Photographs of the racing plates in which
Desert Orchid won his fourth King George VI
Rank Chase at Kempton Park, Boxing Day
1990. The rear plates are reproduced here
actual size. Pieces of Kempton Park mud and
woodshavings still adhering to the plates have
been left in place.